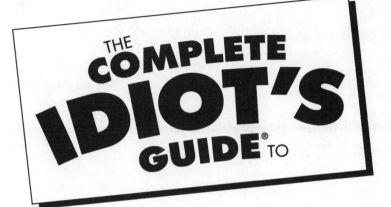

THE COMPLETE IDIOT'S GUIDE® TO

Geocaching

by Jack W. Peters and the Editors and Staff of Geocaching.com

ALPHA

A member of Penguin Group (USA) Inc.

ALPHA BOOKS

Published by the Penguin Group

Penguin Group (USA) Inc., 375 Hudson Street, New York, New York 10014, U.S.A.

Penguin Group (Canada), 10 Alcorn Avenue, Toronto, Ontario, Canada M4V 3B2 (a division of Pearson Penguin Canada Inc.)

Penguin Books Ltd, 80 Strand, London WC2R 0RL, England

Penguin Ireland, 25 St Stephen's Green, Dublin 2, Ireland (a division of Penguin Books Ltd)

Penguin Group (Australia), 250 Camberwell Road, Camberwell, Victoria 3124, Australia (a division of Pearson Australia Group Pty Ltd)

Penguin Books India Pvt Ltd, 11 Community Centre, Panchsheel Park, New Delhi—10 017, India

Penguin Group (NZ), cnr Airborne and Rosedale Roads, Albany, Auckland 1310, New Zealand (a division of Pearson New Zealand Ltd)

Penguin Books (South Africa) (Pty) Ltd, 24 Sturdee Avenue, Rosebank, Johannesburg 2196, South Africa

Penguin Books Ltd, Registered Offices: 80 Strand, London WC2R 0RL, England

International Standard Book Number: 1-59257-235-9
Library of Congress Catalog Card Number: 2004101844

08   8

Interpretation of the printing code: The rightmost number of the first series of numbers is the year of the book's printing; the rightmost number of the second series of numbers is the number of the book's printing. For example, a printing code of 04-1 shows that the first printing occurred in 2004.

Printed in the United States of America

Note: This publication contains the opinions and ideas of its authors. It is intended to provide helpful and informative material on the subject matter covered. It is sold with the understanding that the authors and publisher are not engaged in rendering professional services in the book. If the reader requires personal assistance or advice, a competent professional should be consulted.

The authors and publisher specifically disclaim any responsibility for any liability, loss, or risk, personal or otherwise, which is incurred as a consequence, directly or indirectly, of the use and application of any of the contents of this book.

Most Alpha books are available at special quantity discounts for bulk purchases for sales promotions, premiums, fund-raising, or educational use. Special books, or book excerpts, can also be created to fit specific needs.

For details, write: Special Markets, Alpha Books, 375 Hudson Street, New York, NY 10014.

Publisher: *Marie Butler-Knight*
Product Manager: *Phil Kitchel*
Senior Managing Editor: *Jennifer Chisholm*
Acquisitions Editor: *Mikal Belicove*
Development Editor: *Michael Hall*
Production Editor: *Megan Douglass*
Copy Editor: *Keith Cline*
Illustrator: *Kokoro Kimura*
Cover/Book Designer: *Trina Wurst*
Indexer: *Brad Herriman*
Layout/Proofreading: *Ayanna Lacey, John Etchison*

Contents at a Glance

Contents

Foreword

Congratulations! You found this book, intentionally or not.

It was June 21, 2000, an unusually warm day in the Pacific Northwest. I was brushing the pine needles from a yellow 3×5 card box hidden in the crook of a stump only an hour and a half from Seattle. Inside was a disposable camera, a drink container, and a simple logbook. As I sat there, elated, enjoying the scenery with the logbook open, I realized I had not only discovered my first geocache, I had also stumbled onto the first activity that combined my two interests—technology and the outdoors.

Since the launch of Geocaching.com in August of 2000, the number of hidden containers has grown from 75 to more than 80,000, and the game is now played in more than 195 countries. And in that time, more and more participants have contributed their time and creativity to make geocaching an activity for young and old, for all levels of physical activity. You can choose your own adventure and set your own schedule, spending an afternoon or an entire week on one hunt. Or you can design your own adventure for other participants to enjoy.

I am honored to be part of such a unique and growing activity that has had such an impact on so many lives in such a positive way. We've received letters from parents who have reconnected with their children through geocaching. Search and rescue teams, Boy Scout troops, and 4×4 enthusiasts are using geocaching as part of their group training and activities. Nomadic RVers are traveling the roads in search of that next elusive geocache. You can get lost online for hours just reading the log entries from participants who are documenting their own geocaching adventures around the world.

Jack Peters has written a book on geocaching I wish I could have had that June, while making preparations for my own first cache hunt. His insightful and informative pages will give you a thorough overview of geocaching from the time you pick your first cache to seek to your first find, and get you safely back again. Are you looking to purchase your first GPS receiver? Visit Chapter 9. If you want to get into the guts of the technology and history of GPS, check out Chapter 3.

In today's world when the idea of entertainment normally positions you in front of a television or computer monitor, the sport of geocaching is a refreshing new way to incorporate technology into the outdoors. It is one of the few activities where the Internet makes you stretch your legs, gets your coat, shows you the door and into the great beyond.

Welcome to the world of geocaching! I hope to see you on the trail.

Jeremy Irish

Founder, Geocaching.com

Introduction

Congratulations for taking the time to find this book, *The Complete Idiot's Guide to Geocaching*. Here is your opportunity to learn about one of the most exciting and fastest-growing sports in history. The phenomenon was inevitable. It has been created in a time when the Internet and recreational GPS use continue to spread like wildfire. With this surge of interest in the high-tech, there is also the desire to experience the outdoors. Geocaching has become so popular because it enables you to embrace both technology and the wild.

Our goal was to create the ultimate book on geocaching: one that makes learning about the sport enjoyable and easy to understand. Whether you're new to the sport or a seasoned veteran, we trust you'll find that we covered all of the topics necessary to keep you geocaching successfully and safely every time you hit the trail. To do so is no small feat. Being the first book on the subject, and the official book of Geocaching.com, we felt as if we were breaking new ground covering the sport in its entirety.

What You'll Learn in This Book

In our effort to make this book user-friendly, we have divided the chapters into four parts. In **Part 1, "Welcome to High-Tech Hide-N-Seek,"** we cover the basics of what geocaching is and how it all got started. We go over the game's limited rules and offer information and advice to help you get started. We then give you the rundown on GPS: what it is, how it works, and how accurate it can be. We cover the benefits and limitations so that you can use the gear to its fullest potential.

In **Part 2, "Get Off the Couch and Play!"** we get down to the business of playing the game. We go over the Geocaching.com website to learn how to find caches to seek, and how to post a cache of your own. We also go over the details of playing the game: how to use maps and clues to find your first cache, as well as what to consider when you are placing your own. We then go pro with lots of useful advice on finding the tough caches as well as dealing with potential hazards on the trail. Geocachers are creative and help the sport develop through new variations of playing the game. We go over many of the game options and learn all about hitchhikers and travel bugs.

In **Part 3, "Finding Your Way Around,"** it's time to find yourself with help from above. You'll learn the ins and outs of selecting, setting up, and using GPS. Learn how to save waypoints and track logs and routes so that, hopefully, you never get lost again. It's also back to basics to learn low-tech navigation skills (like how to understand coordinate systems and how to read a map and compass). We also cover how to use computers for geocaching, whether on your desktop or in the field.

In **Part 4, "Welcome to the Community,"** learn about the geocaching community. Although caching is often considered a solitary activity, there are thousands of cachers out there who like to get together online or for events. We cover these get-togethers and discuss how to get involved in competitive events. It's then time to take a look at the many uses of GPS, and how these possibilities fit into geocaching. We look at the brief but explosive growth of the sport, and how GPS games are finding their way into more traditional sports. Finally, we look at the environmental issues and try to determine just how geocaching will evolve in the future.

Extras

We've added these extras to help you navigate through the world of GPS and geocaching. Keep a lookout for *Signal the Groundspeak Frog* for a fun way to learn important tips, language, and warnings.

Eureka!

These provide tips, discoveries, and trivia.

Geo-Lingo

These help define technical or slang terminology.

Navigation Nuggets

These provide useful advice specific to GPS and navigation.

Dead Batteries

These provide a caution or warning to help keep you out of trouble.

Acknowledgments

This project took some help and there are a number of people to thank who helped make this book possible. First of all, a special thanks to Jeremy Irish, Bryan Roth, Elias Alvord, and the rest of the crew at Groundspeak.com, the headquarters for Geocaching.com. Also, thanks to Mikal Belicove, Michael Hall, and the rest of the staff and editors at Penguin Group (USA) Inc./Alpha Books. Their follow-through and patience made this book possible. Thanks to GPS manufacturers Garmin and Magellan. We have to thank a bunch of great geocachers like the group at Emerald Valley Cachers in Eugene, Oregon. This includes Jim Dezotell, Tara Negelhout, Jay and Amy Fox, Lee Shive, and the team of Fractal and Soup. Also, many other geocachers around the country: Dan and Tanja Muret, George Malina, David Pleto, Team Magellan, Markus Wadell, Tracy Galsim, J. Pac, and Kevin Shipley.

Finally, I need to thank my bride, Shari, for her assistance and support, as I'm afraid she has become a writer's widow. Also, thanks to my children, Eric and Mikayla, who would agree we need to go geocaching more often! Everyone's efforts are most appreciated, and it's an honor for me to be involved in this endeavor.

Trademarks

All terms mentioned in this book that are known to be or are suspected of being trademarks or service marks have been appropriately capitalized. Alpha Books and Penguin Group (USA) Inc. cannot attest to the accuracy of this information. Use of a term in this book should not be regarded as affecting the validity of any trademark or service mark.

Part 1

Welcome to High-Tech Hide-N-Seek

All set to hit the trail and search for hidden treasure? First things first! Geocaching has been around just long enough to develop quite a few of its own traditions. And even though GPS technology makes staying found easy enough, it's good to understand how it works before depending on it out in the field.

In Part 1, we cover the basics of geocaching, what it is and how it all got started. We cover how to play the game, what to stash, and how to make your explorations go more smoothly regardless of whether you're a rank newbie or a seasoned pro. We also explain the technology behind geocaching. GPS, the global navigation system provided by the U.S. government, enables us to find our way anywhere in the world and makes geocaching possible. We cover its benefits and limitations so that you can learn to use the gear to its fullest potential.

What Is Geocaching Anyway?

In This Chapter

- ◆ What is this geocaching anyway?
- ◆ How this all got started
- ◆ Why the time is right for a high-tech adventure sport
- ◆ Big family fun on a baby budget
- ◆ Reasons to play and skills to learn
- ◆ What type of caches are out there?

The scientists who developed global positioning satellite (GPS) technology probably never thought it would develop into a sport, but that is exactly what happened. Geocaching is one of the most exciting and quickly growing games in recent history. But is it a game, a sport, or a relaxing and scenic family activity? It is all of these things, depending on how and where you play it and the energy you put into it.

Geocaching is a great sport for many reasons. Not only is it a great way to enjoy the outdoors, it is also a fun way to learn navigation skills. Finding caches will help keep your GPS and navigation skills sharp as you save *waypoints* in a GPS receiver and then find them in the field.

Geo-Lingo

A **waypoint** is a selected point of interest that can be saved, stored, and then recalled from a GPS receiver's memory. It is basically a coordinate address for any location anywhere in the world.

This chapter introduces the game and tells you how it is played. You'll learn why this game is unique in the way it combines high tech with the great outdoors and why now is a perfect time for this type of activity. There are a number of reasons you will enjoy this game; even your kids will think it's great! You'll learn about the geocache community and how the game got started.

This is a typical cache with a logbook and its treasure stored in a watertight container.

Geocaching.com

What Is Geocaching Anyway?

Geocaching combines "*geo*" for geography and "*cache*," a term used for both hidden provisions and, in a more modern sense, data stored on a computer. Put them together and you have the newest and hottest outdoor activity going. Enthusiasm for the game has quickly spread as participants combine their love of the great outdoors with their interest in modern technology. It isn't often when you can tap into an outdoor game that has a government budget of more than half a billion dollars a year!

The sport began after the Clinton administration removed selective availability from the GPS system in May 2000. That was the scrambling technique that made GPS receivers inaccurate up to 100 meters. Now that they're accurate within 15 meters 90 percent of the time, it is possible to save the location of hidden caches with some precision.

As of this writing, geocaching is played in 192 countries. There are approximately 450,000 participants worldwide seeking more than 75,000 actively registered caches. The number of caches continues to grow at a rapid rate as new sites are posted daily from around the world. It's fun to have a look to see how many stashes are located within your wilderness backyard. You might be surprised at the number out there just waiting to be discovered.

Eureka!

Geocaching.com was established in August 2000 with 75 caches posted online. Three years later, there are now more than 75,000 hidden in 192 countries around the world.

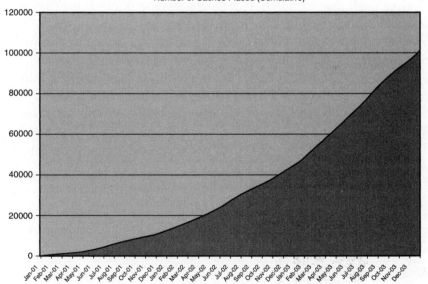

Number of Caches Placed (Cumulative)

This graph shows the popularity explosion of the game since its beginnings in May 2000.

Geocaching.com

The goal of geocaching is to locate hidden treasure from latitude/ longitude coordinates found on websites such as Geocaching.com. The treasure consists of neat stuff in ZipLock bags, stored away in hidden watertight GI ammo cans or plastic boxes. Caches are hidden in the wilderness, parks, or even urban locations accessible to the public. How the stashes are hidden depends on the skill and creativity of the one doing the hiding. Some are easy to find, others take some work. They could be on a cliff, in a cave, hidden in a hollow log, even underwater. Caches include a difficulty rating for finding the cache as well as the terrain to get there.

Treasure can include nearly anything of value. Common items are books, CDs, toys, tools, games, camping gear, and even cash. Successful seekers take something, leave something else, and then sign the cache's logbook. As much fun as it is to find someone's stashed booty, many geocachers find that the reward is more in the challenge of the hunt.

What's the point, you may ask? Doesn't GPS take you to the exact location? Yes and no. Actually finding a location in the outdoors is often more difficult than it sounds. Going to a cache's coordinates will take you to the approximate location, but not exactly, due to the system's inaccuracy. Remember, GPS is only accurate to 15 meters most of the time, assuming the receiver has a clear view of the sky. That's 49 feet on a good day! Also factor in that the receiver of the person who hid the cache is inaccurate, and if it's under tree cover, that throws the equation off further. The bottom line is you may have more than 5,000 square feet of wilderness to cover, and that's a lot of plants, rocks, and trees to look around. In fact (although rarely), some caches are never found!

Websites like Geocaching.com provide you the coordinates of the cache, but not how to get there. The person who hid the first geocache of record, David Ulmer, reminds us that there are 360 ways to get to any one location. Roads on a map may not be accessible, and a map may not show the difficulty of the terrain.

After the cache has been found, or not, seekers can post feedback, or logs describing their geocaching adventure. These postings are fun to read and provide clues to new hunters, and are a way to document previous adventures. Persons posting comments should be careful not to post *spoilers*, giving too much information, making it too easy for the next person, such as saying, "We couldn't find it until we looked on the south side of the big tree!"

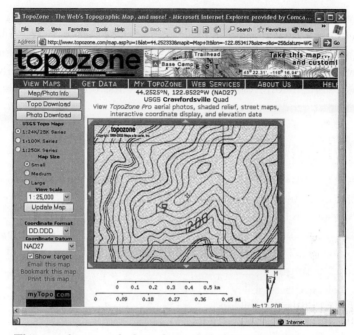

*This map shows a cache located on a dashed line representing an
unimproved road.*

Image courtesy of TopoZone.com and Maps a la carte, Inc.

This map from TopoZone.com is an example of the maps available
from the geocaching websites. This map shows the Shotgun Park geocache stashed by the Oregon Trail Four-Wheel Drive Association.
Finding this cache requires off-road driving or hiking to get to this
remote location.

Geocaching is so new that there are not a lot of rules. People who hide
caches can be as creative as they like, providing cryptic clues to find
them. Outdoor groups and clubs are using various forms of GPS treasure hunting to improve navigation skills as well as to add more excitement to their events.

How It All Got Started

You might be surprised to learn that geocaching has only been around
for a few years. With the limited accuracy of available GPS signals

prior to 2002, geocaching would have been much too difficult. A GPS receiver could only get you so close to the cache and then you'd have to spend a lot of time searching a broad area. After the removal of selective availability in 2002, the resulting increase in accuracy combined with some creative thinking on the part of some individuals led to beginning of geocaching.

GPS Users Get an Instant Upgrade

On May 2, 2000, at approximately midnight, eastern daylight savings time, the great blue switch controlling *selective availability* was pressed. Twenty-four satellites around the globe processed their new orders, and instantly the accuracy of GPS technology improved tenfold. Tens of thousands of GPS receivers around the world had an instant upgrade.

> **Geo-Lingo**
>
> **Selective availability** (SA) was an intentional error in GPS technology. When turned on, accuracy of GPS was around 300 feet. It would be like trying to find and catch a hopping "You are here" sign in an area the size of a football field. Today's accuracy ranges from 6 to 20 feet.

The announcement a day before came as a welcome surprise to everyone who worked with GPS technology. The government had planned to remove selective availability—but had until 2006 to do so. Now, said the White House, anyone could "precisely pinpoint their location or the location of items (such as game) left behind for later recovery." How right they were.

London, Paris, New York, Beaver Creek?

For GPS enthusiasts, this was definitely a cause for celebration. Internet newsgroups suddenly teemed with ideas about how the technology could be used.

On March 3, one such enthusiast, Dave Ulmer, a computer consultant, wanted to test this accuracy by hiding a navigational target in the woods. He called his idea the "Great American GPS Stash Hunt" and posted it on an Internet GPS users' group. The idea was simple: Hide a container out in the woods and note the coordinates with a GPS unit.

The finder would then have to locate the container with only the use of his or her GPS receiver. The rules for the finder were simple: "Take some stuff, leave some stuff."

On May 3, he placed his own container, a black bucket, in the woods near Beaver Creek, Oregon, near Portland. Along with a logbook and pencil, he left various prize items including videos, books, software, and a slingshot. He shared the waypoint of his "stash" with the online community on sci.geo.satellite-nav:

N 45 17.460°   Latitude   W 122 24.800°   Longitude

Within three days, two different readers read about his stash on the Internet, used their own GPS receivers to find the container, and shared their experiences online. Throughout the next week, others excited by the prospect of hiding and finding stashes began hiding their own containers and posting coordinates. Like many new and innovative ideas on the Internet, the concept spread quickly—but this one required *leaving your computer* to participate.

Within the first month, Mike Teague, the first person to find Ulmer's stash, began gathering the online posts of coordinates around the world and documenting them on his personal web page. The "GPS Stash Hunt" mailing list was created to discuss this emerging activity. Names were even tossed about to replace the name "stash" due to the negative connotations of that name. One such name was "geocaching."

The Origins of "Geocaching"

Geocaching, first coined by Matt Stum on the "GPS Stash Hunt" mailing list on May 30, 2000, was the joining of two familiar words. The prefix, *geo*, for Earth, was used to describe the global nature of the activity, but also for its use in familiar topics in GPS such as geography.

Caching, from the word *cache*, has two different uses, which makes it very appropriate for the activity. A French word invented in 1797, the

> **Geo-Lingo**
> Due to the global nature of geocaching, there are various pronunciations of the term. However, the most common pronunciation is jee-oh-kash-ing, like riding in a jeep and cashing a check.

original definition referred to a hiding place someone would use to temporarily store items. The word *cache* stirs up visions of pioneers, gold miners, and even pirates. Today the word is still used in the news to describe hidden weapon locations.

The second use of *cache* has more recently been used in technology. *Memory cache* is computer storage that is used to quickly retrieve frequently used information. Your web browser, for example, stores images on disk so you don't have to retrieve the same image every time you visit similar pages.

The combination of Earth, hiding, and technology made *geocaching* an excellent term for the activity. However, the "GPS Stash Hunt" was the original and most widely used term until Mike Teague passed the torch to Jeremy Irish in September 2000.

The Birth of Geocaching.com

For the first few months, geocaching was confined to existing experienced GPS users who already used the technology for outdoor activities such as backpacking and boating. Most participants had an existing knowledge of GPS and a firm grasp of obscure lingo like datums and WGS84. Due to both the player base and the newness of the activity, players had a steep learning curve before going out on their first cache hunt. Tools were scarce for determining whether a cache was nearby, if one existed at all.

As with most participants, Jeremy Irish, a web developer for a Seattle company, stumbled upon Mike Teague's website in July while doing research on GPS technology. The idea of treasure hunting and using tech-gadgets represents the marriage of two of his biggest interests. Discovering one was hidden nearby, Irish purchased his first GPS unit and went on his first hunt the following weekend.

After experiencing the thrill of finding his first cache, Irish decided to start a hobby site for the activity. Adopting the term geocaching, he created Geocaching.com and applied his professional web skills to create tools to improve the cache-hunting experience. The cache listings were still added by hand, but a database helped to standardize the listings, and features like searching for caches around zip codes made it easier for new players to find listings for nearby caches.

With Mike Teague's valuable input, the new site was completed and announced to the stash-hunting community on September 2, 2000. At the time the site was launched, there were 75 known caches in the world.

If You Hide It, They Will Come

Slashdot, a popular online magazine for techies, reported the new activity on September 25, introducing a larger group of technology professionals to the activity. *The New York Times* picked up the story and featured it in its "Circuits" section in October, starting a domino effect of articles written in magazines, newspapers, and other media outlets around the world. CNN even did a segment in December to profile the new hobby.

However, because there were so few caches in the world, many would-be participants discovered they didn't have a cache listed nearby. Many wondered whether anyone would bother looking for a cache if they hid one in their area. The growing community chanted the mantra "If you hide it, they will come" to the newer players. After some reassurances, pioneers of the hobby started placing caches just to see whether people would go find them. They did.

Eureka!

"SD #1" was hidden on March 3, 2001, in South Dakota, the last state in the United States to get a hidden cache. The eighth finder discovered it in January 2002. After that discovery, the cache went missing and its maintainer retired it. It can still be found in the archives at Geocaching. com.

Through word of mouth, press articles, and even accidental cache discoveries, more and more people have become involved in geocaching. First started by technology and GPS enthusiasts, the ranks of geocachers now include couples, families, and groups from all walks of life. The excitement of the hunt appeals to both the inner (and outer) child. Today you can do a search on just about anywhere in the world and be able to walk, bike, or drive to a nearby hidden cache.

Since Geocaching.com's creation, geocaching has doubled in participants every six months. When the website was launched, the pioneers of the game probably never imagined what an international phenomena caching would become. As they say, the rest is history.

Timing Is Everything

Sometimes, multiple factors have to come together in just the right way at just the right time for a new phenomenon to be created. How else could we explain the immediate popularity of GPS gaming? If you think about it, it all makes sense. Our traditional sports were created around 100 years ago in a low-tech, agricultural, and industrial age. Now children grow up playing video games and operating computers. Most of the population utilizes high technology for work, entertainment, and convenience.

As children, we grow up with a sense of adventure in finding something. From our earliest memories, we recall hunting Easter eggs and hearing stories of pirate's treasure. We enjoy games like hide-and-seek or capture the flag. We live in a unique time when we experience technology that quickly develops from an obscure concept to a daily necessity. Consider the last 15 years, with the rise of personal computers, cell phones, GPS, and the Internet. We can only imagine what's next, and we often wonder how we got by without this gadgetry before.

But along with the rise of technology, we have witnessed the rise of various extreme sports. Adrenaline junkies push themselves to the limits of their abilities and common sense for barroom bragging rights. That is why the time is so right for a game like geocaching. We get to utilize the latest technological advancements in navigation and the web, and challenge our mind, body, and spirit with the childlike excitement of uncovering hidden treasures.

A Hobby, Game, or Sport?

Geocaching is what you make it depending on the player's obsession level. It can be played anytime, as often as you like. You can do it by yourself or with the whole gang. After you get the hang of using GPS and finding caches, you'll enjoy sharing your adventures with fellow cachers on the web, or better yet, in person. When you are really ready to get serious, you can join a team for competitive events. There are annual tournaments around the country and around the world where players get the chance to play for big cash and prizes.

Geo-Lingo
Trade items and **McToys** are common terms used to describe the geo-treasure just waiting to be found.

Cache Me If You Can

Because this game is so innovative and continues to evolve, you cannot expect it to be a one-cache-fits-all kind of game. You need to be aware of a number of different kinds of caches before selecting one to find for yourself. Common cache types include …

- **The standard.** The good ol' watertight container filled with goodies neatly, or not so neatly, organized in ZipLock plastic bags. They're usually weatherproof containers such as GI ammo cans, plastic boxes, or buckets.

- **Microcache.** This is a micro container small enough to hide just about anywhere. Many of these caches are barely large enough to store a logbook. It may be just a sheet of paper to sign in on. Sometimes they provide coordinates or directions to find another cache site. Most likely there will not be enough room for a pen, so be sure to bring your own. Containers are usually film containers or some other kind of small, watertight box. Some have magnets so they can be attached to objects in urban environments.

- **Multi-Cache.** A multi-cache ("multiple") involves two or more locations, the final location being a physical container. There are many variations, but most multi-caches have a hint to find the second cache, and the second cache has hints to the third, and so on. An offset cache (where you go to a location and get hints to the actual cache) is considered a multi-cache.

- **Webcam Cache**. These are caches that use existing web cameras placed by individuals or agencies that monitor various areas like parks or road conditions. The idea is to get yourself in front of the camera to log your visit. The challenging part, however, is that you need to call a friend to look up the website that displays the camera shot. You will need to have them to save the picture to log the cache. If you're a tech-head, you could use your wireless modem and save the image yourself on your laptop.

- ◆ **Virtual cache.** This is usually some form of a unique object existing on the landscape—possibly a monument of some kind with no container to find at all.

- ◆ **Benchmarks.** These are brass markers found in the United States and originally placed by surveyors. Many are at the tops of mountains or near historical landmarks.

More types of caches with new variations are being created all the time. We will get into variations of the game after covering more of the basics.

The Cacher Community

Participants are more than lone individuals in the wilderness. People who play this game—whether alone, with a family, or in a group—consider themselves part of a community. The geocaching community extends from a local bunch of friends and families, across the country and around the world. Clubs and groups have sprung up everywhere. You most likely have a group nearby, or at least in your state. These groups often have elaborate websites, and the members get together frequently for all kinds of events, or at least pizza.

The community is made up of adventurers from all walks of life, races, ages, and sexes, loosely bound to each other by their common interest: to enjoy and promote a sport they love so much. What that means to you is that no matter where you travel, if you are a geocacher, you can always make a new friend and have a cache or two to find.

This is a player-driven and self-regulated sport. Participants take pride in their activity and its positive reputation. It is important to always obtain permission from the landowner or managing agency prior to placing your cache. Also, never place a cache in any area that would be considered a potential environmental hazard, such as in a bed of flowers or rare plants. Caches that are hidden in potentially environment-damaging areas might tarnish the excellent reputation cachers enjoy and make it more difficult for geocachers to work with park agencies and officials to obtain permission for future cache placements.

It is also important to remember this is often a family activity, so nothing should be stashed that is considered harmful, illegal, or in bad taste. Most geocache websites will not knowingly post caches that are in inappropriate areas or are filled with illegal or hazardous contents.

The Complete Idiot's Top Ten Reasons to Go Geocaching

10. It's a great excuse to use that SUV and all that outdoor gear.

9. It's a fun way to learn GPS, navigation, and outdoor skills.

8. It's a great excuse to go hiking in the rain.

7. Finding a remote cache with a loved one can be very romantic.

6. You'll get some exercise, and it's more fun that dieting.

5. You can entertain yourself on the cheap.

4. You can do something together with the whole family.

3. It's a great way to make new friends.

2. You will see places you never new existed.

1. You get to go outside and play!

The Least You Need to Know

- Geocaching involves finding someone else's hidden treasure using a GPS receiver and your detective skills.

- Geocaching has only been around since the middle of 2000, but there are thousands of caches hidden all around the world.

- Caching is a great sport to get you outdoors, anytime, anywhere.

- Caching is fun for the whole family and can be played on a budget.

- Geocachers make up a community of participants from around the world.

Chapter 2

Game Basics

In This Chapter

- ◆ How do you play this game, anyhow?
- ◆ Learn the lingo
- ◆ One man's garage sale is another man's treasure
- ◆ Geocaching environments
- ◆ Grab your gear!

In this chapter, you'll learn the basics of the game and a little about how to speak the language. We'll familiarize you with website features to get you started with your first cache hunt. We'll cover what environments caches are found in and how to prepare for a successful outdoor trip. Did you know that geocachers have designated their own radio frequencies? Read on, you are getting closer to hitting the trail!

Game Basics

So you want to go geocaching? Well you can't play yet until you learn how it's done. Pay attention class, its time for Geocaching 101.

The first rule of the sport is to get out and have fun! Okay, there are more specific rules to play, although they are more like guidelines rather than hard-and-fast rules. That's because geocaching is flexible and tends to evolve in the direction the participants take it in.

We will cover all these procedures in detail, but first, the basics: The idea is that the participants select a cache from a website that posts information on caches to be found. After a cache is selected, the coordinates to the location are entered or downloaded into a GPS receiver. It is then up to the players to use their navigation and detective skills to seek out the hidden container.

This is all possible with help from above. Twenty-four GPS satellites in space broadcast coded signals right to your receiver. After locking on to four of these satellites, your receiver can pinpoint your location by triangulating with the GPS satellites. When your receiver knows its location, you can use it to find the coordinates of the cache. The receiver provides the details needed to find the cache by displaying the cache's distance and *bearing* plus a pointer arrow.

Geo-Lingo

A **bearing** (also known as azimuth), is a compass degree to be followed to find your target. When we go after a geocache, our GPS receiver provides a bearing as one of a compass's 360 degrees.

For example, the receiver might read "Distance: 2.8 miles, Bearing: 185°." But even knowing where the cache is located on the planet is only half the battle. It sounds easy, but as you will discover it may take more work than you think. Not only will you have to navigate uncharted terrain, but when you reach the location it may take some serious searching, depending on the accuracy of the GPS receiver and the craftiness of the hider.

Take Something

Congratulations! You've discovered your first cache. Now what? Well, let's crack it open and see what you have found.

After pulling off the watertight lid, we find a bunch of items all stored in resealable bags. Don't worry, it is not as dubious as it looks. Items are stored in plastic bags to keep those items all clean, organized and dry. Let's see: a Magic Eight Ball, a book on dog training, a windproof lighter, a couple of silver dollars, and a "Best of the '80s" CD. You have worked hard for it, now choose your reward! You snag the CD for the ride home.

Leave Something

If you do take something, don't forget to replace the item with something else for the next lucky visitor to discover. The treasure can be almost anything you might feel is valuable, but try to replace the item you found with something of equal or better value. Because you planned ahead, you assembled your own swag in a plastic bag to leave behind. Placing a cool key chain that includes a compass, a minilight, and a carabiner in the cache, you leave a true treasure for the next person to find.

Sign the Logbook

Did you see a bobcat on your way to the cache? Was it an unusually cool day? Did your dog enjoy a swim in the nearby lake? Make sure to write it all down in the cache logbook. Also write down the date of your visit and the members of your party. If you took anything out of the cache, write down what you took and what item you left. It's also nice to leave a message thanking the person who hid the cache and letting him or her know how much fun you had finding it.

Often the owner will leave a disposable camera. Take a picture of yourself and your group. The cache's owner will enjoy seeing who showed up at the cache. Who knows? Maybe your picture will be posted on a website and seen by people all over the world!

Cache In, Trash Out

Before you head back in, don't forget to give back to the outdoors and leave the area a little cleaner than you found it. *Cache in, trash out* is a geocaching motto adopted to encourage good outdoor civic responsibility. While out on your hunt, carry a trash bag to pack out whatever trash you find along the trail. Doing so not only sets a good example for other hikers, it also improves the looks of the area.

You'll not only feel like a superhero, it's also a great way to camouflage yourself on the last 40 feet to the cache.

Share Your Experience Online

After you return to the warmth and safety of your keyboard, you also have an opportunity to share your experience with others online. Make sure to return to the website and post a log entry for the cache listing, which will inform the online community of your find. If you have any digital photos of the hunt, you can upload them for others to view. Just be careful to avoid giving away too much information in the online logs so others have the same challenge locating the cache.

This is also a great time to inform the owner of the cache if there are any issues with the placement. Is there construction going on in the area? Is the placement of the cache appropriate? Is there a leak in the container? Is the logbook full and in need of replacement? Any feedback that can help update the cache owner on the cache's status is always welcome.

Learn the Language

"Where in the $%@#! is the cache anyway? Is this *&@#! GPS even working?!? &@*%! blackberry bushes and poison oak!"

No, not that language. We're talking about the real terms used by veteran cachers. Of course cachers have their own lingo. You can check out the glossary for a complete list of caching and navigation terms, but here is a quick rundown of cacher slang you might hear, or things you might find on the trail:

- **Chromes.** From the term "crow miles" or "as the crow flies." GPS receivers calculate distances in a direct line to the target. Actual ground travel is often double the distance.

- **Force (The Force).** The ability to instinctively know where a cache is hidden when you get within a certain proximity.

- **Geocoin.** Small minted coins with the geocaching logo on one side and a customized impression on the other. Like travel bugs, they can be tracked through Geocaching.com.

- **Golf ball (used).** The most dreaded and despised trade item in a cache.

- **GPS receiver food.** Batteries.

- **Hitchhiker.** A hitchhiker is an item that is placed in a cache, with instructions to relocate it to other caches. Sometimes they have logbooks attached so you can log their travels. Travel bugs and geocoins are examples of hitchhikers.

- **Neocacher.** An inexperienced geocacher or a "newbie."

- **Spoiler.** Text that gives away too many details of a cache location, spoiling the experience for the next cachers who want to find it. Also used to describe a person who gives away details to other geocachers.

- **Travel bug.** A special hitchhiker, trackable on Geocaching.com.

- **Waypoint.** A selected point of interest location that can be saved, stored, and recalled from the GPS receiver's memory. Cache locations are saved as waypoints.

Log On Before Heading Out

Now you know how the game is played, and you even know a little of the language, but before you hit the trail you'll first need to go online and find a cache in your area.

Geocaching.com is the original and primary international site for geocachers. It includes an extensive list of caches throughout the United States and in more than 190 other countries.

The website includes a great deal of information on how to get started and how to search for caches. It also provides information on what GPS is and how it works. This site also has chat forums and useful links. Surfing around the website is a great way to get up to speed on the activity.

From the website, you can also find links to regional groups and clubs for nearly every state or major area. Many of these groups have websites full of informative local information. Many groups sponsor events, camping, pizza nights, and tournaments that make it easy to keep in touch with fellow cache hunters in your area.

The Best Stuff to Stash

There are many rewards when geocaching, and everyone has his or her own personal favorites. Some thrive on the adventure and excitement of discovery. Others enjoy arriving at a destination they wouldn't have visited without the thrill of the hunt. But many are in it for the treasure—especially the kids.

You're not going to get rich from this treasure, but you're bound to find some unique items along the way. Caches are filled with just about anything that someone might find of value, whether you think so or not! From key chains to stress balls, a cornucopia of unusual treasure is waiting to be found.

For your own personal trade items, use your imagination and have fun. Consider the items you leave as a reflection of yourself. Items don't need to be expensive, but unique prizes that will delight the next finder.

A List of Favorites

Let's be creative and resourceful to raise the bar on cache prizes. "Just use common sense and you should never have to apologize for what you left," says geocacher Jolly B. Good. Here is an example of good swag:

- Antiques
- Baseball cards
- Batteries (AA)
- Books
- Buttons (interesting or political)
- Camping gear
    - Carabiners
    - Compass
    - Emergency blanket
    - Hand and foot warmers
    - Maps

- ◆ Rain ponchos
- ◆ Small flashlights or LED lights
- ◆ Small pocketknife
- ◆ Waterproof matches
- ◆ Windproof lighter
- ◆ Whistle
- ◆ Calculators
- ◆ Cigars
- ◆ Collector items
- ◆ Comic books
- ◆ Computer/video games or software
- ◆ Disposable cameras (but do not take the cache's)
- ◆ Dollar Store stuff
- ◆ CDs, DVDs, or videos
- ◆ Flags
- ◆ Gemstones
- ◆ Gift certificates
- ◆ Geocaching website gear (stickers, hats, pins)
- ◆ Jewelry
- ◆ Rolls of film
- ◆ Money (cash, coins, or silver dollars)
- ◆ Small first-aid kits
- ◆ Stickers
- ◆ Tickets
- ◆ Tools (allen wrenches, pliers, screwdrivers, multitools, or tape measures)
- ◆ Toys

- Action figures, Barbie, or GI Joe

- Crayons or colored chalk

- Decks of cards

- Die-cast cars and trucks

- Plastic army men

- Puzzles

- Games

- Traditional toys like Lego's, Mr. Potato Head, or Magic Eight Balls

Geocacher Signature Items

Many geocachers, after they become more active in the hobby, create their own *signature items*. A signature item is an object of personal meaning that geocachers place in caches for others to find. It's like a calling card to leave behind for others, and in many ways reflects the personality of the owner. Some geocachers use their personal craft skills to create items, like wood carvings, painted stones, or unusual items like chain mail stress balls! Others will make their own stickers or design a stamp for their logbook. Some go as far as designing coins, pens, and other items to place in caches.

Geo-Lingo

A **signature item** is a trademark item used as the cacher's own calling card. These are often custom cards, tags, stickers, or coins bearing the cacher's name and often a favorite phrase or graphic to sum up the cacher's philosophy.

Many of these signature items become collector items for other geocachers. Finding a local geocacher's coin in a cache can sometimes feel like owning a Babe Ruth rookie card.

If you want to create your own signature item, try to imagine something that reflects your own interests. If you're into snowboarding, you could design a stamp with a snowboarder and your username. If you like spiders, create a spider out of wire and attach it to a piece of cardboard with your name. You don't have to spend a lot of money to create a unique item to leave in caches. And other geocachers can get to know you by the items you leave for them.

George and his two sons. "Dad and the Dynamic Duo" have a unique signature item. How long does it take to make a dress shirt out of a dollar bill?

George Malina

What Not to Stash

Geocachers do their best to self-regulate their sport to keep the activity in a positive light. However, as with any activity, there can always be the occasional bad egg. Because this is a family activity, not only should we obey the local laws, we also need to apply common sense to the items placed in a cache. Even so, some items that seem harmless can be inappropriate cache items. The following are just some of the inappropriate cache items:

◆ Alcohol

◆ Ammunition, knives, explosives, or weapons

◆ Drugs or drug paraphernalia

◆ Food

◆ Pornography

Food? We list food because animals can find food even faster than the best cachers. Animals have been known to chew through caches to get the grub. That's the best-case scenario. If it's not found in a reasonable amount of time, it could go bad and make the whole cache nasty.

Areas Where Caches Are Found

Caches can be found almost anywhere, from remote mountain peaks, to city parks, to dense urban jungles. This is the beauty of the game: It can be played anywhere. You can discover caches in a park next to your neighborhood, in another city while on vacation, or in many exotic locations around the world. Here are some advantages to caching in these different environments.

Wide Open Spaces

What makes geocaching truly special is that it will take you to beautifully scenic wilderness areas you would probably never take the time to seek out for yourself. We all enjoy a scenic drive in the country, but how often do we push ourselves to climb up and over that next ridge? Caching in wilderness areas might involve a trip to a waterfall just off the beaten path, rock climbing, or a multiple-day hike. Whichever way, it is not uncommon for the world's natural beauty and the experience of actually being in the middle of it to take your breath away. It is also not uncommon to hear, "Wow, this place is great, I never knew it existed!" You will find special favorite places to return to again. You may share these locations with loved ones, because words alone do not describe the sights, sounds, and feeling of being in the middle of nowhere.

Parks

Okay, so you don't always have time to knock an extra day or two off work and pack up all your gear with extra everything to venture off into the great unknown. In our fast-paced lives, parks are great places to take a breather and relax with the family or fun places to picnic and play with the kids on the playground. They are close to home and easily accessible. Because they are not far, even an hour spent feels like you had a rewarding outing. What a great way to spend the afternoon.

What's even better is that most of these areas include a cache or two. Park caches are typically easy to find, allowing kids of all ages to help take part in the search. These types of areas allow the obsessed geocachers to go on their lunch hour!

Out on a limb for this cache.

Eric Peters

Urban Jungles

A good percentage of our world is made up of concrete and steel. Skyscrapers replace mountains, and wildlife tends to be of the two-legged variety. Don't let that stop you from taking part in the hunt. Caches are hidden in all parts of a city. Some are above or below ground, possibly in abandoned cars or buildings. Microcaches are often used to make them easier to hide. Statues and landmarks may also serve as virtual caches. Remember:

Navigation Nuggets

Outdoor navigation and travel is much easier if you are organized. Keep all of your essential gear in a bag or pack. This saves time and helps to ensure you will not forget anything.

Do not let your location discourage you. Caches can be found nearly anywhere you may live or go.

Hitting the Trail

Finally! You are almost ready to go. You are so close to finding your first cache you can almost feel those elusive prizes in your hand! Not quite yet: First things first. It's time to pack our bags before heading out. You may have your GPS receiver ready, but there is a bit of planning to go before hitting the trail.

Here's an example of a small, easy-to-carry pack with essential gear.

Jack W. Peters

We recommend setting up a bag, waist pack, or small day pack with all the basics neatly organized and always ready to go. This way when the phone rings and it is time to go play, you do not have to search the house, garage, and car for all of your stuff.

Here is the basic list of gear to take with you:

◆ **GPS receiver.** Don't forget the power cord so you can use it in the vehicle on the way there.

- ◆ **Batteries.** Bring a lot of AA's. Not only are they necessary food for your GPS receiver, they are also good to have for your flashlight and camera.

- ◆ **Maps.** Bring general maps of the roadways to get there, and a more detailed topographic map of the area. Waterproof map cases with marking pens are also helpful.

- ◆ **Flashlight.** It can get dark when venturing into the unknown.

- ◆ **Compass.** Get one with a dial-in declination adjustment.

- ◆ **Notepad and pen.** Keep them in a watertight bag.

- ◆ **Map accessories.** A clear, watertight plastic cover with a grease pencil to write on the cover. A map ruler is also helpful for transferring coordinates between a GPS receiver and a topographic map.

- ◆ **Cache repair kit.** It's always good to bring some items to help repair caches you find on your trip. Extra pens, logbooks, sealable sandwich bags, and duct tape are good to repair leaks, protect contents, and replace missing items.

Going Out a Little Farther?

It is not so much survival of the fittest as it is survival of the smartest. If you are going anywhere off the beaten path, there is always a chance of getting lost, being caught in a storm, or, for whatever reason, getting stranded. We recommend you bring the ten essentials:

1. Water
2. Map and compass
3. Flashlight/batteries/bulb
4. Knife
5. First-aid kit

6. Extra clothing
7. Matches/fire starter
8. Sunscreen/sunglasses
9. Signal mirror
10. Whistle

Be sure to take special medications such as insulin for diabetics or prescription eyewear. In any outdoor situation, the best food and water is what you bring with you. Take a little extra of both: Someone else will forget, and you are covered in the event you extend your stay a little longer than expected. Drinking untreated water and eating from nature's salad bar will not provide the calories needed for outdoor activities, and will most likely make you sick.

Navigation Nuggets

If you do remote wilderness travel, consider using a PLB, a personal locator beacon. Now available in the United States, these transmitters broadcast a satellite-based emergency beacon to allow rescuers to find your exact location anywhere in the world.

Be sure to tell someone where you are going. In your car, leave an extra copy of the cache's information page, including the coordinates, or write this information on a travel itinerary. We provide one in the back of this book. Taking the time to do so will pay off big if you have a problem. By taking these precautions, search and rescue crews can provide assistance within hours instead of days.

Dress for Success

There is no bad weather, only inappropriate gear. Just as with packing gear and supplies, extra clothing is better than not enough. In hot or cold climates, it is typically best to cover up with long-sleeve shirts and pants. This protects the skin from scratches, insect bites, and sunburn. Wear clothing and a jacket that will shed water; your apparel should be made of fabrics that wick moisture away from your body. Also wear layers you can remove to prevent overheating. Cotton clothing, such as T-shirts and jeans, absorb water and perspiration, sometimes taking days to dry. If you get wet and cold, it is difficult to regain heat, which increases the risk of hypothermia.

Dead Batteries

Hypothermia is one of the biggest threats to outdoor enthusiasts. It is easy to get caught in a storm, but improper clothing will result in getting soaked through, resulting in the rapid loss of body heat. Keeping dry will go a long way to improve your comfort and survivability.

Don't forget a hat! Wide-brimmed boonie-style hats work great. They provide good cover from the rain and sun. Baseball caps leave the back of your neck exposed. Also wear a good pair of boots that will provide ankle support, and keep an extra pair of socks in your gear bag. Is all of this really important? Not if you're visiting a park for an hour or two. But it is in any wilderness environment. We want you to enjoy your outdoor geocaching experience, not be miserable because you're un-prepared.

Cacher Comms

Can you hear me now? If not, try the right frequency. Yes, cachers use their own radio frequencies on the FRS (Family Radio Service) band in North America and the PMR (Private Mobile Radio) band in Europe. These bands are used in walkie-talkies, which are reasonably inexpensive and do not require a license to operate. The range is limited, however, often to a mile or less depending upon the terrain. On FRS, the community uses channel 2 with channel 12 as an alternative. On the PMR band, use channel 2 with channel 8 as the alternative.

Garmin Rino GPS receiver with FRS and GMRS radio and peer-to-peer tracking.

Image used courtesy of Garmin Ltd. or its affiliates. Copyright Garmin Ltd. or its affiliates.

Garmin International makes a GPS receiver, the Rino, that includes FRS and GMRS (General Mobile Radio Service) radio frequencies. These receivers are unique in that they work as GPS receivers and two-way walkie-talkies, and have a tracking feature that allows others within range using the same model of unit to appear on the screen. This peer-to-peer tracking is a great way to keep track of the group as well as stay in radio communication.

The Least You Need to Know

- ◆ When you find a cache, take something, leave something, and sign the logbook.

- ◆ Visit Geocaching.com to find cache listings in your area.

- ◆ Geocaches are hidden in all types of outdoor environments.

- ◆ The success of your outdoor experience will greatly improve with the right gear and clothing.

Chapter 3

GPS—Rocket Science for the Masses

In This Chapter

♦ Understand what GPS is and how it works

♦ Learn about how accurate the gear can be

♦ Learn what satellite reception is needed for accurate navigation

♦ Limitations of GPS technology, and why it does not replace the map and compass

So now you know enough about geocaching to be dangerous. Let's not forget about the electronic assistance from above that makes this game possible.

In this chapter, you'll learn about the origins of GPS and how it works. You'll get a good understanding of how accurate the gear can be, as well as how to check and improve accuracy to make sure you're on track. After getting to know GPS, you'll understand why it doesn't completely replace traditional navigational methods like the map and compass.

The U.S. government, with an investment of billions of dollars, developed GPS. Now anyone with an investment of $100 can use it. Like cell phones and Hummers, this is military technology that we civilians have adopted for uses both practical and fun, like geocaching. How cool is that? Anyone can use the system after purchasing a GPS device. Read on to learn about everything you wanted to know but were afraid to ask about GPS.

DoD's Gift to Techies

GPS, an acronym for global positioning system, is a gift from the U.S. Department of Defense. Twenty-four satellites, with a couple of spares, broadcast special radio signals down to Earth that are intercepted by GPS receivers. The receivers analyze the signals to determine their exact location anywhere in the world. There has not been such a quantum leap in navigation since the Chinese invented the compass 800 years ago. Imagine: We now have the ability to record our favorite locations and return to them again. Getting lost has never been so much fun. It sounds too good to be true, but, like anything electronic, there are limitations and the possibility of failure.

Eureka!

The inspiration for today's GPS technology resulted from observing the orbit of the Sputnik 1 satellite. Launched by the Soviet Union on October 4, 1957, scientists at Johns Hopkins University's Applied Physics Laboratory developed a theory based on these observations and submitted it as part of a proposal to the Navy Bureau of Ordinance. The proposal became Transit, the precursor to the global positioning system we use today.

Evolution of the GPS Receiver

The origins of GPS began in the 1960s as a concept for a worldwide U.S. military navigation system. By the mid-1970s, it became a joint effort of various branches of the U.S. military and was referred to as Navstar. Despite the official name, GPS is the term that stuck.

The system's first major public debut was in 1991 when it contributed to the overwhelming success in the first Iraqi war, Desert Storm. With the system still in its infancy, only 16 satellites were utilized, with many specifically positioned over the Persian Gulf area. Handheld receivers, primitive by today's standards, helped allied forces navigate and maneuver around enemy positions in an unfamiliar, featureless desert. The system was considered fully operational in 1995.

In the late 1990s, improvements were made to allow receivers to track all 12 satellites simultaneously, instead of the older single-channel units (which were not quite as accurate and much slower in getting a good satellite fix). Also at this time, the prices began to drop to a more reasonable range, allowing more of the public to take advantage of the technology.

The guys scout out a new area for the best place to hide a cache.

Jack W. Peters

Useful Gear for Work and Play

GPS obviously has many applications for the military, engineers, and emergency service agencies, but this is a major development for us technology enthusiasts who love the latest technology gadgets. Even better yet, this is something that is practical enough to actually use.

For those of us who enjoy the outdoors, GPS provides us a little more freedom and confidence in backcountry travel with the reduced risk of getting lost.

With the ability to save locations as waypoints and document your travels with track logs, this technology has, for the most part, removed the uncertainty and guesswork from navigation. For example, we can save the location of a trailhead, venture off in a different direction to hide caches, and still return to the exact location of any saved waypoint. This can be done with traditional navigation skills through dead reckoning, but it's not nearly as efficient or fun as using GPS.

Satellite Signals

A GPS receiver is essentially a computer that receives signals broadcast from GPS satellites. That's why a GPS unit is referred to as a receiver, or GPSr. There are 12 satellites orbiting over each hemisphere. GPS receivers need to read the signals of at least three satellites at a time to "triangulate" the equipment's exact location. Four are needed for a more accurate three-dimensional fix providing elevation and the precise atomic time. The more satellites the receiver can lock on to, the more accurate the position information.

Navigation Nuggets

GPS devices are known as receivers because they intercept special radio signals broadcast from GPS satellites to determine their location on earth. There is often confusion over whether someone else can track the user's position. Recreational GPS gear does not transmit data. No one will know your position unless you have communication equipment adequate enough to tell them.

Triangulation works by a receiver downloading radio signals broadcast from each satellite it can lock on to. The satellites are in a stationary orbit, which allows the GPSr to calculate its location by determining the distance from each overhead satellite. Satellites broadcast their radio signals in a sphere. The unit's computer determines its location by determining where all of the spheres intercept. This is why accuracy readings substantially increase with the more satellites a receiver can lock on to.

The government broadcasts two sets of coded signals. Military equipment can receive both the (P) and (CA) signals for highly accurate readings. Civilian gear only accepts the slightly less accurate (CA) code. Despite this limitation, most receivers with a clear view of the sky will be accurate within 49 feet, (15 meters) more than 90 percent of the time.

Benefits of Using GPS

Modern receivers offer many features, maybe more than you'll ever need or use. All of the buttons and screens can be a bit overwhelming. Despite being a high-tech electronic item, they are actually quite easy to use. The more you practice with the gear, the more your intimidation will turn into interest as your confidence grows. You will enjoy discovering the equipment's features and capabilities and how they can be applied in the field.

Here Is What to Expect

Regardless of the brand, size, or price, GPS receivers are designed to provide the same basic functions. More expensive models provide a greater memory storage capability. They also provide a basemap to display on the receiver's screen. Even the least-expensive models will provide many of the following basic features:

- A display indicating your position anywhere in the world, typically within 49 feet (15 meters) of accuracy. The current location is displayed on a view screen as a pointer icon.

- Receivers record data that is displayed on the view screen and stored in the unit's memory. Such data includes saved points of interest known as *waypoints*, as well as an electronic breadcrumb trail indicating where you have traveled, known as a track log.

- Provide time of day, elevation, speed, compass readings, and ETA.

- Provide a pointer, bearing, distance, and ETA to selected waypoint destinations.

Navigation Nuggets

GPS receivers provide elevation information after acquiring a fix on four or more satellites. This altimeter function is usually not as accurate as the location data, but will most likely get you within 100 feet (27 meters). Some receivers have built-in barometric altimeter to help ensure greater accuracy.

◆ More expensive models provide a built-in basemap. These are electronic maps provided from the manufacturer. A receiver's basemap may include all of North America or the United Kingdom.

◆ More expensive receivers provide additional memory for map storage. This is used to enhance the basemap with topographical map data or other information selected by the user, available online or on a CD-ROM from the manufacturer.

How Accurate Is Accurate?

Accuracy remains about the same regardless of the brand, size, or price of a receiver. Receivers work on line of sight to the overhead satellites, so the whole trick to accuracy is allowing the antenna to get a clear view of the sky. Because the government's selective availability is no longer in effect, a GPS receiver should be able to lock on to its location anywhere in the world within 49 feet (15 meters) more than 90 percent of the time. Not perfect, but somewhere within 50 feet (13 meters) will be close enough to find a cache, your camp, or anything else you might be looking for.

Thankfully, in May 2000, the government eliminated selective availability. This was a military safeguard that deliberately made the GPS signals civilians could receive inaccurate by 100 yards or 91 meters. The government got around the security problem by scrambling the signal around military bases and other sensitive sites. As previously mentioned, this major development allowed caches to be hidden and found again, inspiring the game of geocaching.

Receivers can also provide elevation information. Unfortunately, their altimeter function is not always as accurate as their other location data. Altitude readings may be off as much as 100 yards (91 meters). Special systems have been developed for aviation and boating, for which absolute accuracy is required for autopilot features and for navigating around hazards in low visibility. Accuracy is improved by including radio signal broadcasts that help fine-tune the user's position. There are two systems that increase GPS accuracy, the original differential correction known as DGPS, and WAAS. The DGPS system is primarily used around seaports and waterways and requires an additional differential beacon receiver.

WAAS

Fortunately, a new system that improves accuracy considerably has been developed. Known as the wide-area augmentation system (WAAS), this system typically improves accuracy from 15 meters down to 3. It was created for the aviation industry and includes 25 ground reference stations with a master station on each U.S. coast. These stations monitor and correct GPS signal interference caused by satellite drift and signal delay through the ionosphere. The corrected messages are then broadcast from one of two geostationary satellites. This corrected signal improves accuracy to less than 3 meters 95 percent of the time. Currently WAAS is available only in the United States, although other governments in Europe and Asia are developing similar systems.

Most GPS receivers sold after 2000 are capable of accepting WAAS signals. Luckily, there is no additional cost or equipment needed to use this system. When using your receiver, check the satellite status page to determine whether the system is searching for, or has picked up, WAAS signals. Be aware that the WAAS feature uses more battery power. Your receiver can most likely be set to turn this feature off if battery use is an issue.

Factors That Affect Accuracy

The main cause of inaccuracies in civilian GPS equipment is ionospheric interference. This is caused by the delay of radio waves as they travel through electron fields in the ionosphere. Military receivers send two sets of signals that allow the ionospheric delay to be measured and compensated for. Nothing can be done for civilians to correct this inaccuracy other than DGPS and WAAS. Civilian GPS users must learn to accommodate for the equipment's inaccuracy.

A second problem is multipath interference. This is caused by error from a receiver picking up satellite radio signals that have bounced from terrain obstacles, such as buildings or cliff walls. Civilian receivers cannot distinguish the ricocheting signals from the ones traveling directly from the satellite to the receiver. Water droplets on overhead vegetation can also cause this problem. Be aware of your surroundings and understand that overhead vegetation, especially if it is wet or snow covered, will distort GPS signals considerably.

If you doubt the accuracy of your position, check the satellite status page to determine the current signal strength and quality. You may have to get into a clearing for a better view of the sky. Also be aware that tall buildings and cliff walls will be a factor. Sometimes adjusting the receiver itself will also help. Receivers with built-in antennas work best when held straight up and down.

Getting a Fix

When you fire up the receiver by pressing the power button, the computer begins seeking out satellites. You have a satellite fix when the receiver picks up enough "birds" (satellites) to activate the navigation process. GPS radio signals work on line of sight, meaning they travel to the receiver in a straight line. So we know the signals will not bend around obstacles like heavy tree coverage or cave walls, but fog, dust, rain, or other extreme weather conditions do not affect them.

Depending on the quality of an antenna and a user's position, an average of seven or eight satellites may be locked on at any one time. Under ideal circumstances, like on a hilltop, all 12 may be received. Only picking up three signals will result in a two-dimensional (2D) reading. This operation will provide location information that may be inaccurate by as much as several miles, and no elevation data will be provided. At a minimum, four satellites are needed to obtain a three-dimensional (3D) fix. This will provide reasonably accurate location and elevation data. Accuracy is greatly improved with every additional satellite received.

When in doubt, check the satellite status page on your GPS receiver often to determine what kind of accuracy you can expect. This page provides a great deal of information, including the receiver's working status and the number of signals received at any given time. Through graphs, the signal strength will appear for each satellite. A satellite geometry graph will display how they are positioned overhead. This is important because satellites clumped together or arranged in a straight line will provide poor geometry. The best satellite geometry is provided when there is at least one satellite directly overhead, with several others on the surrounding horizon

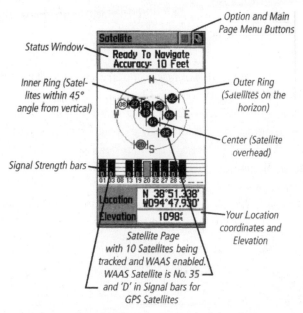

Image used courtesy of Garmin Ltd. or its affiliates. Copyright Garmin Ltd. or its affiliates.

Two different accuracy readings are also provided. There is a signal strength indicator known as the DOP number. This stands for dilution of precision. The smaller the DOP number, the better the satellite geometry. Good satellite reception is represented by the number two or smaller. Readings below the number 3 should provide accuracy within 15 meters. Readings from 4 to 6 could provide inaccuracies up to 100 meters. A reading of 6 indicates that the receiver is failing to maintain a satellite lock.

The other indicator is the EPE, the estimated position error number. This measurement also considers satellite geometry to determine the estimated accuracy in feet or meters. Check out these readings often to determine your level of accuracy and to ensure the antenna and gear are working properly.

Initialization

When you turn on the receiver for the first time, it will not be sure of its location. The gear needs to initialize itself to determine its location. This process is also necessary if the receiver has traveled a few hundred miles away from its home area with the power shut off, like when you take it on vacation. The receiver may initialize automatically, although it may be necessary to point out your approximate location on the receiver's basemap.

To initialize a receiver, go outside to an area with a clear view of the sky and turn the receiver's power on. The unit may prompt you to select an initializing method. If your receiver includes a basemap, choose By Map. Use the cursor arrow to zoom to your current location on the map page and press Enter. The receiver will now start to read satellites from the new location. After satellites are fixed, the present position pointer icon will appear in the center of the map page to show your exact location. When the receiver switches over the map page showing your position, it is an indication that enough satellites are received for the equipment's navigation function to work properly. Now you're ready to go.

Dead Batteries

GPS receivers do not replace the traditional magnetic compass. Although receivers have a compass feature, it does not activate unless the unit is moving at more than 4 miles per hour. Some receivers include an electronic compass to get around this problem.

GPS Limitations

Wow, we can know exactly where we are at any time, anywhere in the world. With that kind of technological power, we can toss out the maps and compass and forget about paying attention to where we are going, right? Not exactly. GPS seems too good to be true, but there are limitations. For one, receivers are electronic just like your cell phone and computer hard drive. You wouldn't trust your life to one of those, would you? Gear can fail. It can also be damaged, lost, waterlogged, or stolen.

The other issue is that it needs power to operate. If you have the equipment set up in your truck, plugged into the cigarette lighter, it's not a problem; you can leave it on all day. For hiking and geocaching, however, the gear has to rely on battery power. A receiver with dead batteries is nothing more than an expensive doorstop. Check the battery gauge. This meter often looks like an E-to-F fuel gauge and is often found on the satellite status page. Always bring spare batteries. Carry at least six or more AA's in a resealable plastic bag. Even if your receiver doesn't run out of power, you may need them for your flashlight or camera.

Even though GPS receivers include a compass feature, they do not replace the traditional compass. This is because the receiver's compass will not work if the gear is in a stationary position. A receiver has to be traveling at least 4 miles per hour before its computer can calculate the direction you are traveling. This is why, when you ask your receiver to navigate to a waypoint, the compass pointer arrow could be off in any direction, which we refer to as "loose bearings." When you start moving, the arrow immediately aligns to the correct bearing.

GPS manufacturers have attempted to get around this problem by adding electronic compasses to receivers. This is a good idea, although they can be a bit cumbersome to use and the feature drains batteries faster. So you still need a good old-fashioned compass. Look at the bright side, though: You will learn how to use it in Chapter 13.

Using GPS, map, and map ruler, Shari plots her location on a topographic map from coordinates saved in the receiver.

Jack W. Peters

Backing Up the Gear

As you can see, as many benefits as GPS provides, one is not the ability to replace the traditional map and compass. Equipment failure and dead batteries are not that uncommon, and getting lost or stranded turns a pleasurable outing into a serious nightmare. Because the consequences could be tragic, these skills are too important not to learn.

Knowing traditional navigation skills will greatly increase your confidence in backcountry travel and allow you to use your GPS receiver to its fullest capacity. Besides, you will need to know how to read a map and compass to go geocaching! Part 3 covers using GPS, maps, and a compass in detail.

The Least You Need to Know

- GPS is a U.S. government technology that anyone can use.

- GPS devices calculate their position by receiving satellite signals.

- GPS receiver accuracy is typically within 15 meters and can be improved further with the aid of WAAS.

- GPS receivers need to lock on a minimum of four satellites to navigate accurately.

- GPS devices have limitations besides their accuracy: They can fail, and their batteries go dead.

- Learning traditional navigation skills backs up the electronic gear and allows you to navigate and geocache more efficiently.

2

Get Off the Couch and Play!

So you've got a basic understanding of how to go out and find a cache, and you understand how GPS works well enough to trust it in the woods. Now it's time to go out and explore everything geocaching has to offer. You might be surprised to learn that there's more to it than just crashing around in the woods: City slickers can geocache without leaving sight of an espresso shop! In this part, you learn about the many geocaching variations. Maybe you'll come up with one of your own!

Enthused about finding your first cache? In Part 2, you'll learn about how to find caches on the web before finding them in the wild. We then cover everything you need to know to find even the toughest caches, and then discuss how to hide your own. It's then time to go over some potential hazards to be sure that you come back from your adventures in one piece.

You'll also discover travel bugs and hitchhikers. These tokens represent their owners, traveling from cache to cache across a country or around the world.

Chapter 4

Navigating Geocaching on the Web

In This Chapter

- ♦ Learn which websites to search for caches
- ♦ Set up your own user profile
- ♦ Learn the many ways to seek out a cache to find
- ♦ What to consider before seeking a cache
- ♦ Use maps and aerial photos
- ♦ Learn how to post your own cache

After learning the basics, at last it's time to go geocaching.

Before we find a cache, we first have to find a cache to seek. In this chapter you'll learn the many ways to select a cache as well as how to get the maps and clues you need to ensure success. Do you use a personal digital assistant (PDA) and need more caches to find? We'll show you how to download lists of caches to take with you. You'll learn about the neat topographic maps and aerial photos available, and we'll show you how to post a cache of your own.

The primary website for geocaching is Geocaching.com. As the head-quarters for geocaching, potential problems and questions have been anticipated for new participants. Spend some time cruising around the site and checking out the various features. The website provides an-swers to frequently asked questions, allowing the greenest of newbies to go out hunting in no time.

Developing Your Cacher Profile

One of the first steps you can take to get involved in geocaching and become a member of its community is to log in and set up your own account. This is your opportunity to provide your cacher name, e-mail address, the area where you're from, a photo or image, and other details you want to share with the community. Other geocachers will be able to access your profile to learn a little more about you and what caches you may have found or hidden. With your new geocache identity, you'll also be able to participate in discussion forums.

Searching for Nearby Caches

Searching for nearby caches is easy. In fact, they're everywhere! You will be surprised to see the number of listings within 100 miles of where you live. The trick is to know how to select the interesting ones to hunt. The following is a list of ways to search for the perfect cache to seek:

♦ **By zip (postal) code.** Postal codes are available in the United States, United Kingdom, Canada, and Australia. On the front page of Geoaching.com, simply type in a zip code and press Enter. A list of caches will appear in order from the nearest to the far-thest from the center of the zip code's region.

♦ **By state/country.** Select a state or country to search. After a state or country has been selected, a menu list of cities or states will appear to narrow your search.

♦ **By keyword.** Search for caches by keyword. This method is ideal for recalling caches, especially if you can't remember the entire name.

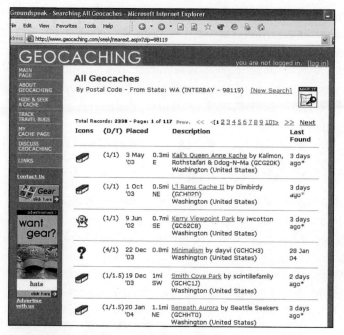

A quick search by zip code provides a long list of caches listed by the distance from the zip code's center.

Geocaching.com

- ◆ **By username.** Search the database for fellow cachers. Select a username and you can get a list of caches found or hidden by this person.

- ◆ **By waypoint name.** When a cache is submitted for posting, the website creates a unique code for the cache listing. Geocaching. com's caches begin with GC followed by letters and numbers, and are six characters or less so they can fit in the waypoint title field on most GPS receivers.

- ◆ **By address (United States only).** Based on a mailing address, the site determines the closest coordinates and does a search. This can be more precise than a zip code search, but the data can be imprecise and become outdated quickly.

- ◆ **By cache type.** Search for caches by their type. Options include All caches, Traditional, Multi, Virtual, Letter box Hybrids, Event, Mystery, and Webcam.

◆ **By coordinate.** This is the most precise query available. Using a specific waypoint, you can do a distance search from your exact position.

As you can see, there are many options to search for that perfect cache. All of these features make it easy to get a list to track down no matter where you may travel.

Paperless Geocaching

After a few geocaching outings, you'll come to realize that printouts of cache listings are one of your more valuable tools on the hunt. The description of the cache location, parking coordinates, and even hidden clues in the name of the cache will often give you that extra bit of information you need to find the more elusive caches. And, of course, any hints provided by the hider will assist you if you ever get stuck!

A cache as it would appear on a PDA using Mobipocket Reader.

Geocaching.com

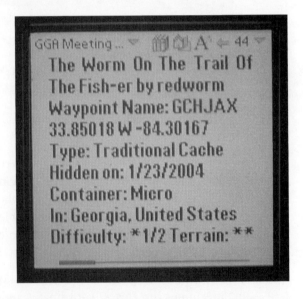

You'll also discover how cumbersome it can be to enter a waypoint for every geocache you want to seek. Hand entering coordinates can sometimes result in accidental errors, perhaps causing your GPS receiver to show a geocache to be 100 feet to 100 miles from its actual location.

Double-checking your coordinates before going out on a hunt will help, but fortunately there are alternatives to hand entering coordinates and carrying reams of cache listings along on your hunts.

As the game has grown, so have the features for both enjoying a paper-free existence and downloading geocache waypoints directly to your GPS unit. With a few simple steps and some free software, you can spontaneously geocache without having to return to your computer.

Downloading Coordinates

Transferring cache coordinates from the Internet to your GPS receiver is easier than you might think. However, you need a computer-to-GPS data cable. These cables are available for most brands and models of GPS receivers with the possible exception of some lower-end GPS units. Some more expensive models even come with their own data cable.

After you have a cable, you need to get a file of caches you want to download to your GPS unit. After you create an account and log in to the website, search for nearby caches. On the page of results, you'll notice there is a check box to the right of every cache listing. Select caches you want to download to your GPS by checking the box next to each listing, and then click the Download Waypoints button at the bottom of the page.

If you haven't agreed to the license agreement, you will be redirected to another page. Otherwise your browser will prompt you to save a file named something like geocaching.loc to your computer. The LOC file format contains a list of coordinates for each selected cache, a web link for the location of the cache description, the name of the cache, and the waypoint name to be downloaded into your GPS unit.

Now that you have your waypoint file, you need a software application to open the file and upload the waypoint information to your GPS receiver. Fortunately, many GPS applications support the LOC file format. A list is always available at www.geocaching.com/waypoints.

The software application will ask you to choose your GPS receiver before uploading your cache list, because different units have distinct ways of downloading information. Now all you need to do is send the waypoints to your GPS receiver.

> **Navigation Nuggets**
>
> If you open up a LOC file, you'll notice that the coordinates differ from the ones you see on the cache listings. They're actually the same coordinates but shown in decimal degrees, a format used by most software applications. Because most GPS receivers come out of the package in the format shown on the cache listings, the website shows them this way to reduce confusion.

Coordinates on your receiver show each cache with a name that starts with GC, for geocache. You can use this waypoint name to look up the details about each geocache on the Geocaching.com website. If you prefer, you can change the name of each cache to something more descriptive before uploading it to your unit.

Pocket Queries

Now that you have the coordinates downloaded to your GPS receiver, wouldn't it be nice to have a copy of each cache listing so you can have more details about each hunt? Although it is straightforward to print out a few cache listings, 10 or more would quickly become impractical. Many geocachers like to hunt on vacation, when lugging a laptop and Internet connection would be difficult, if not impossible. Because normal GPS receivers can store up to 500 waypoints, carrying around a volume of cache listings would kill more than a few trees.

If you own a PDA, like a Palm or PocketPC device, Pocket Queries can be your best geocaching companion. Pocket Queries is a service for premium members of Geocaching.com. It allows you to receive a file that contains a listing of caches tailored to your interests, which you can then upload as an eBook to your PDA. You will also be provided a LOC file of the same cache listings to upload to your GPS unit. Using the search feature in your eBook reader, you can quickly view each cache listing and hints while out on a hunt.

Pocket Queries can be customized to search by cache type, ones you haven't found, caches hidden between dates, and many other alternative searches. It's like having a copy of Geocaching.com in your pocket. Up to five queries can be scheduled to generate as often as on a daily basis, and are e-mailed directly to your e-mail inbox.

If you prefer, you can request an alternate format called GPX, or the GPS eXchange format. Similar to the LOC file format, GPX is a file type that can be read by many GPS applications. It combines the way-point information from LOC files with the eBook cache listings to allow software programs the freedom to provide alternative features for searching, sorting, and viewing cache data.

Check out Chapter 11 for more information about using PDAs and computers with GPS.

Selecting a Cache to Seek

As you can see, the difficulty is not in finding a cache to seek; instead, it may be more challenging to select one from all that are available. So you found a cache that looks interesting? Let's take a closer look to see whether this might be the one to find first. You need to consider a number of things before packing up the crew and hitting the road.

A Land Rover club tracks down a Jeep Club cache. Reaching this remote location will require off-road driving or a long hike.

GPS Navigator Magazine.com

- **Access.** Is the location next to a parking lot? Is it permissible to use bikes, wheelchairs, and horses?

- **Children.** Is the site kid-friendly? Can searchers bring a stroller, and is there a restroom or a playground nearby?

- **Cost.** Some parks charge for admission.

- **Distance.** Check out the distance so that you can plan how to get there. It's great to find caches in park areas within walking distance.

- **Dog-friendly.** Check out any factors that might affect whether Rover can come along.

- **Special equipment.** Does the cache location require a special vehicle or other equipment to reach? This could include rock climbing or scuba gear.

- **Terrain.** Get an idea about how far this cache might be off the beaten path. Should you wear shorts and sandals or long pants with boots? Depending on the location, there could be hazards like poison oak or sticker weeds. Remember that for hiking in brushy areas, more clothing coverage is best.

- **Time consideration.** Is this a cache you can snag on your lunch hour or is it a weekend excursion? Travel time will be a factor in determining how long it will take. Be sure to add a little more time than you think you might need.

- **Weather.** Caches in higher elevations could be snowed in for much of the year.

Cache Difficulty Ratings

When you're ready to report your own cache, you can fill out the questionnaire through a link on the Report a Cache page on Geocaching. com. There you can answer questions about the difficulty of finding your cache, and the program will provide a one- through five-star rating. Even so, giving a score for your cache can be somewhat subjective.

Difficulty

- ★ **Easy.** The cache is in plain sight or can be found in a few minutes of searching.

- ★ ★ **Average.** The average cache hunter will be able to find this in less than 30 minutes of hunting.

- ★ ★ ★ **Challenging.** An experienced cache hunter will find this challenging, and it could take up a good portion of an afternoon.

- ★ ★ ★ ★ **Difficult.** A real challenge for the experienced cache hunter. May require special skills or knowledge or in-depth preparation to find. May require multiple days or trips to complete.

- ★ ★ ★ ★ ★ **Extreme.** A serious mental or physical challenge. Requires specialized knowledge, skills, or equipment to find the cache.

Eureka!

The most extreme geocache ever was placed by Lord British, on July 19, 2002. The inventor of the Ultima Online game series, he placed it using a Russian Mir submersible in the Atlantic Ocean. The cache is more than 1.4 miles underwater, at the bottom of the ocean near a hydrothermal vent. If you ever find it, make sure to retrieve travel bug TB31F1.

Terrain

- ★ **Handicapped accessible.** Terrain is likely to be paved, is relatively flat, and less than a half-mile hike is required.

- ★ ★ **Suitable for small children.** Terrain is generally along marked trails, and there are no steep elevation changes or heavy overgrowth. Less than a 2-mile hike required.

- ★ ★ ★ **Not suitable for small children.** The average adult or older child should be okay depending on physical condition. Terrain is likely off-trail. It may have one or more of the following: some overgrowth, some steep elevation changes, or more than a 2-mile hike.

★ ★ ★ ★ **Experienced outdoor enthusiasts only.** Terrain is probably off-trail. Will have one or more of the following: very heavy overgrowth, very steep elevation (requiring use of hands), or more than a 10-mile hike. It may require an overnight stay.

★ ★ ★ ★ ★ **Requires specialized equipment, knowledge, or experience.** This cache may require a boat, a four-wheel-drive truck, rock climbing, or scuba gear, or is otherwise extremely difficult.

Using Maps and Clues

So you found a cache to seek out that fits your criteria. The distance, accessibility, and difficulty rating are just right. It's time to take a closer look at the cache's page for clues. There are descriptions offered that will probably provide useful information to this elusive stash's whereabouts. Clues might include details of the area and local landmarks. There might also be comments on what you need to bring along and what the cache itself looks like.

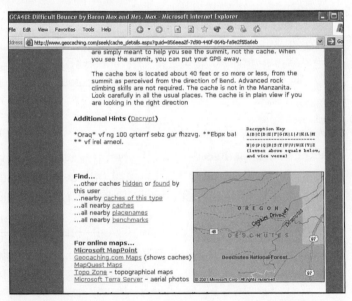

Note the clues that are provided, including the encrypted line.

Geocaching.com

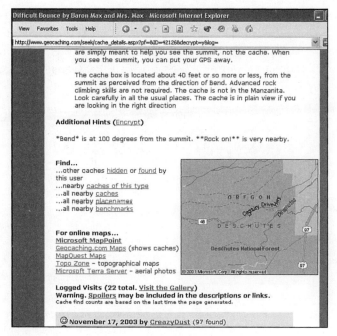

Here is the same page with the clue decrypted.

Geocaching.com

The main clue will most likely be encrypted. To read the clue in the field, you will have to decode the clue using a letter key system that is provided on the cache's web page. To make it even easier, click the Decrypt link to have the clue unscrambled before your very eyes. This clue will probably just about tell you where the cache is hidden, so you may not want to decrypt it unless you really have to.

Geo-Lingo

Contour lines are used to interpret the terrain on topographic maps. These lines provide a three-dimensional aspect of the ground. For example, contour lines on a 1:24,000 scale map typically represent a 40-foot change in elevation.

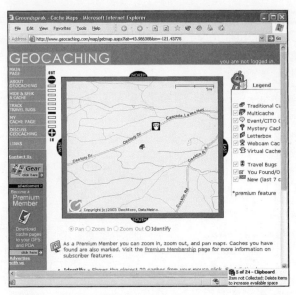

The first map provided is a general one, typically indicating where the cache is located in relation to the nearest city or town.

Geocaching.com

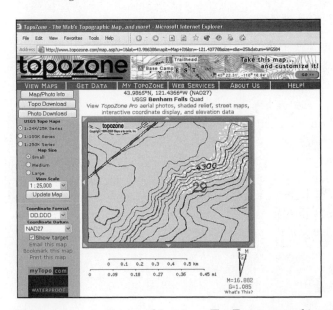

This is the same area zoomed in using a TopoZone topographic map.

TopoZone.com

The cache information page will include an option to select a topographic map. Clicking on the link will bring up a topo map with the cache appearing in the center. You can zoom in or out for as much mapping detail as you like.

Map page options include detailed 1:24,000 topographic maps from Topozone.com. Topographical maps are helpful because their contour lines allow you to analyze the terrain. Arial maps from Microsoft Terra Server are another clever option. These photos literally give you a view from above, making it easier to find roads and trails to access the cache.

The page also includes a map indicating the cache's location, depending on its type. By clicking the map, you can zoom in for more details on a separate map page. From that page, you can identify other nearby caches in case you want to plan ahead for several cache hunts.

Geocaching.com provides a premium membership feature allowing you to pull up a map showing all of the caches within a search area. Caches you have already found are labeled so you can focus on new cache challenges.

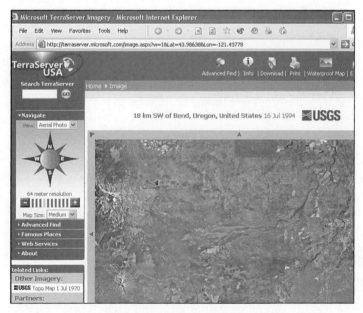

A sky view helps you find ways to access the area.

Microsoft

Navigation Nuggets

Maps are an essential guide, but don't be surprised if the map does not exactly match the ground. Maps are often inaccurate due to changes over time to roads, trails, waterways, and other features.

These maps are important for two reasons. The general small-scale maps often show you how to get to the general location. When you're there, it's time to get serious by studying the topo maps. By analyzing the terrain layout shown on these maps, you should get a good idea about the cache's location. Check out Chapter 14 for complete information about reading topographic maps.

Watching a Cache

Would you like to be notified whenever there is a change to a cache listing, or when a cache is found by another player? Perhaps the cache is in a unique location, or you simply want to be notified when the first finder logs it. Whatever your reason, if you want to be notified of changes to a cache listing you can add it to your watch list.

A watch list is a feature on Geocaching.com that allows you to be notified by e-mail whenever the status of a cache has changed. When you are logged in, this option will become visible for you to select on each cache listing. If you add a listing to your watch list, you can remove it at any time from your account preferences.

Keep in mind that if it is a popular geocache, you may receive a lot of e-mails. Also, there is no need for you to watch your own cache listings because you'll be automatically notified of changes. Sometimes you can tell the popularity of the cache listing by the number of geocachers who watch it.

Posting Your Own Cache

It's easy to report a new cache of your own. Just follow the instructions when filling out the online questionnaire, and cachers will be seeking out your stash in no time. When you are done, click the button at the bottom of the page to send it for review. You will receive a confirmation if your cache report was successfully submitted. After your cache is submitted, you will have the opportunity to post photos.

Features to list when you post your own cache include the following:

- **Type of cache.** Traditional, multistage, virtual, event, etc.
- **Size of cache.** Regular, micro, large, or virtual.
- **Name of cache**
- **Who placed the cache**
- **Date placed**
- **Latitude/longitude coordinates in decimal minutes**
- **Location by country.** Select a country, Afghanistan to the United States, and then select the individual state.
- **Overall difficulty rating.** Select a number between one and five; one being the easiest, five being the hardest.
- **Overall terrain rating.** Select a number between one and five; one being the easiest, five being the hardest.
- **Details.** Provide descriptions or details about location, difficulty, terrain, access, etc.
- **Long description.** Provide additional information about the cache, including contents and what the container looks like.
- **Hints/spoiler info.** This information will be encrypted on the site until a geocacher clicks a link to decrypt it, or decodes it on the trail. Keep your hints short so that decoding it on the trail is easier.
- **Travel bugs.** Got a travel bug? You will need to add a log entry to your cache page.

The final step is agreeing to the cache website's guidelines and user agreement terms. There are a number of do's and don'ts that we will get into in greater detail in the next chapter when we prepare to hide our first cache in the field.

Disabled Caches

After you place a cache, you are responsible for letting the website know whether it becomes missing or you no longer want to manage it. This is important because we do not want to subject other geo-cachers to the frustration of looking for a cache that no longer exists. Geocaching.com shows a cache is disabled by placing a line through the title. This means the cache is currently inactive. It can be made active again if the owner reinstates it or agrees to allow someone else to adopt it.

Geocaching websites rely on player feedback to keep the status of caches updated. If you discover a cache is missing, be sure to log on to the website to let the owner know the cache was not found. A cache owner should check out the location if there are an unusual number of "not found" log entries. The cache can be temporarily disabled to allow the owner time to check on it. If a cache owner cannot be con-tacted, the cache can be adopted or removed completely from the site. If the cache remains disabled or abandoned, it will be archived and removed from the search list altogether.

Posting Photos

Posting photos is a great way to share your adventures of caches you have hidden or found. As the owner of a cache listing or log entry, you have the ability to upload digital photos to the website. Participants in the hobby enjoy viewing the galleries and cache listings to see how other players are enjoying hunts all over the world.

As the cache owner, you may want to provide photo clues to help users find the hiding spot for your cache. After you submit your cache listing, you have the option to upload photos. Some cache owners show pic-tures of the general cache location, or a nice photo of the nearby area to entice players to seek out their cache. Some owners even develop and upload photos from disposable cameras left in their caches, which is often informative and, even more often, humorous.

The Least You Need to Know

◆ Setting up a user profile allows you to join the Geocaching.com community.

◆ Cache data can be downloaded into your GPS and PDA.

◆ Consider the difficulty rating and other factors before seeking a cache.

◆ Maps and aerial photos help you analyze the terrain to get where you want.

Chapter 5

Playing the Game

In This Chapter

- ◆ Get ready, it's time to play!
- ◆ Hitting the trail to find a cache
- ◆ Learn how to hide a cache of your own
- ◆ How to maintain your hidden treasure
- ◆ Learn how to avoid potential problems (by what not to do)

Finally it's time to go outside and play! In this chapter we are getting down to business. In this chapter, you'll learn how to go outside and find a cache or two. After you get that down, its time to hide a cache of your own. You will also learn how to maintain a cache as well as ways to avoid any potential problems.

The Hunt Is On!

At last you've selected a cache to find. You have our GPS receiver and other gear neatly organized in a pack, and everyone is anxiously waiting to go. But wait, you still have some homework to do. Actually, finding a cache is a little like detective work, a case that needs to be solved. After you select a cache, the sleuthing begins. First some research, as you comb the information page for clues. Then some CIA-type analysis as you study maps and decrypt secret codes. Finally, it's time for gumshoeing as you seek to solve the mystery of the uniquely hidden stash you've chosen.

Navigation Nuggets

A confusing issue with using latitude/longitude coordinates is that they can be displayed in two different formats. The full address includes degrees, minutes, and seconds; or the seconds are removed and the minutes are converted to a decimal number. Geocachers have chosen to use decimal minutes because many GPS receivers have a default setting for this format.

Geo-Lingo

A map **datum** is a global survey system that is used to create maps. Each datum may take a slightly different measurement of the earth. Using the wrong datum may result in positions being off by as much as a mile. The most used datum for geocaching is WGS 84, but many older maps use NAD 27.

Data Entry

The first step is to enter the cache coordinates into the GPS receiver. This requires knowing how to save a waypoint. If you do not know how to do this, check out Chapter 9, which covers waypoints in detail.

The standard geographic coordinate system used for geocaching is latitude and longitude. Latitude is a measurement of distance north or south of the equator. Longitude is a measurement of distance east or west of the prime meridian. (The prime meridian is located at Greenwich, England.) Latitude and longitude lines are measured using degrees, minutes, and seconds. More specifically in geocaching, the standard coordinate type is decimal minutes. This means that coordinates are displayed using degrees and decimal minutes instead of a full address of degrees, minutes, and seconds. If this makes no sense to you yet, don't panic! Chapter 11 covers this information in detail.

On the GPS Setup menu, typically under Position, the option will usually appear as hddd°.mm.mmm. Also be sure that the map *datum* is in the

WGS 84 format in North America. On the same Setup Position screen, the option will appear as [WGS 84]. If you are not in North America, be sure to follow the instructions on the geocache website to set your receiver to whatever datum is used for your part of the world.

Image used courtesy of Garmin Ltd. or its affiliates. Copyright Garmin Ltd. or its affiliates.

Okay, so you have the coordinates entered as a waypoint in decimal minutes. The waypoint default number has been changed to a six-digit name that references the cache's title. Print out the cache information page to take along. Use it first to double-check the coordinates to ensure every number is absolutely the same as listed on the sheet. Any data-entry error will give you an address possibly hundreds of miles off.

Dead Batteries

Be sure to double-check the coordinates when entering the data into the GPS receiver. Getting one number wrong could result in being 100 miles from the actual cache location. Don't put yourself through the frustration of searching in the wrong area.

Maps and Clues

Because this may be your first time seeking a geocache, it's okay to read the cache description, look at any pictures, and read about other people's experiences finding it. Some caches may be visible from 20 feet away, whereas others in more trafficked areas may be covered by some rocks or, in one case, in a World War II bunker! The page may also contain clues, the main one being encrypted. You could decrypt the main clue now, or make it more challenging by waiting until you have trouble finding the cache. For the first one, however, decrypt the clue. You might need all the help you can get. Because caches can often be difficult to find, it is helpful to see whether there is a clue to indicate what kind of cache container is used.

Next, check out the many map links on the page and the map shown for the listing. It will be a general map, possibly showing the cache's location in reference to the nearest town or city. Geocaching.com provides you with links to various online map sites, some of which may provide you with turn-by-turn directions to the general area of the cache.

Reviewing the map is important because you have to find the cache area before getting out and actually finding the cache. Often there is more than one way to access the area. A little analysis is required to figure out the best route to take. The road that gets you closest to the cache may not leave you at the best route to take when you get off the road.

One of geocaching's greatest challenges is figuring out how to access the cache site. GPS provides the direction and distance, but not instructions about how to get there. When you know the general area where the cache is located, it's time to check out the topographic maps. They give greater detail of terrain features through the use of contour lines. After reading Chapter 14, you'll be reading maps like a pro. First start with one of the linked online map sites to check out the area. Based on the location and potential difficulty, you can decide whether you need to buy an additional detailed topographic map.

The geocache information page maps allow you to zoom out for reference and zoom in for greater detail. The idea is to study these maps to determine the best way to access the cache. There may be more than one road that reaches the area, although you shouldn't assume the closest road will be the easiest. There could be obstacles that lie between you and that elusive treasure. Waterways, mountains, cliffs, or simply no trail are all examples of potential challenges. Another consideration is the access road itself. A map's collar information should reveal the type of roadway going in. The collar is the section across the bottom of a map that contains the map's reference information. That way you'll know whether you can bring along a Honda Civic or a Land Rover.

Road Trip!

In our case, the maps are printed and the gang is confident they know where they're going. It's time to fire up the GPS. After we get a satellite fix, we ask the receiver to show us the way to the geocache waypoint. Within a moment, the data is revealed. Distance is 21.8 miles at a bearing of 86° east. That doesn't sound so bad, does it?

Remember two important things about GPS data: Distance is measured in a straight line directly from you to the target; and with the turns, hills, and *switchbacks* of ground travel, the actual distance to the cache may often be significantly farther than the distance indicated on your GPS receiver. The compass bearing and pointer arrow also give you a straight shot to the target. Rarely can we ever follow an exact compass bearing unless flying or sailing, because there are fewer obstacles in the open sea and air.

> **Geo-Lingo**
>
> **Switchbacks** are areas on a trail that zig and zag up and down steep slopes. Although indirect, switchbacks help protect the incline from erosion; they also create a more gradual climb to the top of the hill. Always follow switchbacks when hiking.

You are off and running. The GPS is plugged into the cigarette lighter to save batteries. Sure enough, after some time spent driving, the distance slowly starts to tick down. Only 15 miles to go, and when you turn on the main road, the pointer arrow is generally pointing in your direction of travel. Two roads will take us to the general area of the cache. After careful inspection, however, you find a creek runs between the closest road and the cache site. From the map it's difficult to determine how big the creek is. That thin blue line could be anything from a dried up riverbed to a raging river. You decide to take the turnoff that requires hiking a little farther, but that's okay. It's not a race. It's all about the journey, the challenge, and enjoying the outdoors.

When we take the turnoff, the distance changes to 4.1 miles. We keep driving until we are about a mile away. If we continue up the road, the

Navigation Nuggets

A GPS receiver will not provide you with directions to a cache, only distance and compass bearing. Remember there are 360 approaches to each location (one for each compass degree). The shortest distance may not be the most accessible.

distance stops decreasing and starts to increase. So we turn around to park at a turnoff, estimating this is about as close as we are going to get from the road. Sure enough, there is a trail heading off in the general direction of where we need to be, which is also the direction toward the cache as indicated on the GPS receiver. It is now time to grab our gear, including a day-pack with plenty of water, supplies, and spare batteries.

Ground Search

We flip through the GPS receiver's pages to find a helpful one. The trail does not appear on the receiver's basemap. The compass page is selected to provide a large pointer arrow and the distance to the target. In this case, we are .85 miles away with a compass bearing of 290° west. Onward we go, down the dusty, twisted trail as the distance indicator slowly ticks down. For the person holding the receiver and watching its arrow, it is tempting to walk in a direct line, following the pointer arrow, tripping over rocks and brush, even though a neatly groomed path runs right alongside the course.

Geocaching point one: You probably do not need to bushwhack (travel off-trail). This might be necessary when you reach the cache's general location, but not three quarters of a mile away. It's time to start thinking like the person who hid the cache. Would he or she stumble over nature's obstacles for nearly a mile even though a trail leads to the same location? Besides not tripping and falling on your face, there are other good reasons not to bushwhack. Staying on trails makes less of an impact on the local environment. You may be leaving tracks and needlessly breaking tree limbs. Besides, it is not fun to get tangled in trees, thorns, and blackberry bushes. This across-land travel will get you scratched up and make it easier to get lost (as you wander in foliage that may obstruct your view). Even animals know this; that's why they use the trails, too.

This is especially true for off-road driving. Whether on a mountain bike or four-wheel-drive vehicle, traveling off the trail marks the ground and damages foliage. Off-trail travel often leads you to obstacles such as boulders or ravines, which make passage difficult. That is why someone else has already made a trail going to the desired location. Also, if you do need help, taking yourself off the beaten path only makes it more difficult for someone to find and assist you.

So after stumbling around in the weeds and rocks, we decide to use the trail. We are getting closer now, less than a half-mile, but now the trail has switched back and is heading the wrong way. Excitement turns to confusion as the group questions whether we are on the right path.

Geocaching point two: Even though a road or trail veers off in a different direction, it does not mean you are on the wrong path. Often wilderness roads switch back and curve all over to reach their destination. When you are in this situation, you have a choice of two actions to take. One is to check your map to determine where the trail or road ends up. If your path is not mapped, continue to follow it out. Keep a close eye on the distance indicator to see whether you are walking closer to or farther away from the target. If you continually get farther away, it may be time to backtrack and reassess your direction.

In our case, we decide to follow the trail out to see where it goes. Despite its curving, it does continue to lead us closer to the prize. Now, with 320 feet to go, our anticipation builds as we wonder what we'll find. The arrow leads us into a forested area filled with logs and rock outcroppings—many good places to hide a cache. There is overhead tree coverage, and we wonder how good a signal we can get. We wander into a rocky, tree-covered area and continue until we get a reading of 41 feet. Going farther on the trail only increases the distance, so we turn around for another look.

No cache and no big "X" on the ground: This might be a little harder than we thought. Turning back around, we walk until there is a reading of 39 feet. This is still not as

Navigation Nuggets

Check satellite reception often. This will give you a good indication of how accurate the gear is at any given time. Be sure to check the battery gauge while you're there. It is typically located on this page.

close as we would like to be, and the tree coverage is most likely affecting our GPS unit. This is a good time to check satellite reception.

We remember the receiver's satellite status page contains three indicators to check the potential accuracy. First, it indicates the number of satellites received. Under the trees, we only have four. Second, it indicates the EPE, estimated position error number. Our reading indicates that our receiver could be inaccurate up to 42 feet. The third indicator is the DOP, dilution of precision reading. Our number is 3.1. These numbers indicate that the tree coverage is definitely affecting accuracy.

After walking around the area, we narrow the location enough to start a ground search. Eureka! A plastic box is tucked away in a hollow log. In this case, we didn't use the encrypted code. Later, after decoding the message, we see that it reveals that we should look for a hollow log. We are glad we found the cache without the clue. That was a great search. We got to go for a hike and had fun looking around rocks and trees until we found the cache. We congratulate ourselves and take a group picture with the cache's disposable camera. The treasure we liberated was well deserved.

We found it!

Jack W. Peters

After the Hunt

Remember the rules: Take something, leave something, and enter your name and experience in the logbook. You worked hard to find it; it's your right to leave a record of the experience.

Now it's time to seal up the cache and place it back where you found it. If it was hidden in a stump or covered with rocks, place it back the way it was. Do not move the cache or leave it exposed. You want the next person to enjoy finding it also.

When you get home, e-mail the person who hid the cache to announce that you found it! A cache owner is always happy to know the condition of a cache and will be pleased to know that people are looking for it. This is especially important if the cache is damaged, vandalized, or missing. Your e-mail might give the owner a critical heads up that something is wrong with the cache, and give him or her the opportunity to fix it as soon as possible. You can also write a log detailing your experience on the website where you found the cache listing. This will allow future cache seekers to see when it was found and possibly learn from your experience. It may even help other geocachers decide whether this is the type of cache they want to visit.

Rating a Cache

Most geocachers provide feedback on the caches they find; some have even come up with a more elaborate way to rate them. Cacher Grin 'n' Bearit has developed a five green-face-grin approval rating system. The system is based on the following criteria:

1. How interesting is the area the cache is hidden in?

2. What kind of experience did I have finding this cache?

3. How is the cache hidden and camouflaged?

4. What kind of cache container was used?

5. What were the contents of the cache?

This system rates caches from one to five based on these factors:

☺ **Poor cache.** The cache is in plain sight in an area that is not very interesting. The cache is the only reason to visit the location.

☺ ☺ **Fair cache.** Nice park setting or somewhat interesting area. It is fairly well hidden or in a decent hiding spot.

☺ ☺ ☺ **Good cache.** An interesting area with a good hiding spot. The cache was well hidden, and finding it was an enjoyable experience/adventure.

☺ ☺ ☺ ☺ **Great cache.** A very interesting area with a great hiding spot. It was very well hidden, and finding it was a very enjoyable experience/adventure.

☺ ☺ ☺ ☺ ☺ **Awesome cache.** One of the most interesting places I've seen. Most likely, very few people know of this area. The seeker probably would not have ever found this place by just looking at a map. This was one of the most memorable experiences or adventures I have had while geocaching.

Do you have to provide feedback or rate the caches you find? No, of course not, but it is a way of letting the owner know about what you think of his or her cache-hiding ability. Feedback also gives future cache seekers an idea of what to expect; just remember to not give away spoiler information.

Hiding a Cache

So you have found a few caches by now, and it's time to move up the geocaching food chain. No longer just a seeker, you are now ready to join the elite ranks of those who hide geocaches. Great! Read on to learn how to place a geocache that you and fellow seekers will be proud of.

The first step is to research a cache location. Geocaching is just like real estate—location, location, location! When thinking about where to place a cache, keep these things in mind:

◆ **Will it be easy to get to?** If the cache is just placed a couple hundred feet from the highway, there will be a strong chance that someone may plunder it. Try to find a place that will take a bit of time to get to, preferably on foot.

- **Will it be easy to find?** If the cache is too visible, or too close to busy roads or trails, there's a good chance someone will find it by accident. Several of the original caches were discovered this way. Fortunately, most of the people who found them were nice enough to leave them alone, or they started participating themselves. But don't make it too difficult to find! After you hide it well, leave good hints and an encrypted clue on the geocache information page.

- **Will it be on private or public land?** Before hiding a cache on private land, please ask permission! If you place the cache on public land, contact the managing agency to find out about their rules and permission-related requirements.

- **Does it meet Geocaching.com's listing requirements?** During your research, review the guidelines for listing a geocache. Most of these guidelines are listed under Do's and Don'ts.

As the owner of your geocache, you are ultimately responsible for it, so make sure you know the rules for the area where you place your cache.

Finally, place a cache in a place that is unique in some way—a location, possibly challenging and scenic, that will leave a lasting impression on its visitors. Ideally, the site itself will be as great of a reward as finding the cache. Use your imagination and think of some of your favorite outdoor spots. A secret getaway, a prime camping spot, a great viewpoint, or some kind of unusual location are all good places to hide a cache.

Container Considerations

You have many options for containers; the primary requirement is that they hold up to the elements. Depending on your climate, the container will have to hold up to rain, snow, dust, and heat. Often, containers are camouflaged to blend in with the natural environment. This makes them more difficult to find, especially by someone who might stumble across one by accident.

Eureka!
Geocache containers can be nearly anything that is durable and watertight. Ammo cans and plastic boxes work great. They can be as large as a 5-gallon bucket or as small as a film container. Camouflage helps prevent muggles from finding the cache.

Geocachers have had success with various types of plastic buckets and boxes. Tupperware and Rubbermaid containers work well. Military ammo boxes work great because they're strong, watertight, and already painted an elusive olive drab. Again, be creative. Capped-off plumbing pipes work, too, but be careful not to make any container look like it could be a bomb. Microcaches are often plastic film containers or some other type of small waterproof capsules, usually just large enough to contain a small logsheet. Others are made out of fake rocks, mint tins with magnets, and waterproof match cases. To determine which type of container is most appropriate, think about where you will be placing it.

You'll also want to invest in some ZipLoc-style baggies. These help you to organize the cache contents and help protect them if the container leaks. Whichever type of container you choose, be sure to identify your cache so that someone who doesn't play can figure out what it is. Most folks mark the container with "Geocache" or "Geocaching.com," and the name of the cache. It's a great idea to include an information sheet explaining what a geocache is and contact information for if it needs to be moved. This data may help keep it from being ransacked or removed by someone who does not know what it is. Check out the Cache Notification Sheet in Appendix E. Make your own copy to laminate or place in a waterproof bag. Geocaching.com has a list of cache notification pages that have been translated into many different languages for placement in a variety of different countries.

Next you'll need a logbook and a pen or pencil. A small spiral notebook does the trick. If the cache is in an area that will freeze, use a pencil; pens can freeze and refuse to work in the cold. Be sure to place the logbook and pen in a plastic bag. Now it's time to stock the cache with goodies. Chapter 2 included lots of ideas about what to stash.

When you stash the container, never bury it. However, it is okay to cover it up with rocks, bark, moss, and dead branches. Concealing the cache a bit helps keep it from being found by *geo-muggles*. Place the container in a hollow log or stump or secure it with a heavy log or rock to decrease the chances of it blowing, floating, or washing away.

Saving the Coordinates

After the cache has been placed, it is time to save the coordinates as a waypoint. If you haven't already, be sure to come up with a unique name for your cache. You'll use the name

Geo-Lingo

Muggles (or geo-muggles) are nongeo-cachers, usually people on the trail who look suspiciously at a geocacher on the hunt, or who have accidentally found a cache. Geocachers borrowed the term from the *Harry Potter* series, in which it refers to non-magical persons. Geo-muggles are often puzzled but are usually harmless. Geocachers often try to avoid being seen by geo-muggles in order to keep the Geocache safe from curious potential plunderers.

when saving the waypoint. Saving a waypoint is easy. Press and hold the Enter button on your GPS receiver until a new waypoint screen appears. Title the waypoint to match the name of your cache. You will have to abbreviate it because most receivers limit your title to only six digits or letters.

If your receiver has an averaging feature, use it to record the most accurate waypoint possible. This feature allows you to take the waypoint's reading over a span of time, usually a minute or two, to improve accuracy.

If your receiver does not have this option, you can use a couple of tricks to do it anyway. One is to save multiple waypoints of the same area; however, this is more effective if done over time. Selecting the waypoint in the center averages the position. You can use this same technique with the Track Log feature. Leave the receiver on to record a track log. After some time, zoom in to the recorded track log "blob" and save the center as a waypoint.

Just as when you entered a waypoint to find a cache, save your waypoint in the same format. Be sure to use decimal minutes and the WGS 84 map datum in North America. After you have your waypoint, it's not a bad idea to write it in permanent marker on the container and logbook, and make sure you have a copy to bring back with you.

As covered in Chapter 4, it is time to go online to post your new treasure box for the world to find. Don't forget to fill out the cache- and terrain-difficulty rating systems. When you post a cache, it is up to you to make sure all the information is correct. No one from a geocaching website will personally get out to see the site before approval. When a new cache is submitted, it is reviewed for inaccuracies, bad coordinates, and appropriateness before being posted on the web.

If you hide it, will they come? You will find out soon enough.

Care and Feeding of Your Cache

After you place the cache, it is your responsibility to maintain the cache and the area around it. You need to return as often as necessary to ensure that your cache is in good shape and is not having a negative impact on the area. After it has been visited, it is not a bad idea to check with the persons who found it to ask their opinion of its condition and placement. Have a look when you can to make sure it is in good condition and stocked with trade items. If you have concerns about the location, discontinue the cache site and move it to a better location. When the cache is active, it can last as long as you or someone you appoint will manage it.

Ask Permission

When in doubt, ask permission before placing a cache. Most wilderness areas have postings that indicate who owns or manages the area. Especially with private property, be sure to ask the owner first. Chances are they will not know what you're up to or what geocaching even is. It is up to you to make the case that it is a legitimate activity and that they will not regret their decision to allow you to use their property. Getting permission is very important for at least three reasons. Asking to use someone else's property is the right thing to do. Besides that, the property owner will not remove your cache because he or she will know what it is. We also do not want the property owner to think the people looking around on his or her land are trespassing.

Be aware that the United States National Park Service does not allow geocaching on the property it manages. In fact, it considers caches violations of federal regulation. These strict regulations are intended to protect the often fragile, historical, and cultural areas they manage. This does not mean, however, that there are no caches in National Park Service areas. Remember virtual caches? You cannot leave anything behind, but you are allowed to use the monuments and landmarks that are already there.

Dead Batteries

As the cache owner, it is up to you to ensure that its placement and the foot traffic being brought into the area do not cause problems or environmental damage. As soon as you realize the cache is in a poor location, discontinue the site immediately and relocate it to a better location, or remove it entirely.

Cache at the Little Bighorn monument (Crow Agency, Montana).

Jim "Fresh Meat" Dezotell

Do's and Don'ts

As mentioned before, the geocaching community is a self-regulating group. There are no geopolice to ticket you for placing a bad cache or leaving behind inappropriate booty. Something even worse would happen: The game and its participants would start getting a bad reputation for being careless with safety, or possibly damaging to the environment. This type of reputation will do nothing but cause us to be viewed negatively, resulting in bad press and the closure of areas to geocaching. Cachers know this, and, with minimal exception, have gone out of their way to ensure that geocaching goes on without causing concern or problems for others. Here are some important points to remember:

- ◆ Use common sense when thinking about a location for your next cache. Consider the possible impact it may have on the local area. Remember that your cache could attract a number of visitors.

- ◆ Do not place a cache in any area that's home to rare or endangered species and plants. Also avoid areas with delicate ground cover: Consider the number of people walking around the site.

- ◆ Do not place caches on archaeological or historical sites. These areas could be negatively affected by the extra traffic the cache may cause.

- ◆ Do not leave behind any alcohol, tobacco, weapons, or drugs.

- ◆ Do not leave a cache in an area posted "No Trespassing."

- ◆ Do not bury caches or leave them in areas near railroad tracks or military installations.

- ◆ In our age of concerns over terrorism, do not place caches under public structures deemed potential targets.

- ◆ Do not place a cache while on vacation; you need to be available to maintain it.

- ◆ Do not place caches that solicit customers or are perceived to be posted for religious, political, or social agendas. Geocaching is supposed to be a light, fun activity and not a platform for an agenda.

The Least You Need to Know

◆ The decimal minute format is the most commonly used for cache coordinates.

◆ Be sure to use the correct datum to avoid serious error.

◆ Know how to use maps and clues for assistance in finding caches.

◆ Geocachers should keep cache owners up to date on the status of their caches.

◆ Maintaining a cache is a responsibility: You must keep the site where you posted it up to date and you must follow up on reports about its status.

◆ Geocaching on private property without asking permission, or on public lands where it's discouraged, puts the sport in a bad light.

6

Geocaching Tricks and Tips

In This Chapter

◆ Lots of good stuff to know before and during your geo-caching adventure

◆ Learn techniques to find caches like a pro

◆ Learn how to keep yourself safe while on the trail

◆ What to do when encountering nongeocachers

At last you know how to geocache. You've learned how to use the web and how to get outside to seek and then hide your own caches. Hopefully by now you've had the opportunity to experience the thrill of the hunt for yourself. If so, this new activity could go beyond an occasional weekend pastime to a full-blown obsession.

Have you been bitten by the bug to the point that you try to find ways to sneak out to get just one more cache? At night, are you looking around ferns and rocks in your sleep? We thought so. There is just one reasonable thing to do, and it's not therapy or counseling. No, it's time to go pro by learning from the best! We have assembled the best advice we could think of to help you find 'em fast and get you home by dinner.

Good Advice

We're not your mother, and many of you are not accustomed to taking advice, but we are giving it to you anyway. This is an attempt to consolidate the best geo-wisdom, tricks, and tips we could think of to transform you from a stumbling newbie to a seasoned professional.

This chapter covers good, commonsense information that is actually important to know for any outdoor outing. This chapter also offers you specific search techniques that will help make even the toughest caches easier to spot. Because the outdoors is still a wild place, this chapter also provides more information to help you get there and back in one piece. What do you tell nongeocachers you run into while on the trail? This chapter covers that topic, too.

Before You Leave

Tell someone where you are going. Use the travel itinerary in Appendix F to leave vital information on what caches you are going after. Besides leaving the coordinates, let someone know whom you're traveling with, what communication gear you have, and what time you expect to return.

Bring a friend! It's always good to have someone with you when venturing outdoors. It's easy to have car trouble, get lost, or twist an ankle. Having someone with you can help overcome these challenges and get you back home safely. Besides, geocaching and the outdoors are always best when shared with a friend.

Bring along a notepad and camera. You may see awe-inspiring areas that take your breath away. You will visit areas you have never seen before, and may not again if you don't take some notes. In the excitement of the moment, it's easy to forget the names of parks, trailheads, and waterfalls, or the unmarked turnoffs to get you there. Make notes and save lots of waypoints in your receiver. Don't forget extra batteries and film. A lightweight tripod works great to allow everyone to get in the frame if no tourists are about to take a bad shot for you. Taking pictures is a great way to document your trip and enjoy your travels again and again. It's also fun to post your photos on the cache's page to share them with others.

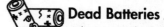

Dead Batteries

When searching for a cache, make sure to give yourself enough time to get there, find it, and get back. Unrealistic trip planning may result in running out of daylight.

Outdoor travel often takes longer that you might think, especially if you are venturing out to unknown territory. When planning your trip, be realistic and give yourself enough time to get there and back.

The problem with being caught outdoors longer than you plan for is that it gets dark. A day trip with a wrong detour can easily turn into a night trip. Always make sure to bring at least one flashlight with a spare bulb and batteries. Have a DD cell for your main pack, a AA cell for your belt or day pack, and a micro or LED light for your key chain.

There is nothing worse than leaving for a trip only to realize you forgot something. Organize your navigation and outdoor gear in the same place. Appendix G is a gear checklist.

Print out the cache's information page and maps to take with you. This is important to check coordinates and clues if you get stumped. Don't forget to bring something of value to leave behind in the cache. Also bring a pen for writing in logbooks.

Don't forget to bring and drink plenty of water.

On the Trail

Do not spend too much time staring into the receiver's screen. If you do, two things will happen: You will miss the beauty of the natural surroundings, and sooner or later you'll crash. Have your passenger check out the screen while driving.

Dead Batteries
    Whether walking, rid-
ing, or driving, taking
your eyes off the road to watch
the receiver's screen too often
could ultimately lead to a
crash. Be careful or your
friends will have to use the
coordinates to call in the para-
medics.

Before heading out on foot for a
remote cache, save your vehicle's
location as a waypoint. It's easy to
get disoriented, even when using
GPS. Having the trailhead saved as
a waypoint provides you a location
to navigate back to.

Pay attention to where you're going
and be aware of the surroundings.
Get a reverse perspective by looking
at the landscape behind you. This
is important because this is what it will look like on your return trip.
Occasionally, stop and make a 360-degree turn to study the landmarks
around you. Besides major ground features, can you see the sun or
moon? Recruit assistance from others to help keep track of where
you're going as well as your location on a map.

Respect the land by treading lightly. Do not leave tracks or break
foliage when not necessary. The best way to travel through outback
areas is by leaving no trace. More

Navigation Nuggets
    A map ruler is useful for
plotting geocache coor-
dinates on a highly detailed
7.5-minute topographic map.

information regarding principles of
leaving no trace may be found at
www.lnt.org.

Carry along a garbage bag to make it
easy to pack trash out.

Map Considerations

Use the general map on the cache information page and a road map to
determine how to reach the cache area. When you're there, it's time to
get serious with highly detailed topographic maps. Topo maps are often
referred to as 7.5-minute maps because the distance they cover is 7.5
minutes long and wide in latitude and longitude, approximately 55
square miles. These maps are typically very detailed in the 1:24,000 or
1:25,000 map scale. For example, in the 1:24,000 scale, 1 inch on the
map equals approximately 2,000 feet on the ground. Book, outdoor, and
travel stores are all great places to find maps. They're a great investment for about $4. The digital topographic maps found on the cache
information page are based on these maps.

After you learn how to read a map, you'll enjoy the challenge of following your position on it. Wilderness roads such as those marked by the U.S. Forest Service use small numbered signs. With a little practice, you can easily match those signs spotted in the field to the roads listed on your map. This proves especially helpful if you're traveling in areas where satellite signals are blocked by overhanging trees or cliff walls.

A map ruler will enable you to plot your coordinates to a paper map, or take coordinates from a map to enter them as a waypoint into the GPS receiver. Also think about a map case to keep your new map dry. These are often clear vinyl sleeves that work great to protect the map and allow you to mark on the cover using a grease pencil or a dry-ink marker. Chapter 14 covers maps in detail.

Keep your magnetic compass handy by having it on a lanyard around your neck or in your front shirt pocket. Remember: A GPS receiver makes a poor compass, and a magnetic compass will not be accurate if used around metal or electronics. If you don't know which end is north, you'll get on track in Chapter 13.

Do Your Homework

If you get stumped trying to find an elusive cache, double-check the clues posted on the cache information page. A bit of overlooked data might just solve the puzzle. Clues are found in the general information about the cache, as well as the primary clue, which is encrypted. Online, you can click the link to decrypt the clue. In the field you can decrypt it manually by matching coded letters. There may be photos to check and spoiler information in the feedback lines that will give you that extra advantage in tracking down the tough ones.

It really helps to know what type and possibly color of container to look for. You know you're looking for a container anyway, but you gain a psychological advantage if you have an idea of what you're looking for.

Search Techniques

Someone new to the sport might ask, how hard could it be? The GPS receiver leads you right to the cache, usually within 15 meters of accuracy. But it is harder than you might think. The problem is the receiver that recorded the cache is inaccurate and your receiver is inaccurate. Poor reception due to overhead tree cover expands the search area further.

Sometimes you can search and search and not find a thing. Seasoned geocachers have been there. In the rain and in the heat, they have spent hours looking around rocks, trees, and foliage only to get stumped. Then when it all looked grim and they were ready to call it a day, their eyes caught something that didn't quite fit in the natural environment—a glimpse of plastic or metal that loomed out from the flora and fauna. You'll experience the same thing when your eye is trained on what to look for.

It helps to think like the person who hid the cache. If you were going to hide a cache in the area, where would you place it? Cache hiders can get very creative, but usually there are standard types of hiding places. Seasoned geocacher Neal "LogScaler," who has found nearly 900 caches, offers this advice: When looking for a cache, ask yourself, "Where would I put it?" In the outdoors, there are typically four main hiding areas: under a log, in a stump, under limbs, or under rocks.

Here are some helpful tips when closing in on the target:

♦ Check the satellite status page when you are within 300 feet. This will give you an idea of your accuracy for approach. Remember the receiver may not direct you to the exact location. Depending on signal strength, 40 feet may be your closest reading.

Geo-Lingo

Loose bearings is the term to describe the loss of accuracy of the GPS pointer arrow from slowing your pace or stopping. The pointer arrow feature requires the receiver to be moving at least 4 miles per hour to function properly.

♦ After you get close, your pointer function will no longer be accurate due to your slowing pace. The GPS receiver's compass feature does not function properly unless traveling more than 4 miles per hour. This is known as *loose bearings*. Because of this factor, when you slow down, disregard the pointer arrow and focus on the distance reading.

Cloverleaf

This is a search technique used when you're close and the pointer arrow feature is no longer operational due to loose bearings. It is a method of narrowing down the search area by using the distance reading.

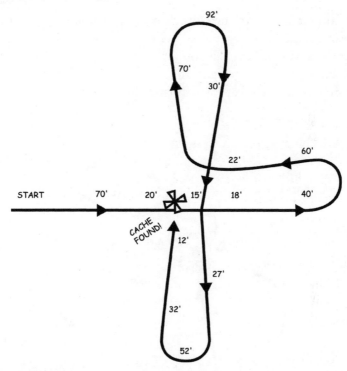

A cloverleaf pattern narrows the search area by moving in and out of the potential search location following the closest distance reading from a receiver.

Groundspeak

As you approach the target, the receiver will indicate a distance at the closest point, typically ranging from 40 feet down to 1 foot. If, as you move through the area, the distance increases, turn around and head back to the area where it decreases. Take off in a different direction until the distance increases, and then turn around and go back through the area that provides the smallest distance number. This method criss-crosses the target area.

Circling around in a cloverleaf pattern narrows the search area further. Moving in and out of the target area reduces the potential search area by confirming the location of the closest reading from at least four different directions.

Triangulation

Triangulation is similar to the cloverleaf except you use a compass to shoot bearings into the target area. When you slow down or stop, the loose bearings will prevent the pointer arrow feature from working properly, although the bearing to the waypoint should still be accurate. This procedure works great for dramatically narrowing down the search area.

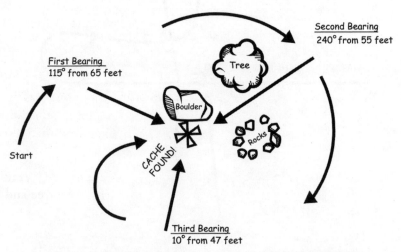

Triangulation narrows the search by taking three or more compass bearings on the target location.

Groundspeak

As you approach the target area, check the bearing degrees and distance. Using your compass, shoot a bearing. Be sure that the magnetic reading of both the GPS receiver and compass match, either true or magnetic north. The receiver will most likely be set as a default to true north, although the receiver can provide bearings on true or magnetic north (an option you can set through the Setup menu). Use the true north setting on your receiver if your compass can be adjusted for declination to indicate true north. If your compass cannot be adjusted, or if you do not know how to make the adjustment, set the receiver to provide bearings in magnetic north. It makes no difference what format you use as long as both the receiver and compass are set the same.

In our example, we approach the cache area and check the receiver data as we get close. We see the following:

> **Dead Batteries**
> Be sure to understand the difference between true and magnetic north. The difference can be greater than 20 degrees. It makes no difference if you use true or magnetic north as long as you and the others in your group agree on the format and adjust receivers and compasses accordingly.

Distance 65 feet, Bearing 115°. Using a compass, we shoot a bearing in that direction. Looking carefully along the bearing, we see that it is just to the right of a large boulder.

We circle the area clockwise to take a second bearing pointing west. The receiver indicates: Distance 55 feet, Bearing 240°. Along this bearing we see the path goes between a tree and rock pile, just to the left of the large boulder.

The third bearing is from the south pointing north: Distance 47 feet, Bearing 10°. From this angle, the bearing is to the left of the tree and appears to be pointing at the large boulder.

From these three bearings, all paths seem to point to the base of the large boulder. Sure enough, we find a plastic tube hidden in rocks exactly where the paths of the three bearings intersected.

In Life There Is No Reset Button

Thankfully, there are still wild and beautiful outdoor places, where Mother Nature and the order of the food chain still rule the day. Most of us have become far too civilized for our own good and we can easily underestimate the power of nature. Safety should always be a major concern, especially if traveling with family, friends, and children. Outdoor skills do not come naturally: They are acquired by education and experience through trial and error.

It is absolutely your responsibility to have the knowledge and equipment to tackle the area you want to travel. This means being realistic about your limits to ensure you're not exceeding your outdoor abilities, putting yourself and others at risk. If you are leading a group, consider their limits, and remember they are relying on your knowledge to get them safely there and back. If you are unsure about wilderness travel, take the time to educate yourself to build the skills and confidence necessary to make each excursion a successful one.

> **Eureka!**
> Wilderness 911?
> Personal locator beacons, PLBs, are ideal for remote travel. If lost or injured, an emergency distress signal is transmitted and received by satellite anywhere in the world. Search and rescue crews are dispatched to the victim's exact location.

The following is a list of potential hazards and how to deal with them. Use common sense, think through challenges, and make the best decisions possible. This is done by not overestimating your abilities and by making choices on the side of caution. Obviously, this book can't provide the exact solution to every potential problem, but here are some guidelines to help get you back in good spirits and in one piece.

Environmental Concerns

The weather is typically the primary concern. Being caught in a storm or in blazing heat unprepared and unprotected will definitely make you uncomfortable. Extended exposure can cause serious health problems and even death. Exposure is one of the leading causes of outdoor-related injury and death.

Hypothermia is caused by extensive heat loss, often caused by extended exposure to freezing temperatures, rain, and wind. The victim's body temperature lowers to dangerous levels, resulting in the body's inability to regain its own heat. It is estimated that hypothermia is responsible for 85 percent of outdoor-related deaths.

Heat exhaustion and eventually heat stroke are risks in warmer climates. The body temperature rises to dangerous levels from ongoing sun exposure and dehydration. In cases of cold and heat exposure, victims are subjected to extreme weather conditions for much longer than their provisions allowed for. They often find themselves in such dire circumstances because they are lost or stranded. Here are some ideas that will help prevent you from finding yourself in a worst-case scenario:

- Tell someone where you are going; give that person your travel itinerary.

- Wear the right clothing for the environment and climate.

- Bring the right gear for the environment and climate.

- Bring communication gear appropriate for the area.

- Bring and consume adequate amounts of food and water.

- Have some form of shelter available capable of protecting you from the elements.

- Take the proper steps necessary to avoid getting lost.

Poison, Stingers, and Fangs

All the stuff a good nightmare is made of: If the weather is not bad enough, we have to worry about being bitten or stung. Out of all the potential outdoor dangers, this is probably the most common and annoying. Okay, getting attacked by a bear would be more annoying, but animal attacks are rare. It's the insects that are more likely to give you fits. Mosquito bites on sunburn, tripping over a hornet's nest, a spider in your boot ... you get the idea.

Eureka!

"Gators" are protective wraps that cover the lower leg from the knee down to the top of your boot. They are ideal for hiking through brush or snow to keep thorns, insects, dirt, and other crud out of your socks and boots. Some are armor-plated to prevent snakebites.

Here's some advice to keep you from scratching your skin away:

- Learn what poison oak and ivy look like and stay away from them.

- Wear pants and long-sleeved clothing, and use insect repellent.

- Carry a first-aid kit that includes a snakebite kit.

 ◆ Always watch where you're walking.

 ◆ Check your sleeping bag, clothing, and boots before slipping into them.

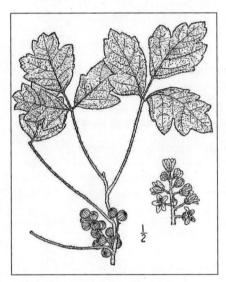 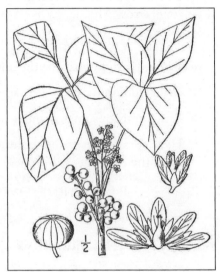

Learn what poison oak and ivy look like and stay away from them.

Pbritt, N.L. & A. Brown, Kentucky Native Plant Society

Dangerous People

Sometimes the most troublesome critters are of the two-legged variety. Without exception, most people you meet in the outdoors are friendly and would go out of their way to help you. There is a very small percentage whose intentions are unclear. Maybe they are opportunists who might steal your gear or mess with you if they really felt they could get away with it. An even smaller percentage of people are downright outlaws. They use the woods to hide out and for illegal dumping or drug operations.

Sometimes you might run across one or more people who appear to be a little shady. Long-term campers and land squatters often look rough, but might be perfectly harmless. If you are unsure about anyone you meet, the best thing is to just smile, wave, and leave. Don't be rude or tell them anything unnecessary like, for instance, that you're traveling alone. Regardless of what kind of jungle you find yourself in, criminals typically do not attack people who do not appear to be easy targets or victims.

If you run across what looks like an illegal activity, immediately turn around and leave the way you came in. Remember the location and report it to the local authorities. Do not investigate the scene. Drug labs and dumpsites contain hazardous chemicals. Drug labs and marijuana crop locations are sometimes booby-trapped. Wilderness management agencies have their own law enforcement divisions for investigating such crimes. It is critical to report these crimes for a number of reasons. This activity is a serious threat to others and the environment. Such activity gives land owners and managers good cause to deny access to wilderness areas. Here is some information to help keep you safe:

- Pepper spray is nonlethal and is very effective against humans and animals.

- If you run across someone who may be unfriendly, just leave.

- Most criminals do not mess with people who look aware, confident, and capable of defending themselves.

- Immediately back out of any areas where criminal activities are taking place and report them to the police.

How Not to Look Weird

When you're geocaching, you are on a serious mission. You have a cold look of determination in your eye as you shake off the elements and obstacles that get in your way. Others who are on a nice quiet scenic getaway might not share your enthusiasm—not because what you're doing is wrong, just because they have no clue as to what you're doing. Curious onlookers may wonder why anyone would so intently look around the same area when nothing appears to be there. You will undoubtedly run across nongeocachers. They're everywhere. At some point, depending on their interest level, you may have some explaining to do.

Some geocachers are happy to share the geo-gospel with everyone they meet, enthusiastically explaining what they are doing and how to play the game. Many people find the idea as interesting as you first did, and who knows, maybe you just created a new cacher. Others like to be a little more discreet. For them, part of the challenge is to get in and out without anyone else even knowing they were there.

Whatever you do, keeping a low profile is good. People do visit outdoor areas for peace and quiet, and there is no reason to disturb anyone else's tranquility. There is also no harm done in explaining what you're doing. Even if you do not want to take the time to do so, it's better than having others become suspicious of your behavior. Some geocachers have developed creative ways to mask their activity. They've used excuses ranging from being agricultural inspectors to doing some kind of research. Other cachers have suddenly pretended that their GPS receiver is a cell phone and they are just having a phone conversation.

Does this sneakiness help or just increase suspicion? Remember that what you're doing is a legitimate activity, but that you do not want to cause anyone alarm. Here are some ideas about dealing with nongeo-cachers:

♦ Be prepared to quickly and politely explain what geocaching is. Most people receive the information with great interest.

♦ It's good to remain low key. There is no reason to disturb anyone or make anyone wonder what you're doing.

♦ Do not say or do anything that would make you appear as if you are doing anything suspicious or illegal.

♦ Be careful about how you use your receiver. In some countries, under certain circumstances, you could be considered a spy.

Finally, the most effective activity is to take out your trash bag and pick up whatever litter you find around the cache area as you search. Passers-by will generally ignore you, and if you're approached the conversation will most likely start on a positive note.

The Least You Need to Know

◆ Save time and reduce potential problems by learning tips from seasoned geocachers.

◆ Find caches like a pro by using the cloverleaf search pattern and triangulation.

◆ Take responsibility to learn outdoor skills and try not to exceed your abilities.

◆ Be diplomatic with nongeocachers you meet on the trail.

Chapter 7

Game Variations

In This Chapter

◆ Many ways to go geocaching

◆ Some of the more common geocaching variations

◆ How to liven up outdoor events with geocaching games

Geocaching is too large and dynamic an activity to ever limit itself to only one way to play. The geocaching community continues to evolve the sport into new variations and activities, giving the original game many new twists. "Basic geocaching is the stepping-stone to other games as the players come up with new ideas," says Geocaching.com president Jeremy Irish. He credits much of the game's popularity to its ability to evolve on an ongoing basis as new variations of the sport emerge.

In this chapter, you'll learn a sampling of the many games currently available. Who knows, maybe you'll be inspired to make up a game of your own.

Auto Rallies

Would you like to do your geocaching a little faster? Auto and off-road event promoters have made their events more exciting by adding geocache challenges. Many motor-sport events are based upon traveling from point A to point B as fast as possible or within a specific time element. Many auto events already require the use of GPS; it only seems natural to add a few navigational challenges along the way. Instead of a cache container, there may be flags to find with some form of punch card or digital photo system to verify the participants found the target.

Off-road events are great if you like to challenge yourself to geocaching on the move.

Jack W. Peters

A good example is Oregon's four-wheel-drive event, the annual Team Trophy Challenge. Promoter Doug Shipman has incorporated a night navigation exercise in this grueling weekend event. Twenty-one targets are hidden throughout the mountains of the Tillamook Forest.

Targets that would be challenging enough to find during the day are extra difficult to find at night. The positions are concealed well, up and down hills, with only a vague description of their location. A typical event may include latitude/longitude coordinates for 10 out of 21 flags, with others including somewhat vague directions based on the previous target, like "NW of top, 250 yards, through brush, tree."

Another exciting event is the annual Hungarian GPS Challenge.

Planning on being in Europe this December with your GPS and well-equipped four-wheel-drive vehicle? If so, don't miss this opportunity to see Hungary by chasing all over the countryside looking for waypoints within a 48-hour period. This event is held between December 28th and 30th and is based from Budapest, Hungary.

Drivers attempt to score points by locating as many of the 100 way-point targets as possible. It will be nearly impossible to find all 100, so drivers and co-drivers will have to use strategy to find the most they can within 48 hours. Many of the waypoints will be on rough roads with snowdrifts. If a truck becomes stuck, the team can call a central dispatch number for help. A team rescuing another will get three bonus points. The team needing the rescuing will lose three points. Other areas will be so difficult they can be reached only on foot.

Besides being a challenging navigation and driving event, it's a sightsee-ing tour that includes the most beautiful areas of Hungary. After the event, participants stay and party through New Year's Day.

Under the pressure of competition, events like these definitely sharpen navigation skills by requiring participants to work quickly under often adverse conditions. Racing across unknown territory, GPS is needed just to keep from getting lost. Teams often use two GPS receivers, one mounted in the truck, the other to take on the run.

Benchmarks

Benchmark hunting is searching for survey markers from a list main-tained by the United States National Geodetic Survey (NGS). *Benchmarks* are geodetic control points that are permanently affixed objects at various locations throughout the United States. They are used for land surveying, civil engineering, and mapping. The NGS maintains a database of these loca-tions, and each benchmark control point marker has a permanent identifier number (PID) and a datasheet of information about it. Many of these markers are old, and much of the descriptive data used to find them is outdated. There are, however, more than 700,000 of these markers within the United States, and they are still used today for the ongoing process of surveying our country.

Eureka!

There are more than a 700,000 benchmarks to find in the United States. Tracking down these markers is like finding a small piece of American history. As of this writing, the Geocaching.com site indicates that there are 42,670 markers found and another 693,755 still out there waiting to be logged.

There are two general types of benchmark control points:

♦ **Vertical control points.** They establish the precise elevation at their placement point. They are typically small brass or aluminum discs, concrete posts, iron pins, or bolts permanently attached to a stable foundation.

♦ **Horizontal control points.** There are several names for these control points: triangulation stations, traverse stations, trilateration stations, GPS stations, and intersection stations. These, too, can be a small brass or aluminum disc, concrete post, iron pin, or bolt similar to the vertical control points. They can also be other features such as radio towers, water towers, church spires, mountaintops, or any other objects that can be identified from a distance.

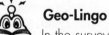

Geo-Lingo

In the surveying profession, the term **benchmark** is applied only to the vertical control type; for benchmark hunting, however, we use the term for both vertical and horizontal control points.

A BLM marker found. Markers like this are used by land management agencies to mark locations and elevation.

Mark Fisher

Searching for Benchmarks

Searching for benchmarks to find is easy. On the Geocaching.com website, pull up a cache and click the link for *all nearby benchmarks*. A list of benchmarks will appear from the nearest to the farthest. Searches can also be made by zip code, latitude/longitude, or by permanent identifier number (PID).

The unique thing about benchmark hunting is that it does not require GPS. A receiver is helpful to get you in the right area, but then it's up to you to interpret the instructions on the benchmark's datasheet. Benchmark information pages from the Geocaching.com site do provide coordinates and directions.

Part of the challenge is that the coordinates are usually not very accurate. They may be within only a couple hundred feet of the marker, requiring the need to study the description to find it.

This is because most were planted before the use of GPS, requiring the coordinates to be plotted from a map. This method is confirmed if the word *SCALED* is under the marker's coordinate.

If the benchmark page indicates the location is *ADJUSTED*, you are looking for a horizontal control point that most likely has been plotted with highly accurate surveying-grade GPS equipment.

Finding a Benchmark

When you find a marker, do not tamper with it or take it. These markers are protected by law because they are public property and still actively used in surveying. Take pictures of the marker and the surrounding area, and then get back on the website and log your find. Upload the photos to the website's gallery.

Some listings describe things like radio towers, church steeples, and smokestacks. These kinds of "large-object" station markers are known as *intersection stations*. They are usually landmarks taller than any surrounding objects, allowing them to be seen from many miles away in several directions. This makes them valuable points of reference for surveying.

When logging these benchmarks, keep in mind that in very unusual cases there is a benchmark disc, surveying nail, or other small object that can't be seen from the ground, the top of the tower, steeple, or smokestack. The datasheet will specify such a marker if this is the case. If not, simply log your find, and if you have a camera, take a picture of the structure from the ground. For safety reasons, it is obviously best not to climb these structures.

Logging a Benchmark

When logging a benchmark, the choices are *Found it!*, *Couldn't find it!*, and *Post a Note*. When you find a marker, be sure to check the description and datasheet to confirm it's the right one.

> **Dead Batteries**
>
> Use caution when seeking benchmarks. Some are located on private property or in hazardous areas. Also remember these markers are very important for surveyors, engineers, and others, so do not tamper with them or take them.

It's not unusual to find benchmarks that are not in the NGS database. This is because there are survey markers everywhere and the NGS is not the only organization that creates and uses benchmarks. Other agencies include the U.S. Army Corps of Engineers (USACE), the Bureau of Land Management (BLM), and other federal agencies, along with highway departments, county and private surveyors, and engineers.

You may log an official report to the NGS if any of these three points are met:

- When the description of how to get to the station marker has significantly changed.

- When a station marker has not been visited in a long time: 30 years or longer.

- When the station marker is obviously destroyed. "Destroyed," to the NGS, means that you found the marker and that it is obviously out of its installed position. If you cannot find the marker for any reason, don't report it to the NGS as destroyed.

Make sure that the control's history has not changed in the official database of the NGS before planning your report. Also, do not report benchmark coordinates to the NGS for any reason. The existing coordinates on the NGS datasheets cannot be changed, except through very rigorous mathematical procedures. Geocaching.com has its own agency code for reporting to the NGS. It is *GEOCAC*. They also ask for your initials.

Navigation Nuggets

The NGS website (www.ngs.noaa.gov/) is an excellent resource for learning how to read datasheets. Review samples by clicking Datasheets.

Degree Confluence Project

The goal of the Degree Confluence Project is for participants to visit each of the latitude and longitude degree intersections around the world. There is a confluence every 49 miles, or 79 kilometers. Even after eliminating confluences in the oceans and some near the poles, there are still 13,539 left to be found.

Each intersection is photographed and the photos and stories are posted on the Degree Confluence website.

For more information, visit www.confluence.org.

Geodashing

Here's a game where "getting there is all the fun." In each game, a large number of waypoints from around the world are posted on the Geodashing website. These waypoints are known as dashpoints. Dashpoint locations are chosen at random by computer, and are located in wilderness and urban locations.

After the dashpoints are posted, the race is on to see who can reach the most dashpoints before the end-of-game deadline.

For more information, go to www.seaotters.net/~scout/Geodashing/.

Letterboxing

Just when you thought geocaching was a new idea, we find out the Brits have been playing a similar game in England (without GPS) for the past 150 years. The game originated in Dartmoor National Park in Devon, England, and now there are thousands of letterboxes hidden around the world, including across North America. Like geocaching, letterboxing is a mix of treasure hunting, navigation, and exploring with an artful flair.

> **Geo-Lingo**
>
> **Pacing** is used to determine distances in the outdoors using the stride of one's footsteps. With a little practice, distances can be measured very accurately. Chapter 12 covers pacing in detail.

A waterproof box is hidden, ideally in a scenic or unique location. The box contains a logbook and a carved rubber stamp. Directions are provided that might be straightforward or cryptic. The clues involve directions that might include map coordinates, but are primarily based on compass bearings and distances in *paces.*

Persons hiding a letterbox do so as creatively as they can; after all, selecting a location and writing the clues is considered an art.

Letterbox hunters use the clues, maps, and tools needed to solve the mystery and find the box. When the box is found, the hunter stamps the letterbox's logbook with a personal stamp, and then stamps a personal logbook with the stamp in the box. Players have their own unique rubber stamps to document their visit, similar to how signature items are used in geocaching. In fact, many geocachers create their own stamps to use when logging geocaches.

You can find listings of letterboxes in the United States on the Letterboxing North America (LbNA) website at www.letterboxing.org/.

Multistage Caches

Multiple caches are hidden. Contents of a first cache contain clues to lead to the next cache, that cache contains clues to the next one, and so on until the final cache is found. Clues in the first cache might include coordinates or clues like a compass bearing and distance to the next.

MinuteWar

MinuteWar is a GPS-based capture-the-flag game using the world as the playing field. Every player uses a local map, but all the maps are combined, allowing all players to compete against each other regardless of their location in the world.

The game maps are divided into squares one minute of longitude wide and one minute of latitude long. Each square contains a virtual flag. Players capture virtual flags by going to their locations in the minute-by-minute squares. Games can vary, but the object is to capture and hold the most flags or to find hidden flags.

For more information, go to www.seaotters.net/~scout/MinuteWar/.

Moving Caches

This is a cache you *can* take with you as long as you hide it somewhere else. A moving cache travels around via each person who finds it. When a geocacher finds the cache, he or she moves it to a different location and then posts the new coordinates.

Mystery or Puzzle Caches

The "catch-all" of cache types, this form of cache can involve complicated puzzles you must solve to determine the coordinates.

This form of cache is developed by those creative enough to really try to stump you. They require a puzzle, problem, or mathematical equation to be solved to acquire the cache's coordinates. The only commonality of this cache type is that the coordinates listed are not of the actual cache location but a general reference point, such as a nearby parking location. Due to the increasing creativity of geocaching, this becomes the staging ground for new and unique challenges.

Offset Caches

These caches are unique in that they bring you to an interesting landmark such as a historical monument, a plaque, or even a benchmark that the person hiding the cache would like you to visit. Then it's up to you to decipher clues to find a nearby cache container. Clues may be included in the numbers or markings contained at the landmark.

Virtual Caches

These caches are intended to bring you to a unique location, not to find a cache container. The location itself is the "cache." These sites are typically some type of unique landmark or historical monument. There are no containers, so nothing is traded except photos and experiences. Cache finders prove they were there by answering a question like "what are the dates on the tombstone?"

Webcam Caches

Webcam caches use existing webcams placed by individuals or agencies that monitor various areas like parks or roads. The idea is to get yourself in front of the camera to log your visit. The challenging part, however, it that you need to call a friend to look up the website that displays the camera shot. You must ask that friend to save the picture to log the cache. If you're a tech-head, you could use your wireless modem and save the image yourself on your laptop.

Eureka!
Geocaching is an effective way to learn GPS because it involves the use of the primary functions the GPS offers, like saving, entering, and finding waypoints.

Adding Geocaching Games to Your Events

The possibilities for adding geocaching-style games to outdoor events are as endless as there are caches to find. Families, clubs, companies, and all kinds of organizations can liven up their picnics and events. This is being done now by a wide variety of organizations, ranging from Boy Scout troops to search-and-rescue teams to church groups. Outdoor skills trainers are also recognizing the benefit of these games as a practical and fun way to teach GPS and navigation.

A volunteer four-wheel-drive search-and-rescue team on a training mission seeks out an unknown waypoint. When at the location, they search for clues to find a missing couple. Some clues will lead to new clues similar to a multi-stage cache search.

Jack W. Peters

Adding geocaching-style games to your next event is a great idea for a number of reasons:

◆ First, it's fun. Remember that? In our busy lives, especially in a corporate or organizational setting, how often do we really get the opportunity to enjoy ourselves? It gives everyone something to do other than sit around and eat. It will intrigue your guests, leaving them with a positive experience they will be talking about later.

◆ Second, it will expose people to GPS, navigation, and outdoor skills who otherwise would not have learned it on their own. This includes children and others who have always wanted to learn about GPS, or have been fascinated by the technology. This provides an introduction to these skills, allowing them to determine whether they want to pursue the activity further.

◆ Third, geocaching is simply a great way to teach GPS navigation skills. Let's face it, rocket science and computer technology can be a little dull or intimidating. Adding the "let's go treasure hunting element" helps build real enthusiasm to learn this information.

Adding geocaching games to your events might be easier than you think. There are a couple of ways to do this. Do a search for caches in the area and bring the information along with you. Most parks, picnic areas, and camp locations have caches hidden in and around them. The other option is to hide a few of your own. Caches could be filled with prizes or gift certificates that would have special meaning to the group. Be creative: A day-off pass would be popular at a company picnic, for instance.

Navigation trainer John Miller uses geocaching for his GPS classes at Lane Community College in Eugene, Oregon. After a number of class-room sessions covering map and compass basics, it's time to use the gear in the field. Classmates break into two teams to find navigational targets by pacing off distances along compass bearings, like what is done for letterboxing. Then it's time to fire up GPS receivers to find a number of hidden waypoints around the Mount Pisgah area. Each way-point target includes a challenge like checking the receiver for an eleva-tion reading or taking a compass bearing to a radio tower. The class ends with the finding of the final cache of donuts and coffee.

A GPS class finds a cache of donuts and coffee—a welcome reward after tracking down a number of compass bearing targets and waypoints.

Jack W. Peters

The Least You Need to Know

◆ Benchmark Hunting is a unique variation of the game that allows participants to seek previously established caches with historical significance. Remember to leave the benchmarks themselves alone.

◆ Trying new variations keeps the game interesting, and you can always come up with variations of your own.

◆ Geocaching-style games will liven up your next picnic or outdoor event.

Chapter 8

Travel Bugs and Hitchhikers

In This Chapter

- ◆ What are hitchhikers and travel bugs?
- ◆ Learn what to do when you find one
- ◆ Learn how to place one of your own

Travel bugs and hitchhikers add a unique twist to geocaching. In this chapter, you'll learn all about these neat traveling objects and how far they can go. You will learn what to do if you find one and how much fun it is to send one off into the wild.

Message in a Bottle Revised

Like a bottle drifting in the ocean, hitchhikers are objects that find their way around by drifting from cache to cache. They are usually some form of toy, symbol, or trinket that has meaning to the person placing the item. Hitchhikers include instructions for transport, either random or to a specific destination.

It's up to the owner of the hitchhiker to give it a travel goal or no goal at all. The person who finds it might be asked to relocate it to another cache, take it somewhere special, or help it complete a journey. Hitchhikers can have goals to visit cities or countries, possibly traveling around the world. They get to travel to a variety of places, and with each move a story is added to the adventure. Each hitchhiker's journey is unique, and they can take on a life of their own. A Darth Vader figurine hitchhiker, for example, accompanied a U.S. Air Force pilot on combat missions over Afghanistan.

Unlike a traditional message in a bottle that is never seen by the owner again, the neat thing about hitchhikers is that their adventures can be tracked online. When someone finds and relocates a hitchhiker, he or she logs the find and shares the story that goes along with the move. It is a unique thrill to receive news that your traveler has moved and read the logs posted by those who have helped it along on its journey.

Hitchhiker Origins and Types

In the early days of geocaching, it was not uncommon for players to move trade items from one cache to another. Players would trade the same item in the next cache, and after a while items would jump long distances with the movements of just a small group of geocachers. At the same time, people would create their own signature items and ask other players to move them along to other caches, often with an e-mail address to contact the original owner to let him or her know how far the object had gone.

As with many good ideas in geocaching, the concept spread throughout the community, and more people created their own versions of hitchhikers. They ranged from low-tech notes to inform the owner of the hitchhiker's status to websites dedicated to each object and its movements.

Hitchhikers can be nearly anything. Almost like a signature item, it's something that has meaning to you. They are often action figures or toy animals or cars. Jason the Dinosaur Hunter uses plastic dinosaurs. They are like a bit of your personality that gets to travel about, even when you don't get to.

Have you seen one of these in a cache? This is a travel bug dog tag with a unique serial number. It can be attached to an object for identification and tracking purposes as it travels from cache to cache.

Groundspeak Inc./ Geocaching.com

With the popularity of hitchhikers, the guys at Geocaching.com came up with the idea of having geocachers attach dog tags with unique serial numbers to the items that move around. Serial numbers provided a much more efficient way to track their travels, and the *travel bug* was born.

Travel Bugs

A travel bug is a metal tag with a unique tracking number available for lookup at Geocaching.com. It is usually attached to a hitchhiker, but can be used by itself. These bugs can be easily tracked on the Geocaching.com site through their number. Geocachers who find travel bugs log information on how they're found and where they've been moved so that the person who hid the bug can check on its current whereabouts.

Travel bugs are metal tags stamped with the travel bug bar code logo and their individual serial number. Each bug includes an exact copy and a chain. Keep the copy as a memento and a quick way to check up on your bug's status. The copy makes a neat necklace for hard-core geo-heads, a great key chain, or possibly the ultimate accessory for your pet's collar.

Travel bugs are usually attached to a hitchhiker, which is an object the owner thought would be neat to travel around from person to person, and to who knows where. Besides the hitchhiker, which is often reflective of the owner's personality, travel

Geo-Lingo

Travel bug is a term coined by Jeremy Irish in July 2001, inspired by everyone's "travel bug," or desire to travel.

bugs take on an identity of their own. They are named, have travel goals, and get their own web page at Geocaching.com. Here is an example of a recently placed bug:

Name: All American Pastime

Released: Thursday, September 25, 2003, by Seal Rock George

Origin: Oregon, United States

Recently spotted: In the geocache: Danielle's Delight

Current goal: The All American Pastime travel bug wants to celebrate baseball. Visit stadiums; meet players (young and old); share in the thrill of wood hitting the ball, the smells, the sounds, and the memories.

About this item: Please take this bug if you are willing to take the responsibility to move this along. Take pictures of yourself with it, or pics of where it travels—and load them onto this site. Also, take a few minutes and share your own baseball stories with us. In other words, just have fun with this—but don't keep it too long—there are others who want to share the fun! Also, attached to this bug is an American Cancer Society Relay for Life tag. If you're interested in helping fight cancer (travel bugs hate cancer), you can contact the ACS using the info on the tag.

Recent sightings: Monday, September 29, 2003

Seal Rock George placed it in Danielle's Delight by Gone_Bananas

Finding Travel Bugs

If you find a travel bug in the wild, check to see whether the owner attached any instructions. Log on to Geocaching.com and go to the cache's page. Log your find, and then click the travel bug name link in the upper-right corner of the page. Note that travel bugs are named. In this example, it's name is All American Pastime.

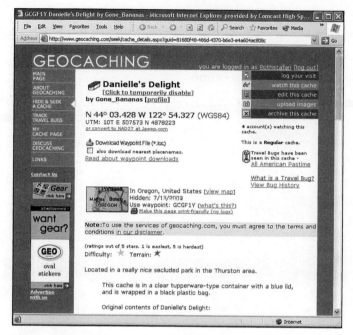

The travel bug link is in the upper-right corner.

Groundspeak.com

Clicking the travel bug link brings up the bug's home page. On this page, you can read all about the bug, including the owner's name and travel goals, as in the preceding example. Click the Found it? Log it! link to enter the details of finding the bug.

This will bring up the travel bug tracking page that will allow you to log that a bug has been found and moved. This requires you to enter the bug's tracking number.

After you have electronically claimed a travel bug, it goes into the online inventory on your personal account page. The next time you log that a cache has been found, there will be an option to select the bug from your inventory list and post it to the new cache.

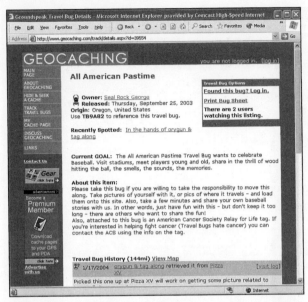

This page contains the bug's information, such as its name, owner, and travel goal. Click the Found it? Log it! link in the upper-right corner.

Groundspeak.com

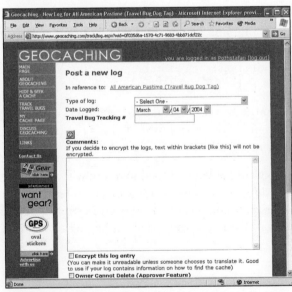

This page enables you to log a found travel bug after entering its tracking number.

Groundspeak.com

Relocating Travel Bugs

When you move a travel bug to a new cache, log on to Geocaching.com and go to the new cache's page. When you log the cache as found, you'll see a drop-down menu at the bottom of the page that provides an option to select the bug from your inventory list and "attach" it to the new cache. When you submit your log entry, the bug will appear on the new cache's page. Don't forget to upload an image.

> **Eureka!**
> The first travel bug, Deadly Duck—Envy, was placed on August 31, 2001. As of this writing, there are approximately 25,000 bugs in play.

Starting Your Own Travel Bug

So sending a bug on its way sounds like fun? Here's the rundown on the care and feeding of your travel bug.

The first thing you need to do is activate the bug. Log on to Geocaching.com and click the Track Travel Bugs link. Enter the bug's tracking number under the Travel Bug icon. If it is a new bug, you must activate it.

The activation code is printed on a sticker on the travel bug package. Successfully entering the tracking number and activation code will bring up the travel bug's home page. Click to assign the bug to you. Congratulations, it's all yours. Use the Edit link in the upper-right corner of the page to give your bug a name, description, and travel goals.

Whether you are relocating a bug or activating a new one, you have an opportunity to upload images to a travel bug page. Click the Upload Image link. If you are the bug's owner and have loaded multiple images, open the bug's Edit page and a drop-down box will appear with a list of the images loaded. Select your favorite picture and it will become the image for your bug's home page and entry in the travel bug photo gallery.

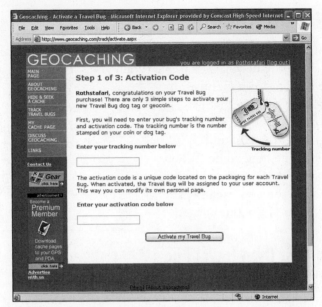

New travel bugs are brought to life by entering the tracking number and the activation code.

Groundspeak.com

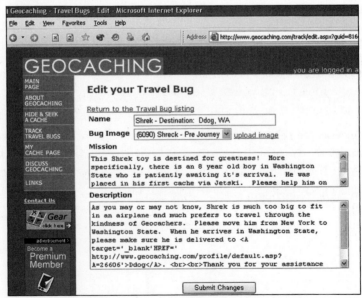

The edit page enables you to name your bug as well as to list a description and travel goals.

Groundspeak.com

Shari displays Mikayla's bug. It's attached to a pouch containing a disposable camera with instructions to "Take me to Australia!" Each person who finds the bug is to take a picture until it reaches its destination. The Aussie who sends the camera back to the United States gets a special thanks and reimbursement for the shipping.

Jack W. Peters

Travel Bug Stories

Travel bug and hitchhiker owners enjoy seeing their creations travel from place to place, each developing a story of its own. Some bugs unfortunately get exterminated by being taken and never placed again, whereas others travel across many countries, from cache to cache, for thousands of miles.

Some of these bugs begin to stand out thanks to lofty goals or distance traveled. Here are examples of travel bugs that have found their way around.

Cannonball Run

This is the official logo from the Cannonball Run website created by J. Pac and company.

J. Pac

In 1971, Brock Yates assembled a group of racers to compete in a timed coast-to-coast race on the freeways across the United States. On November 15, 1971, six hotrod cars screamed out of the Red Ball Garage and onto the streets of New York City, racing west to California. Thirty-five hours, 54 minutes and 2,863 miles later, Yates and his co-driver Dan Gurney won the race by being the first to reach Redondo Beach, California. This race inspired a great B movie, many speeding tickets, and a new race across the county. This time it's known as the 1st Annual Cannonball Run Travel Bug Race!

The rules are simple: Travel bugs are to move only one state at a time, and states must share a common border. Any bug that skips a state, intentionally or not, is required to backtrack to the last contiguous state it was in. Racers are allowed to attach any type of information or map to the bug they think will help accomplish its goal.

Racers cannot possess the bug of any other racer. However, in the spirit of the original Cannonball Run, good-natured interference is allowed. You may ask other cachers to either help your bug along or delay someone else's bug. The first racer to be logged in Pheromone Cache in Ripon, California, is the winner!

J. Pac, one of the first organizers of the event, estimated that there might be 10 to 12 entries. In the beginning, it didn't seem like there was much enthusiasm for the race. The date was set back a month to allow more time for entries to come in … and that they did. On the starting date of March 8, 2003, there were 71 bugs ready to go. This has got to be some kind of a geocaching record! "Gentlemen, please start your travel bugs!"

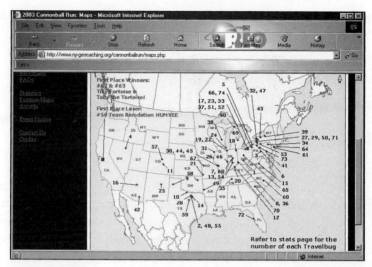

The map shows 71 racing travel bugs making their way from New York to California.

NY-Geocaching.org

On July 7th, four months after the start, the travel bug pair of Tilly and Toby Tortoise tied for first place. Other awards are given for the following categories:

- **First Place Loser.** Second place

- **Last Place Winner.** The last racer to make it to the destination cache before the start of next year's race

- **Most Unique Cachers.** The racer handled by the most unique cachers

- **Fewest Number of Caches.** The racer that has traveled through the fewest caches

- **Most Number of Caches.** The racer that has traveled through the most caches

- **Most Mileage.** The racer that has traveled the most miles

- **Directionally Challenged.** The racer going in the completely wrong direction

- **First Missing.** The first racer to go missing

An award will also be given to the cache owner who has the most number of racers travel through his or her cache.

The Cannonball Travel Bug Race is sponsored by the New York Geocaching Organization. Check out www.ny-geocaching.org/cannonballrun/about.php.

Darth Vader TB 1

This is a typical-looking bug, a tag attached to a Star Wars toy. Its mission is also typical enough: "Darth is on a mission to find other Jedi out in the geocaching universe. Please help him get to as many states as possible by the end of the year. Alaska would be a really cool place to visit, as Darth's master has always wanted to go there, but he will take a trip to any exotic location anywhere in the geocaching world."

This bug, however, has got to be one of farthest-traveled bugs going. We're not sure whether it ever made it to Alaska, but it has been around the world: 17,534.64 miles as of October 2003.

On a combat mission over Afghanistan with a Navy fighter escort.

The captain

After Captain Prozac retrieved the bug, he took it along to the Gulf to fly seven combat missions over Afghanistan. After its share of combat service, it enjoyed a stop in the United Kingdom before returning to the United States. Of course, the bug accompanied the captain at a couple of pub stops along the way. The cool weather was a nice relief from the 100+ degree heat of Afghanistan. After a little R-and-R in the states, Darth Vader TB 1 will be released again.

> **Eureka!**
> Travel bugs have really caught on as a fun way to enhance the sport. Some cachers really have bug fever, including a few like Centris, Feathers, and TH&C, who have found more than 500 each.

Message in a Bottle

Tracy "CameraThyme," from the state of Washington, came up with the idea of a media bug. The bug's goal is to travel to the NBC studios at Rockefeller Plaza in Manhattan. It is to be delivered to Matt and Katie on the *Today Show*. Inside the bottle is a message to Katie and Matt, asking them to contact Jeremy Irish for an interview regarding the sport of geocaching.

Despite its impressive travel distance of 11,869.02 miles, it seems the bug is currently on hiatus. It's been snatched without being replanted. We hope it gets back on track for lights, camera, and action in New York.

> **Dead Batteries**
> Use good geo-sportsmanship when it comes to travel bugs and hitch-hikers. It is considered bad etiquette to remove one from a cache and not move it along to the next cache. E-mail the owner if you keep an item longer than a couple of weeks. Also, do not mail items to a destination. If you do, what's the point? The point of hitch-hikers is to give them the most interesting journey possible.

Tigger

On September 14, 2001, only days after the September 11th tragedy, geocacher bigkid sent a travel bug on a special mission to the site of the World Trade Center. Its goal, "The wonderful thing about Tiggers is their power to heal and make fun. My name is Tigger Travel Bug and I'd like to go to New York City and help the people around the WTC by making them smile. Can you please take my picture at the location of the WTC? Then perhaps I can make my way back to Seattle."

On February 16, 2002, after thousands of miles of travel through the goodwill of geocachers, Tigger stood at the memorial viewing platform at Ground Zero in the hands of geocacher Perfect Tommy.

Tigger's travel bug page contains many touching photos and logs from his journey. Tigger finally returned home to Seattle 16 months after he left. He was attached to a Ground Zero 9-11-01 NYC knit cap. Tigger had traveled 7,022 miles and touched the hearts of many.

The Least You Need to Know

◆ Travel bugs and hitchhikers are special trade items that are designed to move from cache to cache, and occasionally over great distances.

◆ Travel bugs are hitchhikers with serial numbers that allow them to be tracked on cache and user profile pages at the Geocaching.com website.

◆ Placing a travel bug of your own is as easy as registering its owner's name, the bug's name, and its traveling goals or purpose.

◆ Do not take a travel bug or hitchhiker if you cannot place it in another cache soon.

Part 3

Finding Your Way Around

High-tech gear is not just for techno-dudes. Using GPS will provide you more travel freedom into unknown territory than you can imagine. Up to this point, you've probably been using just a few of the features on your GPS receiver, and you might be feeling like there's more you could learn about finding caches or just finding your way around. That's what Part 3 is for.

In the next few chapters, we give you the rundown on the GPS receiver options available so that you can buy the right gear the first time. Then it will be time to set up your gear by finding out what all of those buttons are for.

As good as using GPS can be, it doesn't replace the traditional map and compass. After you get your grid lines and true north figured out, it's time for some serious high-tech fun by exploring the use of GPS mapping and computers.

Chapter 9

GPS Gear Selection

In This Chapter

- Learn what features and options are available before you buy
- Choose the right type of receiver for your application
- Learn to select the right antenna
- Everything you ever wanted to know about batteries
- Check out our recommendations for great geo-gear!

Because geocaching is based on using a GPS receiver, we recommend you do a little research and get the right gear. With so many options and prices, it can be confusing. This chapter gives you a rundown of all the primary features so you'll know what to look for when reading the specifications sheet for each unit.

There are now a number of options to convert your PDA (a personal data assistant, like a Palm or Pocket PC) into a GPS receiver. Neat idea, but will it work for geocaching? There are also accessories like antennas and batteries to think about. This chapter covers the features available and makes recommendations depending on how much money you're willing to part with.

GPS Receivers

GPS receivers are manufactured in various shapes and sizes, with as many features and prices. GPS technology is used for so many different applications it is confusing to know what to buy and how much money to spend to get the features you need for your application. Buying the right gear will be a worthy investment. Getting the wrong gear will be a disappointing waste of money.

Eureka!

Keep your gear longer by securing it with those key-keeper-style coiled lanyards. They are great for attaching receivers, cameras, and radios. If you drop your gear, it may spring back before crashing on the ground. They're great for keeping gear from becoming lost or stolen in wilderness or urban environments.

Fortunately, modern receivers share many of the same features, regardless of price. Nearly any GPS receiver will work for geocaching, but some work better than others. Understanding the available features will allow you to make an informed purchasing decision and enable you to use the equipment to its fullest potential. We understand that when you purchase a receiver you will probably use it for more than just geocaching. Here is a list of the common features available. Learn how they may be applied to geocaching and other applications.

Primary Features

◆ **Accuracy.** Fortunately, accuracy is consistent in most receivers regardless of the style or cost.

◆ **Address finder.** Allows an exact address to be located within a basemap database.

◆ **Alarms.** An alarm notifies the user of an approaching waypoint. Text alarms flash a message on the screen, audible alarms sound a tone.

◆ **Altimeter.** A 3D, four-satellite fix provides elevation information, although satellite-based altimeters are not known for being very accurate. Some units provide a built-in barometric altimeter for accurate elevation readings independent of a satellite connection.

◆ **Antenna jack.** This feature allows for a remote antenna if the gear is mounted within a vehicle with no clear view of the sky.

   You can also bring it along with you on a hunt to get better signals under heavy tree cover.

◆ **Auto routing.** Provides turn-by-turn directions to a waypoint. Directions may be in the form of arrows or automated voice commands.

◆ **Basemap.** Most recent-model receivers include a map database stored within their memory. Basemaps include general information on cities, roadways, and waterways. Basemaps typically include such large geographic areas as North America and the United Kingdom.

◆ **Battery duration.** Battery life is important for extended hikes with no other power source available. Receivers are rated for battery life duration for both continuous use and power-saver modes.

◆ **Channels.** Make sure your receiver is capable of 12 parallel channels. Most units sold after 1997 are equipped with this feature; however, the first receivers available were all single channel. The older single-channel equipment processes information much slower from each individual satellite, one at a time through a single channel.

◆ **Clock and timer.** Receivers provide precise atomic time in either a 12- or 24-hour display. Various timer features include date, time traveled, and estimated time of arrival.

◆ **Computer interface.** Data in/out capability allows the unit to receive (upload) data from a computer or send (download) data to a computer. This information includes digital maps, track logs, waypoints, and routes. NMEA, the National Marine Electronics Association, ensures that data can be exchanged with other electronic devices. If you plan to do more than a few cache hunts, make sure your receiver has this interface capability.

♦ **Electronic compass.** Although receivers provide compass data, the feature will not work in a stationary position. This feature is available to provide compass data independent of satellite reception. However, this feature will drain batteries faster than standard GPS use.

♦ **Memory.** For receivers with a basemap, memory is used to store additional mapping data. GPS manufacturers provide greater detailed maps on CD-ROM exclusively for their brand. Map details, especially topo contour lines, use a great deal of memory. Two megabytes will allow the storage of a few small areas. Eight megabytes may allow the storage of the primary areas of a home state. Ideally, a receiver will have a minimum of eight megabytes of memory. Some models use memory cards, allowing virtually unlimited storage with high-capacity cards (or by storing multiple maps on more than one card). On some units, additional memory will enable you to store additional waypoints.

♦ **Routes.** A series of waypoints listed in sequence from start to finish. Routes typically contain up to 30 waypoints. Designed to guide to a destination, they can also be inverted or reversed to track back from the destination to the starting point.

♦ **Sun/moon position.** Provides sun and moon positions, including sunrise and sunset.

♦ **Tide page.** Provides times for high and low tides. Some caches are hidden on islands that can be accessed only by foot at low tide.

♦ **Track log.** Plots an electronic breadcrumb trail as a sequence of dots or trackpoints, showing a path traveled. Various brands and models provide different numbers of trackpoints that can be used. A backtrack feature automatically establishes a route from the last track log to provide a series of waypoints to follow on the way out.

♦ **WAAS ready.** These receivers are capable of accepting radio signals, which can increase accuracy to within 3 meters. However, this feature will drain batteries faster than standard GPS use.

♦ **Water resistance.** Receivers are rated for their resistance to water. Water-resistant usually means the equipment can be splashed or briefly dunked (a rating of IPX4). Waterproof means the equipment can be submerged for a specific amount of time, such as 30 minutes, before damage occurs (a rating of IPX7). Regardless of rating, use a watertight box or bag if you use your receiver around water. Saltwater can kill electronics instantly.

◆ **Waypoints.** Specifically recorded locations stored within a receiver's memory. Saved waypoints enable you to return to exact locations. Various brands and models enable you to store different numbers of waypoints. Most modern receivers enable you to store at least 500.

◆ **Waypoint averaging.** A standard feature on most receivers. Waypoint averaging provides greater accuracy of saved waypoints because you actually record the position over a period of time. This is ideal for placing caches.

> **Dead Batteries**
>
> Using a receiver without a basemap database requires the ability to read and plot map coordinates. Coordinates alone are virtually useless without the ability to transfer their actual location to a map. The pointer arrow feature, however, is adequate to find most caches.

Types and Application

GPS receivers come in a variety of sizes and prices and provide various features. Recreational gear is grouped into the following four categories.

Handheld Without a Basemap Database

Magellan Sportrak.

Magellan

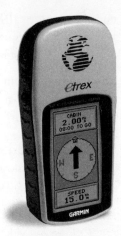

Garmin eTrex.

*Image used courtesy of Garmin
Ltd. or its affiliates. Copyright
Garmin Ltd. or its affiliates.*

Garmin GPS 76.

*Image used courtesy of Garmin
Ltd. or its affiliates. Copyright
Garmin Ltd. or its affiliates.*

These models are examples of low-cost, entry-level receivers. All work
well and are capable of the same accuracy and provide the same features
as more expensive models. These basic receivers are about the size of a
TV remote control, with an approximate 2-inch view screen. They
include built-in antennas and will most likely not include a remote
antenna jack.

♦ **Price.** $99 to $199.

♦ **Pro.** Low cost, small and lightweight, many features, and simple
to operate.

♦ **Con.** No basemap, points of interest only, which makes the
receiver more difficult to use and requires the ability to read and
plot map coordinates. Receivers without a rocker keypad are cumbersome to use. They might not work well in a vehicle unless they
accept a remote antenna. They will have little or no data storage
capacity for additional points of interest, and might not include a
computer-cable data port.

♦ **Application.** Ideal for hiking and biking where size and weight
are important. Purchase this type of receiver if low cost is a primary consideration.

Handheld with a Basemap Database

Magellan Meridian Color.

Magellan

Garmin GPSMAP 76S.

Image used courtesy of Garmin Ltd. or its affiliates. Copyright Garmin Ltd. or its affiliates.

Lorance iFinder Basic.

Lorance

The next step up, these receivers include an electronic basemap.

They may include other features such as memory or the capability to accept a memory card to store additional mapping data.

- ◆ **Price.** $195 to $499.

- ◆ **Pro.** Electronic basemap provides a useful reference. Additional features may include external jacks for a remote antenna and a computer data cable. Memory storage capacity allows the use of the manufacturer's maps on CD-ROM. Some models may also include an electronic compass and altimeter capable of functioning independently of satellite reception.

- ◆ **Con.** Screen size works well for general handheld use, but the screens are difficult to read in a moving vehicle. Occasional users may find the higher price prohibitive.

- ◆ **Application.** Ideal for all-around recreational use. Works well in vehicles through the use of a remote antenna.

Vehicle-Based Receivers

Various models of vehicle-based receivers are available. Their larger screens are ideal for RV or marine use. They are typically mounted with a swivel bracket and hard-wired, eliminating the need for batteries. These receivers are more expensive, averaging $500 to $1,000.

This type of unit works great for traveling around, but is not much good for geocaching if you can't take it with you on foot. You can take some of these larger models with you, such as the Garmin Street Pilot or 176C. The large color screen is great but can be a bit heavy and bulky for field use. You might decide that a larger-sized receiver is fine if you primarily use it mounted in a vehicle, but you can still take it with you when you go out on the trail.

Computers and PDAs

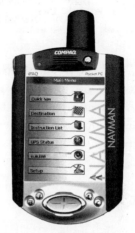

Garmin iQue 3600, a GPS PDA using a Palm operating system.

Image used courtesy of Garmin Ltd. or its affiliates. Copyright Garmin Ltd. or its affiliates.

Navman GPS 3450 for Compaq iPaq.

Navman

If you're already packing around a portable computer, there are options to convert it to a GPS receiver. Digital assistants, PDAs, or laptop computers can be used this way through the combination of software and an antenna. Handheld PDAs use an adapter sleeve with an antenna that plugs into an expansion slot. Laptops use a dash-mounted remote antenna.

Real-time tracking is another neat way to combine the use of receivers and computers. Various brands of mapping software will accept a GPS receiver's signal to display a user's location indicated as an icon centered on a PDA or laptop screen. Chapter 11 covers computers and real-time tracking.

- ◆ **Price.** $150 to $350 (software and antenna).

- ◆ **Pro.** Great way to utilize computer equipment and save money by using electronics already owned. PCs accept high-quality mapping software. Larger screen size with a greater memory capability at a lower cost.

- **Con.** Often a poor choice for geocaching because they are not as durable or weather resistant as regular GPS receivers. Laptops are limited to vehicle-based use due to size and power requirements. Unless you rig up a stand, a passenger is needed to hold the computer; in addition, the power and data cords are cumbersome.

- **Application.** Computers are an excellent complement to traditional GPS gear. They are great for trip planning and managing waypoints and routes. Ideal for vehicle-based use. Perfect for executives and road travelers who already use mobile computer equipment.

Antennas

Would you watch a big-screen TV with poor reception? Imagine sitting through the big game or favorite movie with a fuzzy picture and bad sound. You'll want good reception on your GPS receivers, too. No matter how good the equipment is, it will not function well without strong satellite reception.

As mentioned before, tree coverage, buildings, and cliff walls can stop reception dead in its tracks. Using a receiver on the dashboard of your vehicle usually doesn't work that great either. Mounting a receiver or PDA on the dash or using a suction cup to attach it to a windshield will obstruct your view. Some windshield safety glass is lined with metallic substances that block radio signals.

Here's a rundown of the different types of antennas and how they are best used:

Patch or microstrip. Most handheld receivers include this form of built-in antenna. The antenna is in the nose of the unit, which makes it the most compact and durable. This type is better at locking on to satellites overhead than to satellites on the horizon. For best accuracy, hold the receiver vertically.

- **Pro.** Durable, compact, and lightweight.

- **Con.** Reception might not be quite as good as the other options. A receiver with this antenna might not have a remote antenna jack.

Quadrifilar helix. This is a tube-style, detachable antenna that has been used by Garmin. It provides greater accuracy and can lock on to more satellites on the horizon. Best accuracy is achieved by adjusting the antenna straight up. Because the antenna is detachable, a jack is provided to plug in a remote antenna; you can also make the existing antenna a remote one with the use of a coax patch cable.

♦ **Pro.** Improved reception for increased accuracy. It ensures an antenna jack for going remote.

♦ **Con.** Can be more easily lost or broken.

External. Necessary for applications where equipment is mounted inside a vehicle. Most are powered, or "active." The amplified signal increases the ability to lock on to more satellites and compensates for signal loss due to an increased coax cable length. Use an antenna that is active. Passive, nonamplified antennas do not perform as well and can conflict with an internal antenna. Remote antennas can also be used on top of helmets or shoulder straps, allowing the GPS to be stored safely in packs. This helps protect the gear from being lost or damaged and frees up your hands. Under ideal conditions, a quality active antenna can pick up 11 or 12 satellites.

♦ **Pro.** Ideal for vehicle use. Active antennas provide the greatest potential to lock on to the most satellites possible.

♦ **Con.** They need to be securely mounted to prevent damage. They also need to be backed up with a standard antenna in case of failure.

 Eureka!

It helps to use cameras, flashlights, radios, and other gear that use the same AA batteries as your GPS unit. Solar chargers are available to keep batteries charged during longer stays in the field.

Batteries

Batteries are the lifeblood of geocaching. Not only do you need extras, but when it's time to purchase them, there are more options than you might think. Choosing the right type will help squeeze a little extra mileage out of them and possibly save a little money, too. Here are the basics:

- **Alkaline.** These are typically the most common and economical to use. A quality set of these batteries will last 12 or more hours in a receiver. They are also sold in bulk to reduce the cost further. Power is considerably reduced in freezing temperatures.

- **Alkaline rechargeable.** They will only last approximately 60 percent of the life of a regular alkaline, but they can be recharged effectively up to 25 times. Most rechargeable batteries have memory. Batteries will last longer if they are completely drained before charging.

- **Lithium.** These batteries are more expensive, but may last more than 30 hours in a receiver. A set of four costs approximately $10. This style is ideal for low-temperature use.

- **NiCad.** These batteries may only have a life span approximately 33 percent of alkaline, but they can be recharged around 500 times. Economical to use, but plan on changing them every 7 hours.

- **Nickel metal-hydride (NiMH).** Similar to NiCads, but with an increased life span of approximately 75 percent of alkaline. The greatest benefit is that they do not need to be drained before recharging.

Eureka!

Batteries can be lightly greased to prevent corrosion. This is ideal for longer-term storage applications, such as in flashlights, or any use where the gear is exposed to moisture.

To save batteries, turn the receiver off when you're not using it. Using the screen's backlight burns power faster. Backlights are typically on a timer that can be programmed to stay on a reduced amount of time. Check the equipment's battery-level gauge frequently to avoid having gear go dead.

Special Considerations for Geocaching

Fortunately for geocaching, expensive and elaborate gear is not required. More importantly, it should be easy to use, accessible, and durable. Outdoor gear gets seriously abused. Gear can get smashed in bags and packs, rained on, frozen, dropped in an icy river, and so forth. You get the idea. Luckily, most receivers are built to military specs to withstand a lot of electronic killing factors like moisture, dust, and vibration.

Here's a list of feature considerations for good geocaching GPS gear:

- ◆ **Basemap.** This is highly recommended. The additional cost is marginal, and the increase in the equipment's usefulness is substantial.

- ◆ **Channels.** Use a receiver with 12 parallel channels. This should include most manufactured after 1997. Older, single-channel receivers are much slower and might not be as accurate.

- ◆ **External antenna jack.** This allows the equipment to be mounted inside a vehicle. It is not always possible to obtain good satellite coverage through a front windshield. Even backpackers will benefit from the ability to safely store the receiver inside a pack with an antenna attached to backpack shoulder straps.

- ◆ **Interface.** If using the receiver with a computer, be sure that it includes both data in/out ports, and make sure it's NMEA compatible.

- ◆ **Memory.** This is used to load detailed topographic or street-level digital maps into the receiver. Topo maps use up a great deal of memory. Capacity should be at least 8 megabytes, or the receiver should include the ability to accept a memory card for as much memory as needed.

- ◆ **Power source.** Use a cigarette lighter power cable whenever possible. If you're only using batteries, make sure to carry spares and use a solar charger for extended field use.

- ◆ **Rocker keypad.** Using a receiver without a rocker keypad is like using a computer without a mouse.

- ◆ **Screen size.** For visual ease of operation, use a receiver with the largest screen that can be realistically carried. Screen size is measured diagonally. Color is great and helps define map features, although it does burn battery power.

◆ **Waterproof.** Sooner or later the gear will get submerged. Get gear that is at least water-resistant. Plastic bags and boxes give electronics a little additional protection.

The Least You Need to Know

◆ Consider how you will be using your gear and take the time to learn about all the various features and options available.

◆ Geocachers should shop for receivers that are durable, waterproof, and compact.

◆ Receivers with built-in maps, external antenna jacks, and power cords are typically worth the extra cost.

◆ Making an informed buying decision will save time, money, and aggravation.

Chapter 10

GPS Setup and Features

In This Chapter

- ◆ Learn what those buttons and screens do

- ◆ Do your homework to learn how to set up a new receiver properly

- ◆ Learn how to use the simulator mode to program the various options without wasting battery power

- ◆ Get around easier by learning how to use waypoints, track logs, and routes

Once you own a GPS receiver, it's time to actually learn how to use the thing. You have thoroughly read the owner's manual, right? We thought so. We also tried reading ours—with mixed results. The information in this chapter will in no way replace the owner's manual, but we hope to help by showing you what all those buttons and screens are for.

After that, it's time to get into the Setup menu to program the gear to play. After the basics are out of the way, we can get down to the meat of using GPS and saving waypoints, track logs, and routes.

Learning Your Way Around Your Receiver

As much as we love high-tech gear, it can be intimidating, especially at first glance: There are so many buttons and screens. We enjoy the entertainment center, but who wants to figure out every button on the remote control? Learning how to use GPS technology is similar. Most electronics have more features than you will ever use. That's fine, but you still need to learn the basics. Besides, learning how to use a receiver is fun and easy. Every new function opens up new possibilities, and familiarizing yourself with the unit will quickly increase your confidence in backcountry travel.

Dead Batteries

This information is not intended to replace your equipment's owner manual. Take the time to study the operation of your gear enough to comfortably know how to use it. Read this chapter side by side with your receiver's manual before you head out, and take the manual along in a waterproof bag.

Fortunately, the major brands of GPS receivers share most of the same features and commands, although they may work a little differently. Studying this information with your product's instruction manual will provide an understanding of how your gear works, with its many capabilities.

Spend some time getting to know the purpose of each button and screen and practice using its features before relying on the gear in the field.

Which Button Does What?

You can expect to find several kinds of buttons on most GPS receivers. Here's a list:

◆ **Enter.** This button is used to select options from menus and to save waypoints.

◆ **GoTo or Nav.** This button allows the selection of a waypoint from a list of waypoints saved within the receiver's memory. Holding this button down in an emergency saves a "man overboard" (MOB) waypoint.

◆ **Page.** This button scrolls through the receiver's set of data screens.

◆ **Power.** This button turns the equipment on and off and may be used to adjust the screen's backlight.

◆ **Rocker keypad.** This button is used to move around on the map page and to select options from menus.

◆ **Zoom.** This button is used to change the viewing scale on the map page. "In" provides a more detailed smaller-scale view. "Out" provides a larger-scale view.

Navigation Nuggets

When using steering-guidance screens or pointer arrows, it is nearly impossible to maintain the exact bearing unless traveling by air or water. Roads and trails usually require you to truck in different directions before reaching the destination. They are helpful, however, to determine if you're on track, and are the major indicator used in geocaching.

Common Pages

There are several types of pages you can expect to encounter on your GPS receiver. Here are some common ones:

◆ Active Route Page: Once a route is selected, it displays the list of waypoints in the route and indicates which waypoint is currently activated.

◆ Compass Page: Used for steering guidance, this page provides a compass ring and pointer arrow. If a waypoint is selected, the arrow will point to its bearing. An arrow pointing straight up indicates you are on course to reach the waypoint. The compass ring typically indicates the track, the direction actually being traveled. The compass reading will not be accurate unless the receiver is moving at least four miles per hour.

In a stationary position, a bearing number should be accurate, although a regular compass is needed to determine the bearing's direction.

The compass page, with its large pointer arrow, is the primary screen used to find a cache.

♦ Highway Page:

Also used for steering guidance. A picture of a moving highway runs down the page indicating an upcoming waypoint, or group of waypoints if using a route. To stay on course, keep the highway down the center of the screen. This screen is most helpful when straight-line navigation is possible.

The Compass and Highway pages are both guidance screens. They provide direct bearing to a geocache or anywhere else you might like to go.

Images used courtesy of Garmin Ltd. or its affiliates. Copyright Garmin Ltd. or its affiliates.

◆ Information or   Multiple data fields providing what-
Position Page: ever information is programmed to
                         appear. A wide variety of data can be
                         programmed to appear in a series of
                         fields. Take the time to review the
                         various information available to
                         determine what data is the most use-
                         ful to your application. The follow-
                         ing are some typical data fields:

  ◆ Altitude   Average speed

  ◆ Bearing   Course

  ◆ Current coordinates Distance to next

  ◆ ETA to next   Pointer arrow

  ◆ Speed   Sunrise/sunset

  ◆ Time of day   Time to next

  ◆ Track   Trip odometer

  ◆ Trip timer   User timer

  ◆ Map Page: Primary display page that indicates
                         your location with a *present position
                         pointer icon* pointing to your direction
                         of travel. The screen shows your
                         movement in real-time with a history
                         in the form of a track log. The screen
                         may be orientated to be displayed
                         with the top of the page indicating
                         north or the direction of travel.

◆ Satellite Status Page: Provides the number and signal
                         strength of the satellites received.
                         Includes EPE and DOP number
                         readings to estimate accuracy.
                         Provides current navigation status
                         such as: Searching, Acquiring, Poor
                         Coverage, 2-D Navigation or 3-D
                         Navigation. It also typically includes
                         a battery level gauge.

The best way to familiarize yourself with new gear is to simply turn it on and check the features. Go outside and get a satellite fix, then scroll through the pages. One of the most commonly used pages is the Map page. Your current location will be displayed in the center of the page by a present position arrow icon.

If your receiver has a rocker keypad, use it to move the cursor arrow around the map screen. A data field box will display changing coordinates and the distance from your current location. This is useful for finding approximate distances to nearby locations. Scroll to a nearby city and check out the bearing and distance. The distances provided are direct as the crow flies. Unless traveling in a straight line, mileage needs to be increased to estimate actual distance on the ground.

If your receiver includes an electronic basemap, it is viewed in greater or less detail by using a Zoom feature. When initially viewing the Map page, the present position arrow icon will be in the center of the screen. The bottom of the screen will include a distance indicator, showing the scale of the current map. Zooming in will increase the map's detail. Roads and waterways and their names will appear as an area of the map is zoomed into. The zoom range may go from 2,000 miles to 500 feet.

Setup

Before using the gear in the field, take time to carefully review the owner's manual to make some choices. The following sections summarize what to consider when selecting setup options.

Alarms

Alarms can be set for a specific time, waypoint arrival, and to notify if off-course. When the alarm activates, a text message will appear on the screen.

Backlight Timer

The backlighting on the map screen uses a good deal of power. If operating on batteries, set the light to remain on just long enough to view the screen. When using a direct power source, it is helpful to keep the light on.

Battery Type

Enter the type of battery used to ensure the greatest level of accuracy from the battery-level gauge. Installing batteries also resets the battery-use timer.

Coordinates

This setting determines how coordinates will be displayed. There are various options available based on your location and preference. The two primary geographic coordinate systems are latitude/longitude and Universal Transverse Mercator (UTM).

Latitude/longitude is displayed in degrees, minutes, and seconds. The selection may look like HDDD° MM' SS.S". The standard for geocaching is the minutes displayed with a decimal point without the use of seconds. This display looks like HDDD° MM.MMM".

UTM is metric and displays in meters. Its selection looks like [UPS/UTM]. The UPS is the UTM's system to grid the North and South Poles.

Distance Measurement

Distance and speed can be measured in statute or nautical miles. The receiver may also display metric kilometers. Note that a nautical mile is equal to 1.15 of a regular statute mile. A kilometer is equal to .62 of a statute mile, and a statute mile is equal to 1.6 kilometers. Based on your selection, altitude will display in either feet or meters.

Map Datum

The receiver will have been set as a default to one of the common map datums such as the one used for geocaching, WGS 84. In North

Navigation Nuggets

Remember, if working within a group, be sure everyone is speaking the same navigational language. Agree in advance on the following, and then set your GPS to the correct values:

1. Map coordinates, lat/long or UTM? If lat/long, full address or decimal point?

2. Which north, true or magnetic?

3. Which map datum?

America, other common datums include NAD27 CONUS and NAD83. Remember to set the receiver's datum to match topographic maps. Note that there are a number of options for NAD27. The primary datum used in North America is CONUS.

Map-Page Orientation

This sets the direction of the map page. North Up orients the top of the page to north despite the direction of travel. Track Up changes the top of the page to the direction of travel.

North

The type of north can be selected for your preference. The following are the options available:

◆ **Auto Mag Var.** Magnetic north automatically adjusts for local declination (the same reading as a compass).

◆ **True.** True north.

◆ **User Mag Var.** Adjustable to any degree of declination.

Time

Time of day is adjusted to display regular 12-hour time or 24-hour "military" time. The time provided is exact and set to your local time when you enter your time zone, or how many hours before or after UTC time (also known as Greenwich mean time or "Zulu time") your location happens to be.

Timers

A trip computer can be used to track average speed, or minimum speed, or provide an odometer for your overall travels or for a particular trip. Timer features also include a user timer and a battery-use timer. Remember to reset these fields before setting off on a new trip.

Navigation Nuggets
Most GPS receivers provide a Trip Computer feature. Set the computer before your next trek to check out interesting data. This includes trip odometer, average speed, trip timer, and maximum speed.

Save Your Batteries with Simulation, Demo, or GPS Off Mode

This mode saves valuable batter power by allowing you to review and program information without the receiver searching for satellites. This proves helpful when learning how to use the gear indoors; you can learn without the gear trying to obtain a constant satellite fix. Without the receiver searching for satellites, the battery power requirement is reduced by nearly half.

You can review, demonstrate, and program the receiver's various functions and features. It is ideal for transferring data with a computer and for updating and entering waypoints and routes. Despite not using a satellite fix, navigation calculations can still be made. For example, waypoints can be entered as a route to determine the bearing and distance between waypoints.

Unfortunately, the Satellite Status page may appear as if satellites are being received. This is only an example of what the Satellite Status page looks like under normal operating conditions. The unit's location will most likely appear as the last area for which the receiver obtained a real satellite fix. Be sure you are not in simulation mode during normal navigation operation.

Saving Waypoints

One of the primary reasons to use GPS is to save and travel to waypoints. A waypoint is a selected location of interest that is stored in the receiver's memory. This, of course, is the whole basis of geocaching; the cache's coordinates are saved as a waypoint.

Besides telling us the distance and compass bearing, the receiver's computer can provide neat information we have never had access to before. An estimated time of arrival (ETA) is provided based upon our current speed.

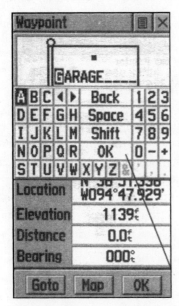 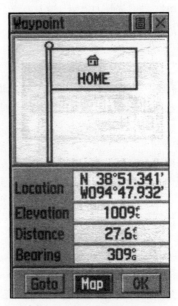

The best waypoint to save first is your own home location. The above Garmin screens show the waypoint name and symbol being selected.

Images used courtesy of Garmin Ltd. or its affiliates. Copyright Garmin Ltd. or its affiliates.

The first waypoint to save is your home. This is helpful, because regardless of where you are in the world, the waypoint can be recalled to determine how far in distance and time to return. Venture out to the yard for a satellite fix.

The present position pointer icon appears in the center of the Map page. Holding down the Enter/Mark button will give the option to save the current location as a waypoint. A mark waypoint screen appears and provides a new number such as 001. Using the rocker keypad or up/down buttons, select the letters to change the default number to the name "Home." You must press the Enter button between each letter or number saved. Most receivers provide at least six characters, letters, or numbers for saving waypoint names. This screen also displays the date the waypoint was created and the coordinates of the location. A symbol can also be selected, which is helpful to label and organize waypoints. In the preceding example, the house symbol that will appear on the Map page screen is selected.

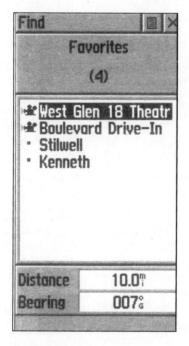

The waypoint screen shows a list of locations saved.

Image used courtesy of Garmin Ltd. or its affiliates. Copyright Garmin Ltd. or its affiliates.

Saving waypoints is important because it gives you a perspective of your travel area. Save lots of waypoints; your receiver will probably allow you to store 200 to 500, and you can always delete old ones. Save your campsite, the trailhead, where you park your truck, and your favorite picnic area or swimming hole. If you ever do get turned around, select the nearest waypoint you need to navigate to. You can select the waypoint page and select a waypoint, or press the GoTo or Nav button, and the screen will ask you what waypoint you want to go to, possibly the nearest or most recently saved. It's that simple; getting lost has never been so much fun. Even in a worst-case scenario with your batteries going dead, you can use your compass and hike out on the bearing provided with the selected waypoint.

Saving waypoints is a fun way to document your travels. Better yet, you can share them with others. There are a number of ways to save waypoints. Here is a list of seven:

♦ **Entered manually.** Geocaching style, the numeral coordinates are entered manually using the rocker keypad or up/down buttons.

♦ **Marking the current position.** This is one of the most common and easiest methods. Holding down the Enter/Mark button, as in the home example, saves the current position.

♦ **Selecting from a basemap.** Using the rocker keypad, the cursor arrow is moved to a desired location and then saved with the Enter/Mark button. Note that holding down the button too long may result in saving the current location instead of the planned position. Double-check the coordinates to ensure you did not save the current location. Using this same method with a Garmin unit and pressing the GoTo button will result in a waypoint titled "Map." This option puts the receiver into a GoTo navigation function to this location.

♦ **From a computer.** Geocaching style number two, previously saved waypoints and routes are loaded from a computer to the receiver. This is done through selecting a computer interface data-transfer option within the receiver and the use of a data cable.

♦ **Name search.** Most receivers provide the option for a name search of towns and cities. When the location is selected, pressing the GoTo or Nav button creates the location as a waypoint.

♦ **Mark a MOB position.** On many receivers, holding down the GoTo button saves a "man overboard" waypoint. This is a quick one-button method ideal for emergency situations, as indicated by the method's name.

♦ **Enter a projected position.** Compass bearing and distance information is entered in the reference fields on a new waypoint screen. This data can be entered from a current position or any other waypoint. From these values, the receiver projects the new location and saves it as a waypoint. Some of the more difficult caches require this function.

After waypoints have been saved, the data can be modified at any time. The name, symbol, and coordinates can be manually changed or deleted.

> **Navigation Nuggets**
>
> Holding down the GoTo or MOB button on most receivers saves the current location as a "man overboard" waypoint. This feature is designed as a one-button method for immediately marking and navigating back to a location.

Waypoint Averaging

As mentioned before, it is helpful when hiding a cache to improve the accuracy of the coordinates you provide for it by averaging a waypoint. After saving a waypoint, press the Menu button. If your receiver includes this function, a menu will appear asking whether you want to average this waypoint. Press Yes and a numbered counter will appear. This indicates how many seconds of averaging has taken place. Obviously, the longer you average, the greater the accuracy. You may want to set the receiver down and let it do its thing. Then come back in a few minutes and press Enter. The screen will provide an estimate of accuracy within feet or meters.

Track Logs

A track log is an electronic "breadcrumb" trail that is stored and displayed by the receiver. This log indicates the path you have traveled, greatly reducing the chance of becoming lost. Following a previously stored electronic track allows you to literally retrace your steps to backtrack to a previous position. This feature requires two elements to work properly. First, there must be a continual satellite fix for the duration of the track. If coverage is broken, blanks will appear on the track, which will most likely be represented as straight lines. The second element is that adequate memory be available to record the track.

Most receivers are somewhat limited in storage capacity. Depending on the unit's setting, one of two things will happen if the track log memory becomes full. The receiver will stop recording or it will automatically delete older track data. Most receivers provide the option of programming the track log as follows:

◆ **Fill.** This option records track log data until the memory is full. A text warning message may appear when the memory is full. This option is useful when returning to a starting position is most important.

◆ **Wrap.** Under this option, data is continually recorded. This is done by recording over the earliest saved data. This option is useful when the latest saved data is most important.

◆ **Off.** This may be useful to prevent recording excessive tracks to be saved on a log. Shutting this feature off presents a risk because no tracks will be recorded if you fail to turn it back on.

> **Navigation Nuggets**
>
> Track log data is valuable to geocachers because it does such a good job of documenting your travels. Zooming in on the Map page will show tracks in greater detail, which may help you to find a cache by indicating that you have circled a target area.

Another variable is how often a track will be recorded. This is known as the interval value. This adjusts the distance between each trackpoint to fit the user's application. Most receivers default to some form of automatic or resolution method where a track is recorded based on the user going into a turn or traveling approximately 80 feet in a straight line. This option works best for most applications. A user-defined distance or time can also adjust the interval. Adjusting the tracks to record by distance or time may be necessary due to most receivers' limited memory to store trackpoints.

Depending on the brand and model, the storage capacity typically averages between 1,000 and 3,000 trackpoints. To extend the range of a track log, a sailboat user traveling a long distance records a trackpoint every 400 feet. A hiker on a twisty mountain trail requires more detail, so a trackpoint is recorded every 40 feet. A good distance for a road trip is 184 feet or approximately 50 meters.

Saving Track Logs

Tracks being saved as a track log.

Image used courtesy of Garmin Ltd. or its affiliates. Copyright Garmin Ltd. or its affiliates.

Track logs are saved just as waypoints and routes. First, clear any previously saved unnecessary track log data. If necessary, adjust the interval value, the distance between each trackpoint, for your application. Select the Fill or Wrap option if the new track log may be longer than what the receiver can store. After the trip, select to record the track log. Most receivers will then save the track log in a reduced number of trackpoints and title the log with the current date. Like a waypoint, the log can be renamed at any time. To avoid a memory problem, users on longer-distance trips can record their travels with multiple saved track logs.

Remember the following points when saving a track log:

♦ Clear the track log at the starting point of the new trip.

♦ Save the track log at the completion of the trip.

♦ Be sure that the receiver is operational during the entire time of the trip. Lost satellite signals or power will result in a discontinuous log. The log will still be recorded, although broken. Non-operational time will be recorded as a gap or a straight line between recorded tracks.

TracBack Route

Garmin has developed a TracBack feature that automatically creates a return or inverted route with 30 waypoints from the most recently saved track log. This feature allows you to return to the starting position with an easy route to follow. After a track log is recorded, simply select the TracBack option for the route conversion.

Routes

A route is a series of waypoints that are listed in the order of start to finish. Routes may contain up to 30 waypoints depending on the capacity of the receiver. Each section between two waypoints is a leg. To create a route, select a series of waypoints in the sequence they are to be followed.

Garmin screen shows an active route.

Image used courtesy of Garmin Ltd. or its affiliates. Copyright Garmin Ltd. or its affiliates.

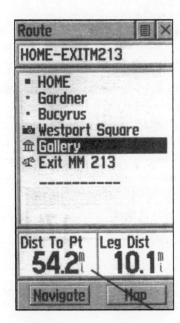

Routes are beneficial because, unless you're flying or sailing, it's difficult to travel in a straight line. Obstacles require us to travel indirect
paths until we reach our destination. This feature provides direction by
organizing waypoints in the flow
of travel. Following a route not
only makes navigation easier, it
also reduces the risk of error.
Multiple waypoints like cabin, stand,
camp, and fish, may not mean much
by themselves, but when saved in a
route they are given order, making
an easy sequence to follow. Routes
also help designate points of interest,
including locations to stop for camping, eating, or refueling.

Navigation Nuggets

Routes are beneficial to
geocachers because
they allow a series of caches
to be saved in a sequence.
Those of you who like going
after multiple caches in the
same day can be easily
directed from one to the other,
with the distance provided
between each cache.

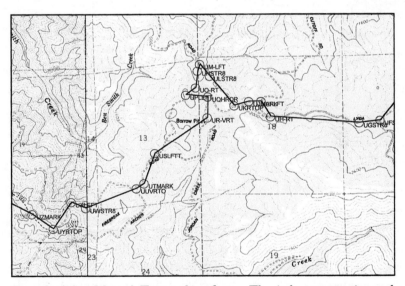

*Route loaded on Maptech Topographic software. The circles are waypoints and
the solid lines indicate route legs.*

Maptech

Saving Routes

There are at least six ways to save routes:

- **Entered while traveling.** One of the easiest ways to create a route is by saving waypoints along the way. These waypoints are selected and added to a route.

- **Manually selected.** Previously saved waypoints are manually selected from the receiver's database in the order they are to appear in the route.

- **Loaded from a computer.** Previously recorded routes can be loaded into a receiver through the use of mapping software and a data cable.

- **From a saved track log.** Using the map pointer arrow, select key locations to save as waypoints along a track log.

- **Use the TracBack feature.** Activating this option creates a 30-waypoint route from the most recently saved track log.

- **Automatic routing.** Newer receivers can automatically create a route to a selected location within the unit's software database.

When a route is saved, data is displayed on the active route page. It includes the distance between each waypoint and the total distance of the route. Detailed information is available for each leg of the trip, including the distance between waypoints, compass bearing, and ETA. Routes can also be easily edited by adding or deleting waypoints. Most receivers have the capacity to store 30 to 50 waypoints for each route.

When a route is saved, the default name will be the date it was created. The route can be renamed at any time. One of the main benefits of using routes is that they are reversible. After the last waypoint destination is reached, the route is reversed by an Invert command to backtrack to the starting point.

Auto Routing

As GPS receivers become more advanced, standard features will include the capability to search for addresses, intersections, and businesses from a built-in or loaded software database. Automatic routing refers to the ability of the receiver to automatically create a route to a selected location within its database.

Using a Find feature creates these automatic routes. The receiver searches for the location and then establishes a route based on user-defined criteria such as reaching the location in the fastest time, in the shortest distance, or in a direct line in an off-road mode.

Navigation gets even easier with new guidance features that provide pop-up screens and audible alarms for next-turn directions. Text screens display a directional arrow prior to each new turn in a route.

This latest technology is ideal for business travelers, emergency vehicle drivers, and anyone who needs to find unfamiliar addresses fast. These types of routing features will not always be completely accurate, but they do work reasonably well. The main problem is that software is not updated fast enough to reflect street changes. Programs can also have difficulty distinguishing between one-way and two-way streets. This feature will become more useful as mapping software continues to improve.

The Least You Need to Know

- Take the time to learn the buttons and screens.
- Carefully go through the setup options to ensure your receiver is programmed properly.
- Know how to enter waypoint coordinates manually.
- Know how to find, recall, and go to waypoints.
- Understand track logs and routes and how they may be helpful to your application.
- Check out the autorouting features available; they might just be on your next receiver.

Chapter 11

Navigation System and Compass Basics

In This Chapter

- ◆ Learn the difference between latitude/longitude and the UTM systems
- ◆ How to select the best system for your application
- ◆ Learn the difference between true and magnetic north
- ◆ How to take compass bearings like a Boy Scout

It's easy to think that all of our navigation worries are over after spending a wad of hard-earned cash for a new GPS receiver. It's true that GPS does provide more navigation freedom than we have ever had before, but that doesn't mean you don't have to learn the basics. As mentioned before, knowing the basics is important to back up your electronic gear as well as use it to its fullest capacity.

Learning to understand navigation systems and how to use a compass is the whole basis of navigation, whether you're using GPS or not. GPS is not some magical system that just automatically gives you all the data you need to tell you where you are, where you're going, and how to get there. Well, actually it is, but it functions on the basic navigation systems that have been used for hundreds of years.

This chapter explains what all those numbers mean in those geocache coordinates you've learned to enter into your receiver. This chapter covers the latitude/longitude system and the UTM system. After that, it's time to find your bearing the old-fashion way, with a compass.

Degrees or Meters?

The two primary geographic coordinate systems used around the world are latitude/longitude and Universal Transverse Mercator (UTM). Most North American GPS units are programmed to default to latitude/longitude. UTM or any other system can be easily selected in the Setup menu. Either system provides a numeric set of coordinates for any location in the world.

UTM is often considered easier to read because it is based on the metric system, using kilometers and meters instead of degrees, minutes, and seconds. Unfortunately, in North America most maps do not include UTM grids or tick marks (except for detailed topographic maps).

Neither system is difficult to learn, but both require some homework. At first glance they can seem confusing because each system seems to function in an opposite manner from the other. The other problem is that we do not think of distances in degrees, minutes, and seconds. In the United States, we use miles and football fields, which means we do not think of distances in kilometers and meters.

For general navigation it's important to have an understanding of the latitude/longitude system. For doing detailed groundwork on topographic maps (like while geocaching), it is easier to use the UTM system. Read on to get on track with both.

Latitude/Longitude

Latitude lines run horizontally around the globe and parallel the earth's equator. The equator separates the globe in northern and southern hemispheres. The equator is 0° with lines stacked horizontally north and south to 90° at each pole. These parallel lines measure north/south coordinates. "Latitude/flatitude" is a way to remember that these lines run horizontally. They are also referred to as "parallels" because they are parallel to the equator.

Longitude lines circle the globe vertically, intersecting the North and South Poles to measure east/west coordinates. The starting point is 0° at Greenwich, England, and these lines wrap around the earth east and west to 180°. The way to remember these lines is by "longitude/ longertude." These lines are the longest because they do not narrow at the poles as latitude lines do. They are also referred to as "meridians," the prime meridian beginning in Greenwich, England.

◆ Latitude lines are horizontal and measure north/south coordinates.

◆ Longitude lines are vertical and measure east/west coordinates.

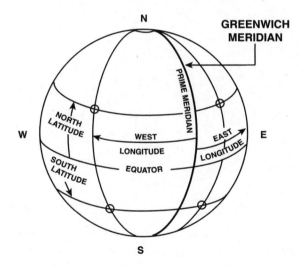

A globe showing latitude/ longitude lines in conjunction with the prime meridian and the equator. Note that latitude lines are horizontal and longitude lines are vertical.

U.S. Army

This system uses degrees, minutes, and seconds. One degree equals 60 minutes, and each minute equals 60 seconds.

1° = 60' (minutes), 1' (minute) = 60" (seconds).

That is how latitude/longitude coordinates are written, in degrees °, minutes ' and, seconds ".

Distance

◆ One degree = 69.05 *statute miles.*

◆ One minute = 1 *nautical mile* or 1.15 statute ground miles.

◆ One second = 100 feet.

These distances are for latitude, but accurate for longitude only at the equator. This is because the distance between the longitude lines narrow as they approach the North and South Poles. Because of this factor, the longitude distance decreases as the lines of longitude reach the poles. This is why latitude/longitude grids are rectangular instead of square.

A globe showing lines of longitude narrowing as they reach the North Pole.

Dawn Wright, OSU

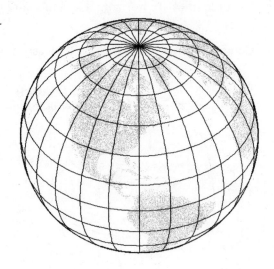

Geo-Lingo

Statute vs. nautical mile—It's true: There are two versions of a mile. A standard ground mile is known as a statute mile, with a distance of 5,280 feet. Sailors use the nautical mile. Its length is 6,080 feet, which is also the length of a minute. Officially, the nautical mile has been declared obsolete as of January 1, 2000, although it is still a distance measurement option on your GPS receiver.

Coordinate Address

A confusing issue with use of this system is that the same address can be displayed in three different formats. The following three addresses are all for the same longitude coordinate.

1. **Full address showing degrees, minutes, and seconds.** In a GPS receiver, this setting looks like HDDD° MM' SS'S".

   N 43° 41' 58.9"   W 122° 49' 10.7"

2. **Decimal minutes, which eliminates the seconds.** In a GPS receiver, this setting looks like HDDD° MM.MMM'.

   N 43° 41.982'   W 122° 49.178'

3. **Decimal degrees, which eliminates minutes and seconds.** In a GPS receiver, this setting looks like HDDD.DDDDD°.

   N 43.69970°   W 122.81963°

Latitude is listed first, measuring the north/south position. This address is north of the equator by 43 degrees, 41 minutes, and 58.9 seconds.

Longitude is listed second, measuring the east/west position. This address is west of Greenwich, England, by 122 degrees, 49 minutes, and 10.7 seconds.

Coordinates are listed with directional letters or positive/negative signs. Latitude numbers north of the equator are positive numbers. Longitude numbers west of the prime meridian are negative numbers.

> **Navigation Nuggets**
> It can be a little confusing going back and forth between the standard and metric systems. Remember that one mile equals 1.609 kilometers, and one kilometer (1,000 meters) equals .62 miles. Also, a meter is just slightly longer than a yard, equaling 3.28 feet.

+ 43° 41' 58.9"   −122° 49' 10.7"

Mils, which really aren't used in geocaching, are used for greater detail, by dividing each degree into 17.7 parts:

A 360° circle = 6,400 mils   One mil = .05625°

One degree = 17.778 mils

Navigation Nuggets

It is pretty straightforward that latitude should start from the equator, because the equator is the middle of the planet. But how did Greenwich, England, become the origin of 0° longitude?

In 1506, mapmaker Pedro Reinel was the first to draw the starting point for measuring longitude. Until the nineteenth century, the world calculated longitude from the Portuguese Madeira Islands or, in many cases, used their own country's capitol city as a reference point for zero longitude. You can imagine how confusing it could get for merchant ships!

The rise of British dominance on the high seas resulted in the European conference changing the location of 0° longitude to Greenwich, England, in 1884. We now use Greenwich for both the origin of longitude in navigation and for setting our clocks all over the world.

Universal Transverse Mercator (UTM)

The UTM system uses the metric system of kilometers and meters instead of degrees, minutes, and seconds. Remember the name of this system by the initials of "**U T**alkin to **M**e?" On the top of each cache information page, you will see these coordinates under the traditional latitude/longitude address.

The UTM world grid divides the globe into 60 equal sections called zones, 6° wide. Each zone is numbered 1 through 60, beginning at 180° longitude, wrapping around the globe to the east. This system covers between 84° N and 80° S. The area above and below these latitudes, the North and South Poles, are covered by the universal polar stereographic (UPS) grid system. This system is listed in the GPS receiver's Setup menu as UPS/GPS.

Each 6° zone has horizontal and vertical reference lines. A vertical line, known as the zone meridian, splits the section into two 3° halves. Vertical and horizontal grid lines are 1,000 meters or 1 kilometer apart. Coordinates indicate the number of meters east from the beginning zone line, easting, and how many meters north or south from the equator, northing. This is how the coordinates are always read, to the right, easting, and then up, northing.

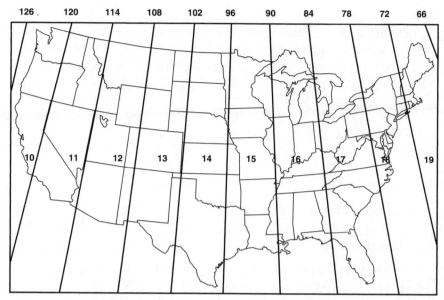

UTM zones across the United States.

U.S. Geological Survey

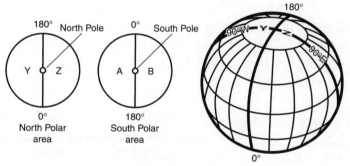

UPS grids cover the poles in the UTM system.

U.S. Army

Easting is the horizontal east/west measurement that indicates the number of kilometers and meters the coordinate is east from the start of the zone line. The numbers increase moving left to right, west to east. Each zone's meridian begins with 500,000.

Northing is the vertical north/south measurement that indicates the number of kilometers and meters the coordinate is north or south of the equator. The number at the equator in the northern hemisphere is 0000000. This number increases moving north. In the southern hemisphere, the number at the equator begins with 10000000, and decreases moving south.

Here is a set of UTM coordinates:

10 T   0624301 E, 4859317 N

This is how UTM coordinates are broken down:

◆ (10) indicates the coordinates are in the tenth world zone. Note on the previous U.S. graph, this vertical zone covers the western United States.

◆ (T) indicates the world zone designator. This horizontal zone covers the northern United States.

◆ (0624301) is the easting as indicated by the (e) at the end of the number. Each zone's meridian begins with 500,000; therefore, this location is 124,301 meters, or 124.3 kilometers east of the zone's meridian.

◆ (4859317) is the northing as indicated by the (n) at the end of the number. The equator in the northern hemisphere is 0000000, therefore, this location is 4,859,317 meters or 4,859.3 kilometers north of the equator.

Navigation Nuggets

UTM coordinates are often considered easier to use because they're based on kilometer grids. It can be confusing, however, to mix the metric system with miles. Remember: A meter is just longer than a yard (39.37 inches), and 1,000 meters (a kilometer) equals .62 of a mile.

The larger two numbers are called the principal digit. These correspond with the coordinates that run along the top, bottom, and sides of the map. The principal digit numbers are 1 kilometer, or 1,000 meters, apart. This is what makes UTM coordinates easier to read, knowing that map grid lines are in 1,000 meter blocks.

This system is often considered easier to use for the following reasons:

♦ There are no negative or decimal-point coordinates.

♦ The grids are square, allowing coordinates to be more easily measured.

♦ Coordinates translate directly into a more recognizable measurement format of kilometers and meters.

♦ Points on a map can be selected by site with accuracy within 50 meters.

Selecting a Coordinate System

The system you decide to use should be based on the type of navigating you're doing. Here are some issues to consider:

♦ If you are working within a group, a primary factor should be to use whatever system the group is using.

♦ The latitude/longitude system is preferred by long-range travelers such as pilots and sailors.

♦ The UTM system is best for detailed groundwork, such as in geo-caching. The system is typically limited to detailed topographic maps from 1:24,000 to 1:250,000.

♦ Often the maps available will dictate what system you use. United States Geological Survey (USGS) topographic maps include a number of systems. Other less-detailed maps often include latitude/longitude tick marks, but not for UTM.

Other Coordinate Systems

A couple of other systems are commonly used in land navigation. You will not use these systems in geocaching, but there's no harm in knowing what they are when you run across them later. Here's a quick run-down on each.

Military Grid Reference System (MGRS)

The U.S. military uses the military grid reference system, which is based upon UTM/UPS grids. The difference is that each zone is divided horizontally into 20 west/east section rows. Each row is 8° north to south, except for the farthest north section, which is 12°. Each row is assigned a letter of the alphabet. This is referred to as the grid zone designation. The sections are lettered from south to north, with the letters C to X, eliminating the I and O. On the UPS grid, letters A and B are used for the South Pole, and Y and Z are used for the North Pole.

The zone number is listed first, and then the letter: Zone 15, Row S or 15S. In this system, be sure not to confuse the S with south, because it is in the northern hemisphere. Each 8° × 6° or 8° × 12° row is 100,000 square meters. The grids are further divided into smaller sections identified by the combination of two letters. These letters make a location unique from any other address in the world. Of these sets of double letters, the first is the column designation, and the section is the row designation.

Township, Range, and Section

The federal township, range, and section (TRS) grids are used in the United States primarily west of Ohio. This system was developed by the U.S. government as early as 1784 as a more accurate and standardized system to survey land.

This system divides land into 36 approximately square-mile units called townships. Each township has a township and range designation to define its 36-square-mile area. The horizontal rows are the township designation. Township coordinates are numbered and listed as north or south from a selected latitude baseline. The vertical rows are the range designation. Range coordinates are numbered and listed as west or east of a selected principal meridian of longitude.

Townships are divided into 36 one-square-mile, 640-acre parcels called sections. The sections are numbered from 1 to 36 within the township. Section one begins in the northeast corner as the numbers proceed west, then east, alternately down each row, ending with 36 in the southeast corner.

Sections are divided into quarters, which are further quartered to describe a property location. For example, the legal description for the Utah Geological Survey's former office on Foothill Drive is written SE [1/4], NW [1/4], Section 23, T.1 S., R.1 E., of the Salt Lake Base Line. This system is good for finding a general direction but lacks serious accuracy without further description. A quarter of the section is 166 acres. To get within 40 acres, a section must be divided two more times, such as the NW [1/4] of the SW [1/4].

Metal yellow section markers or location posters that specify TRS coordinates can be found in the field. The township and range coordinates of this 36-square-mile township are indicated on the top. Wilderness roads are often numbered to correspond to this system. For example, a road numbered 10N59 may indicate that it began in Township 10 North.

The TRS system can appear outdated and confusing, although it is important to know because it is still so commonly used in plotting real property from residences to mining claims. Most topographic and U.S. Forest Service maps include the grid and coordinates, which appear in red. Range numbers are on the top and bottom of a map, and township numbers are on the left and right sides.

Navigation Nuggets

The TRS system is helpful in many ways. First, the numbered section squares on a topo map make a useful reference because they are approximately 1 square mile. In the field, you can find markers where these sections meet. If you find a marker, you can easily plot your position on a map. The third benefit is that wilderness roads are sometimes numbered based on this system, allowing a road to be traced back to its origins.

The Compass

Now that you know your way through degrees and kilometers, let's make sure you're heading in the right direction. So why does a modern GPS user need to use an old-fashioned compass? GPS receivers do not replace the compass because they do not provide directional information when they're stationary.

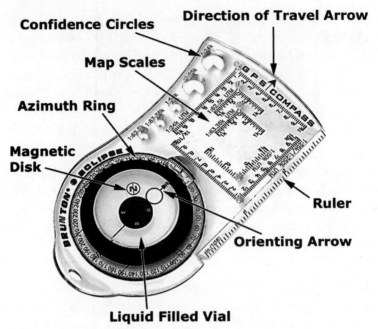

Confidence Circles

Direction of Travel Arrow

Map Scales

Azimuth Ring

Magnetic Disk

Ruler

Orienting Arrow

Liquid Filled Vial

This is a diagram of a standard orienteering compass. Note that the azimuth ring or bezel includes the cardinal points N, E, W, and S, north being 0 or 360 degrees.

Brunton Company

Most of us own at least one compass, but have we ever taken the time to learn how to actually use it? We know the needle points north, but here is where it gets a little technical. Have you ever picked up a compass and thought a direction was a little more the other way? Well, it probably is. The earth's magnetic poles do not line up exactly with the earth's North and South Poles. The magnetic North Pole is offset from the "true" North Pole, and its location varies over time. Because magnetic north and true north are not the same, compass degrees require adjustment to compensate for the difference. This difference is called *declination*. An imaginary line, known as the agonic line, vertically circles the globe. Only at this line are magnetic north and true north the same.

Geo-Lingo

Declination is the difference between true north and magnetic north. The difference varies around the globe, and it is important to know for setting your compass accordingly.

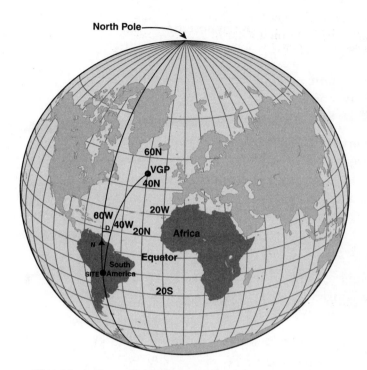

The globe indicates the difference between the North Pole and magnetic north, known as the virtual geomagnetic pole.

Cornell University Geological Sciences

How Many Norths Are There?

In the United States, the agonic line runs through the Great Lakes down to the east of Florida. To the west of this line, the declination is to the east, requiring degrees of declination to be increased. To the east, the declination is to the west, requiring degrees to be subtracted. For example, declination in Oregon averages 18° east. Eighteen degrees needs to be added to any magnetic needle bearing to convert it to a true north bearing.

Dead Batteries

A satellite-based GPS compass will not provide a directional reading in a stationary position. An accurate reading requires the receiver to be moving approximately 4 miles per hour.

Here's a list of the north variations:

◆ **True north.** Direction to the actual North Pole

◆ **Magnetic north.** Direction of compass needle as it points to magnetic north

◆ **Grid north.** Vertical map grid lines that may deviate from true north (usually not enough difference to consider)

The best way to determine declination is by simply checking the bottom of a local map. Note that if the map is more than 30 years old, the value may have changed slightly. GPS receivers automatically make this adjustment and can be programmed to display either true or magnetic north.

Remember to convert magnetic north to true north before using compass readings with a map. For example, in the United States ...

> **Navigation Nuggets**
> Finding the declination for your area is easy. On the receiver's Setup menu, you can set up your receiver to tell you true or magnetic north. Another way is to check the declination scale at the bottom of your map.

◆ Declination is eastern if you're west of the agonic line (western United States). Magnetic bearings are converted to true north by adding the number of declination degrees.

◆ Declination is western if you're east of the agonic line (eastern United States). Magnetic bearings are converted to true north by subtracting the number of declination degrees.

Example:

◆ 60° bearing, declination is 13° east: $60° + 13° = 73°$ for true north

◆ 60° bearing, declination is 17° west: $60° - 17° = 43°$ for true north

◆ The procedure is reversed to convert true north to magnetic north.

- Remember the direction does not change, only the bearing number.

Finding True North

In the field. Using the example of the above topographic map, declination is 17.5° east. This means that true north is left of magnetic north. Rotating the compass (not the bezel) until the magnetic needle, azimuth ring or bezel, and the travel arrow all align provides a magnetic north direction at 0°. To find true north, rotate the compass to the left until the magnetic needle is pointing at 17.5°. The travel and orienteering arrows are now pointing at true north, with the magnetic needle pointing at 17.5°.

The procedure is to add the amount of declination to the bearing. Using a bearing of 0° makes the math simple. Regardless of the magnetic bearing, simply add or subtract the amount of declination. Using the compass's declination scale makes this task even easier. Note that it is difficult to adjust for the half of a degree. With the compass used in this example, each small tick mark on the bezel is 2 degrees. Under the circumstances, a half of a degree is not distinguishable, and we would round up to 18°. If you do not want to bother with doing the calculations, get a compass that can be mechanically set to indicate true north.

On a map. There are two ways to find true north on a map. The first is by rotating the map to set it to true north. This orientation helps reference landmarks while in the field.

The second method is by simply using the map's grid lines. The declination chart indicates the grid lines are off to the right by only .13°. These lines are not exactly to true north; being only a fraction of a degree off, however, they are close enough. Within the compass bezel there are a series of north/south lines that run parallel to the orienteering arrow. These north/south lines are

Eureka!

Special compasses can be purchased that can be mechanically set for local declination. We highly recommend that you purchase a compass that can be adjusted so that you don't have to make the declination calculation yourself. Remember to reset the declination adjustment if traveling outside your local area.

simply aligned with the map's vertical grid lines. The west/east points on the bezel can also be aligned with the horizontal lines. Regardless of the map's orientation, the compass is referenced to true north. When using grid lines, double-check that you are not referencing township and range lines, which often do not run straight. These lines are often angled and are usually red.

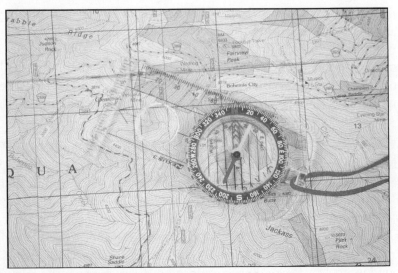

The north/south lines on the compass's bezel are aligned with the vertical grid lines on the map. Regardless of which way the map is really facing, the user obtains a true north bearing of 294° in this example.

Jack W. Peters

Important Terms

- ◆ **Attack points.** One or more landmarks used to reach a navigation target.

- ◆ **Back bearing.** Reversing a bearing for a return trip. It is 180° in the opposite direction.

- ◆ **Bearing.** A direction measured by a compass degree needed to travel to stay on a course. Also known as an azimuth.

◆ **Cardinal points.** The primary compass points: N, E, S, and W. The intercardinal points are NE, SE, SW, and NW.

◆ **Course.** The direction between two points, or to reach a navigation target.

◆ **Navigation or "nav" target.** A destination or waypoint to be reached.

◆ **Track.** The actual direction currently being traveled to reach a navigation target.

Shooting a bearing with an orienteering compass. Taking careful aim with this center-hold technique reduces error.

Jack W. Peters

Shooting a Bearing

The whole point of packing around a compass is that it enables you to determine direction and find a bearing. The compass indicates a direction relative to magnetic north. From this information, we can determine what bearing degree to travel to reach a navigational target. Compass navigation is based on moving from one landmark to another until the final destination is reached. Here is how it is done:

Dead Batteries
Compasses will not work accurately around metal or electricity. Take bearings away from vehicles and power lines.

1. Find an "attack point" landmark like a large tree, rock, or mountain.

2. Hold the compass close to the body and flat, and rotate the body to align with the landmark. Do not hold the compass in front of a metal belt buckle.

3. Rotate the compass bezel ring until the north-sided needle is "boxed" by the orienteering arrow. A rhyme to remember is "put the red in the shed."

4. Check the degree on the bezel ring that aligns with the travel arrow.

5. Take a few readings for accuracy (shifting your eyes from the compass to the target and back about three times), making final adjustments as the compass is being sighted to the attack point.

6. If using magnetic north, don't forget to adjust the bearing, plus or minus, for declination. Remember the direction does not change, just the bearing.

Try it, it is easier than it sounds, and it's fun to practice. From the porch, shoot a bearing to the mailbox. Then to the neighbor's fence. Now back to the garage and back to the porch. In the field, it is wise to write down the bearings traveled to enable you to repeat or backtrack the route. A back bearing is reversing a bearing for a return trip. It is 180° in the opposite direction. For example, a bearing of 5° north would require a back or return bearing of 185° south.

Navigation Nuggets
Compasses are magnetized differently for northern and southern hemispheres. If you travel north or south of the equator, remember that each hemisphere requires a specifically magnetized compass.

Compass Accuracy

The importance of degree accuracy depends on the distance to be traveled. Using a handheld compass, it would be expected that a user might be a few degrees off. Moving a few miles from one target point to another, using landmarks, a user will

hopefully be close enough to find
the desired location. It is clear that
by not making the declination
adjustment, the user could easily
miss the target without major landmarks to serve as a guide. Try walking across the front yard to the
mailbox in a bearing 18° off. You will
miss the target; by using the mailbox
as a landmark, however, you can
reach it by walking an extra 10 feet.

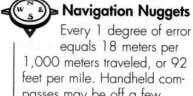 **Navigation Nuggets**

Every 1 degree of error
equals 18 meters per
1,000 meters traveled, or 92
feet per mile. Handheld compasses may be off a few
degrees anyway, so landmarks
are used to help keep you on
track.

Now magnify this effect over many miles. Every degree of error equals
18 meters per 1,000 meters traveled, or 92 feet per mile. With no
major landmarks to assist, the user will be too far off course to reach
the target.

Which Compass?

A number of styles are available that are all variations from the original
design of a magnetized needle floating within a degree ring. More advanced models have pop-up sights and mirrors. A good compass does
not have to be complicated or expensive.

A simple orienteering compass works best for backcountry navigation.
Readings can be taken quickly and easily with one hand. A good orienteering compass can be purchased for about $20. Desired features
include built-in map rulers and glow-in-the-dark markings. Stay clear
of electronic models because they need batteries. Be sure to use a compass that has a declination adjustment scale or, ideally, one that allows
the declination to be mechanically set.

The Least You Need to Know

◆ Understand the basics of the latitude/longitude and the UTM
  systems.

◆ Understand the pros and cons of each system and select the best
  one for your application.

♦ Understand declination and how to determine both true and magnetic north.

♦ If you are using the wrong north, your bearings could be more than 20 degrees off.

♦ Know how to get around by shooting compass bearings from point to point.

12

Maps

In This Chapter

- Learn all about map basics
- Learn why detailed topographic maps are ideal for geo-caching
- Learn how to interpret the terrain through contour lines
- Learn to determine distance and navigate like a professional
- Learn how to use a map ruler to plot cache coordinates on a topo map
- Learn the navigation tricks and tips of the pros

Map reading is the cornerstone of navigation. Whether using GPS or not, your ability to get around in unknown territory will depend on how well you can read a map. Maps come in all shapes and sizes, both paper and electronic. Map-reading skills are consistent regardless of the form of map you use.

This chapter covers map basics to ensure you use the right one with the right scale for the job. You'll find out why detailed topo maps are great for geocaching, and then you'll learn how to read them. This chapter also shows you how to determine distance in the field and how to plot GPS coordinates on a paper map. Finally, this chapter provides some navigation tips that will keep you trekking like a pro.

Map Basics

From highway to topographic, from paper to the increasingly popular electronic formats, maps come in a number of different scales and sizes. Many GPS receivers include electronic basemaps, but that does not mean they will replace a traditional paper map. It is important to have an understanding of the map options available to help ensure that you use the correct maps for the job.

When viewing a map, check out the information along the bottom before trying to find your position in the middle. This "collar" area is full of reference information that will provide aid in its reading. This information includes the scale, legend, distance indicators, color codes, magnetic declination, map datum, and the year the map was published. The gridlines and tick marks around the edges determine what coordinates are provided. Reviewing this information will help ensure the selection of a map in the scale and detail appropriate for your application.

Geo-Lingo

Maps are referred to as small or large **scale**. Small-scale maps cover a limited area in great detail. Small-scale maps range from 1:24,000 to 1:65,500. Large-scale maps are like state or highway maps that show a larger area in less detail.

Map Scales

The *map scale* is the ratio between the distance displayed on a map relative to the actual distance on the ground. The state road map kept in a glove box might be a 1:500,000 scale. Used as a highway reference, an entire state fits on one side, where 1 inch equals approximately 8 miles. When you're performing detailed ground navigation, like when geocaching, the greater the detail the map provides, the easier it will be for you to navigate the terrain.

The primary map used for short-range detail is the 1:24,000 scale 7.5-minute topographic. In this highly detailed scale, 1 inch equals 2,000 feet. The key to choosing the right map is to choose a map that covers enough area with adequate detail to prevent you from traveling outside of its boundary.

Map Name Series	Scale	1 inch represents	1 centimeter represents	Map area (approximate square miles)
Puerto Rico 7.5 minute	1:20,000	1,667 feet	200 meters	71
7.5-minute	1:24,000	2,000 feet	240 meters	40 to 70
7.5- by 15-minute	1:25,000	2,083 feet	250 meters (about)	98 to 140
Alaska	1:63,360	1 mile	634 meters (about)	207 to 281
Intermediate	1:50,000	0.8 mile	500 meters (about)	County
Intermediate	1:100,000	1.6 mile	1 kilometer (about)	1,568 to 2,240
United States	1:250,000	4 miles	2. 5 kilometers (about)	4,580 to 8,669

United States Geological Survey map scale chart.

U.S. Geological Survey

Topographic Maps

In the United States, the most detailed standard map used in the back-country is the U.S. Geological Survey (USGS) 7.5-minute topographic map. These maps can be purchased for about $4 at outdoor stores or from the USGS. They are called 7.5-minute maps because they cover 7.5 minutes of latitude and longitude. That's an area approximately 6.5 miles wide, 8.5 miles long, and 55 square miles. These maps, often referred to as "topo maps" or "topos," provide a three-dimensional perspective of the ground. This perspective is provided using "contour lines," which indicate terrain shape and elevation. Topographic maps also include the primary geographic coordinate systems of latitude/longitude, UTM, and township, range, and section.

Topographic maps are created from aerial photographs.

U.S. Army

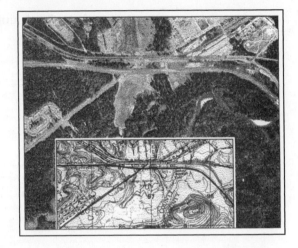

Map Reading

Map-reading skills are universally applicable, regardless of the map's scale or type. Map reading is essentially the interpretation of lines, features, landmarks, and symbols on a map. It helps to think about the map in a three-dimensional way, instead of just a flat sheet of paper. This is done by focusing on major landmarks and high- and low-elevation features. *Contour lines* on topographic maps make this easier, because the lines profile the terrain.

It is helpful to maintain the "big picture" of the area in which you are traveling by keeping major landmarks in perspective. Prominent features, being man-made or natural, include all major landmarks such as mountains, highways, waterways, and bridges. Prominent features are good to use as a reference in conjunction with a map to determine your general location. Baseline features are linear reference points such as roads, rivers, and power lines. These natural boundaries are ideal to follow or use as a return point.

Navigation Nuggets

Map reading is easier if you mark prominent features with highlighter pens. Use a different color for major elevation changes, prominent and baseline features, as well as for your intended route.

In the field, maps are easier to read if they are set to the terrain, matching the prominent and baseline features on the map with those on the ground. This is known as "terrain association." This helps reference landmarks and gives the user a better understanding of what lies ahead. This is done with the assistance of a compass by rotating the map until the top faces true north.

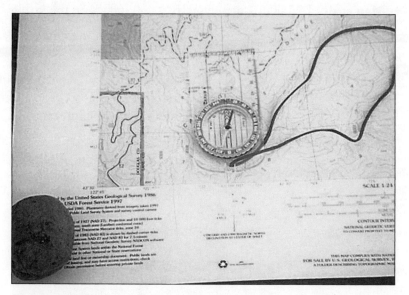

The map is set to the terrain by rotating it until it faces true north.

Jack W. Peters

Reading Topographic Maps

Our example is a 7.5-minute topo map of the Bohemia mining district, south of Cottage Grove, Oregon. This map was located by reviewing a state of Oregon USGS map coverage index to find the map of our exact area of interest. The state index map is divided into titled 7.5-minute sections. Our map is titled Fairview Peak Quadrangle-Oregon. The bottom section of the map gives details that include the following:

◆ **Map date.** Produced in 1986, revised in 1997. Topographic information is from 1980.

◆ **Datum.** North American Datum of 1927 (NAD 27). The datum is the global survey system used to create the map. This is important because GPS receivers need to be programmed to the same datum used to create the map.

♦ **Declination diagram.** The scale indicating the degree a compass is adjusted to correct magnetic north to true north. This map's declination is 17.5° as of 1999.

♦ **Map scale.** 1:24,000; 1 inch equals 24,000 inches on the ground.

> **Geo-Lingo**
>
> **Contour lines** are the curvy brown lines on a topographic map that indicate the shape of the terrain. Every fifth darker brown line is the elevation index line. This line indicates the elevation in feet or meters.

♦ **Mileage scale.** One mile equals about 2⅝ inches.

♦ **Contour interval.** The elevation lines are 40 feet apart, every fifth darker brown line indicates the elevation in feet.

♦ **Misc. information.** Where this map is located in relation to the state, map names surrounding this map, and a list of symbols for highways and roads.

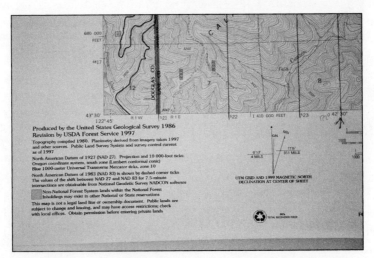

The "collar" area of a topographic map provides the information you need to read the map accurately.

Jack W. Peters

Check the Datum

When using GPS with any map, be sure to program the GPS receiver to the correct datum used on the map. Many U.S. topo maps use North American Datum 1927 (NAD 27 CONUS), or possibly the datum used in geocaching, World Geodetic System 1984 (WGS 84). In Europe, it is the Ordnance Survey Great Britain (OSGB). The receiver is set to a default datum: Check the Setup menu to ensure it is the correct one for your application. Failing to make this adjustment can cause errors of as much as 1,000 meters.

Grid Lock

Notice from the corner of this topographic map that there are tick marks, lines, and numbers everywhere. Besides latitude/longitude and UTM coordinates, there are grids to indicate township, range, and section. To confuse matters further, there are also six-digit numbers with "FEET" behind them. This is a State Plane Coordinate (SPC) system, which is similar to UTM but uses feet rather than meters. When referencing numbers and tick marks, be sure you are referencing the correct markings before taking any readings.

Look at topographic maps carefully to ensure you are reading the correct grid line for the geographic system you are using. Seven-and-one-half-minute topographic maps like this one often include four different geographic systems.

Jack W. Peters

The preceding map includes all of the following coordinates:

- 4818 UTM Northing

- 4817000mN Full UTM Northing

- 529000mE Full UTM Easting (lower left)

- 43° 30' 43° Latitude

- 122° 37' 30" 122° Longitude (lower right)

- 1 and 12 are (TRS) sections

Map Colors and Symbols

Topographic maps are color-coded and are covered with symbols and markings. Fortunately, most are relatively self-explanatory. For example, on the color codes black is used to designate roads, buildings, and other man-made objects. Blue is used to designate waterways, and brown is used for the contour lines. For a complete list of map symbols, check with the U.S. Geological Survey or whoever produces your favorite paper maps.

Contour Lines

Contour lines show the map's topography by indicating the shape of the terrain and its elevation. These lines make it possible to determine the height of the terrain and the depths of bodies of water. These lines do not cross each other because they join points of equal elevation. Every fifth line is darker and is known as an *index line*. The index lines provide the specific elevation listed in feet or meters above sea level. On our example topo, the elevation is listed in feet. There is a distance of 40 feet between each line, equaling 200 feet between each index line. The amount of distance between each line is known as the *contour interval*.

Contour lines provide a low-tech way for a map to come alive by providing a three-dimensional view of the terrain. Reading these lines is simple: The closer the lines are together, the steeper the terrain. Open-spaced contoured areas are flat, heavily lined areas are steep or cliff walls. With V-shaped contours, the tip of the V points uphill, as seen with creeks and rivers. U-shaped contours typically point downhill. The following are typical terrain features:

A. V-shaped lines point to upriver. In this example, a creek is flowing down into a larger river.

B. Mountain peak, indicated by the way the interval between circular contour lines becomes narrower toward the top.

C. Spurs, most likely caused by an ancient creek.

D. Saddle, where a plateau joins two mountain peaks.

E. Cliff wall, as indicated by a concentration of contour lines.

F. U-shaped lines point downhill.

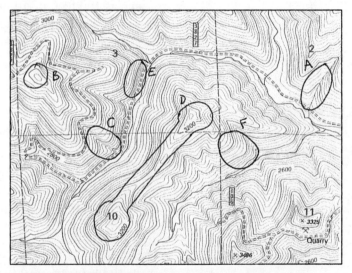

Each topographic map contour line represents a change in elevation. On most 7.5-minute maps this elevation measurement is 40 feet. Remember that contour lines may not indicate cliffs or crevasses that will make travel difficult.

Jack W. Peters

Pacing

Some geocaches and GPS challenges require the ability to measure distance in the field. Pacing is a reasonably accurate way to do so by knowing the distance of your stride. A "stride" is two steps, the distance between where the same foot hits the ground twice. Tally strides by counting every time the same foot hits the ground.

To use this system, you have to know the distance of your stride. To determine the distance of your stride, measure off a predetermined distance, such as 100 feet, or 50 meters, and count the strides it takes to cover that distance.

Here are some points to consider while pacing:

- One stride (two steps) equals approximately 60 inches or 5 feet.

- Know how many of your strides are in 100 feet or 50 meters, whichever system is used.

- Each person's stride varies with his or her own height and the terrain.

- Compensate for travel conditions that shorten strides (for instance, weather, mud, snow, wind, visibility, and backpacks).

Dead Batteries

Be aware that maps can be inaccurate, even detailed topos. The data can be outdated and errors are made during the interpretation of the aerial photographs. Not surprisingly, locations on the ground often look entirely different from what you might think they would look like from a map.

Navigation Nuggets

Keeping track of pacing distances is easier with the aid of "pace beads" or handheld punch counters. Pace beads are used by sliding a bead over a string after a set number of paces. These aids really reduce the chance for error and allow you to concentrate on counting paces instead of trying to remember distances.

Plotting GPS Coordinates

Have you ever thought of how great it would be to transfer cache coordinates from a GPS receiver to a paper topographic map? Well, it is possible through the use of a map ruler. This calculation is easily done through mapping software that automatically provides the coordinates wherever a cursor is placed on a map. With paper maps, however, it requires the ability to measure the target's location with a special map ruler.

With a little practice, waypoint locations can be plotted on a map, or the coordinates can be obtained for a location of interest on a map. If you can master this skill, you will have reached a pinnacle of ability in map and GPS use. The ability to know your location on a paper map provides you with real freedom to travel while keeping your location and the surrounding landmarks in perspective. For geocachers, this is a great tool for plotting groups of caches on a detailed topo map.

 **Navigation Nuggets**

Using a map ruler will allow you to transfer coordinates from a map to a GPS receiver. Coordinates can be measured from a map and then entered as a waypoint into a receiver, or a waypoint from a receiver can be plotted on a map.

Map rulers are available to measure both latitude/longitude and UTM coordinates. Using either system requires preparing the map by using a long ruler to connect the geographic coordinate tick marks. Turn the map into a grid by connecting the tick marks from side to side and top to bottom. USGS 7.5-minute maps include both the latitude/longitude and UTM system. For latitude/longitude, there are two tick marks on each side of the map every 2.5 minutes apart. Connecting these creates a nine-section grid that resembles a tick-tack-toe board. These maps are approximately 10 kilometers wide and 14 kilometers long. Connecting the blue UTM tick marks creates 140, 1,000-meter or 1-kilometer sections.

The grid lines represent a known coordinate location. A map ruler measures the distance between the known location at the grid line to the target. This is where the UTM system really shines through.

Finding a location within a 1,000-meter section is much easier than trying to find a location with degrees, minutes, and seconds. This is because UTM grids are square, representing 1,000 meters or 1 kilometer in height and width. To find the coordinates, it's just a matter of counting meters east and north to the target.

Measuring latitude/longitude is a little trickier because these grids are not square. Remember, grid lines are compressed as they get closer to the North and South Poles. This factor, except at the Equator, makes the grids rectangular. Measurements are still easy to do, but taking the longitude reading requires an extra step. Here's a rundown on taking measurements with each coordinate system.

UTM System

Using the UTM system is the way to go for detailed groundwork. One simple measurement will get you the coordinates within a few meters of accuracy. Here are the steps involved in taking a measurement:

1. Grid the map by connecting the UTM tick marks, creating 1-kilometer sections.

2. Find the grid section that contains the target.

3. Use a map ruler UTM scale that matches the map you are using. Placing the beginning end of the ruler on the grid line, take a measurement from left to right to the target. You are measuring east for the Easting coordinate.

4. Determine the number of meters from the grid line to the target and write them down. Next take a measurement from the bottom grid line and measure north for the Northing coordinate. Determine the meters and write them down. Now simply add the Easting and Northing meters to the baseline coordinates.

When plotting coordinates on a map, you follow the same procedure. Mark the map where the Easting and Northing numbers come together to find the target.

In the preceding example, a measurement is taken of the Puddin Rock Road staging area.

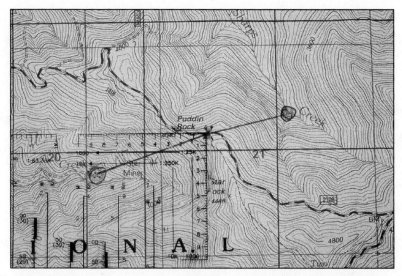

*Using UTM, one quick measurement provides both Easting and Northing
coordinates.*

Jack W. Peters

Remember, the UTM coordinates increase from bottom to top and
from left to right. The target is in the grid of **524** and **525** Easting, and
4823 and **4824** Northing. The ruler is used to measure the number of
meters from the baseline to the target.

Easting is the first measurement. The number increases from left to
right. Measure from the left grid line **524**; the target is an additional
480 meters. Add the number for the coordinate of **524**480 E.

The next measurement is Northing. The target is about 127 meters
north of the **4823** baseline. Adding the meters provides the coordinate
of **4823**127 N.

Latitude/Longitude System

Map rulers are available to measure latitude/longitude in the full
address of degrees, minutes, and seconds or in decimal minutes. In this
example, we will be measuring in degrees, minutes, and seconds. Here
are the steps to take a measurement:

1. Grid the map by connecting the tick marks every 2.5 minutes
   apart, creating 9 2.5-minute sections.

2. Find the grid section that contains the target.

3. Use a map ruler scale that matches the scale of your map. The first measurement is north/south measurement of latitude. From the grid line below the target, measure straight up counting the minutes and seconds to the target.

4. Finding longitude is a different procedure because the distance between these grid lines decreases as they become closer to the North and South Poles. This requires placing the beginning of the ruler at the lower-right corner of the grid section. Bring the other side of the ruler up and over to the opposing grid line to the left of the target. The ruler will be at approximately a 45° angle.

5. Slide the ruler up until the target intersects with the ruler. When taking a measurement, be sure that both ends of the ruler are touching the dividing grid lines.

6. Measure the minutes and seconds from the lower-right corner to the target, and then add the distance to the longitude baseline.

To plot coordinates on a map, you follow the same procedure. Mark the map where the latitude and longitude coordinates come together. The intersecting lines mark the target.

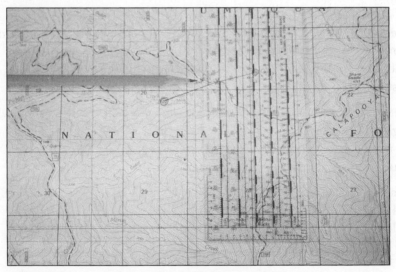

Measure minutes and seconds up from the base grid line.

Jack W. Peters

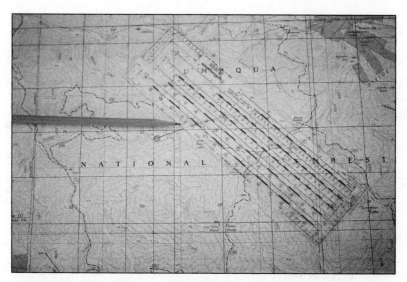

Measure minutes and seconds over from the east base grid line at an angle (because of the compression of longitude lines).

Jack W. Peters

In the preceding example, a measurement is taken of the same Puddin Rock Road staging area.

The 2.5-minute × 2.5-minute section the target is located in is north of 32' 30'' latitude, and to the west of 40' longitude. The first measurement is latitude. Remember, latitude numbers increase from south to north. We've started the ruler on the 32' 30'' baseline. The minutes and seconds up to the target are 1 minute and 15 seconds. Now add the distance to the latitude baseline of 32' 30''. The latitude is 43° 33' 45''.

In finding longitude, place the beginning end of the ruler at the lower-right corner (the 40' line). Bring the other side of the ruler up and over to match the vertical dividing line to the left of the target (the 42' 30'' line). Remember, longitude increases from east to west.

Place each end of the ruler on the vertical grid lines, at approximately a 45° angle. Slide the ruler up until the target intersects with the ruler. The minutes and seconds over to the target are 1 minute and 50 seconds. Add this distance to the 40' baseline. The longitude is 122° 41' 50''.

Navigation Tips

Combining the traditional map and compass skills with a few tips will have you navigating like a professional. Understanding these skills also enables you to use your GPS receiver to its fullest potential. Here's a list of useful navigation skills to help keep you on track.

> **Navigation Nuggets**
>
> Be sure to write down any coordinates that are being plotted. Check and double-check your work to avoid any errors. Remember, one wrong number could take you more than 100 miles off track.

♦ **Aiming off.** This is traveling on a compass bearing in an indirect path to your target. This is done to bypass an obstacle, or to help find a target on a linear feature. For example, you believe your truck is parked on a roadway straight ahead at about 5°. You cannot see the vehicle because of dense vegetation, so you aim off slightly to the right at 15° knowing that when you reach the roadway, the truck will be to your left.

♦ **Calculate map distances.** Keep a small piece of wire in your navigation kit for measuring distances on a map. Bend the wire to follow a road or trail, and then straighten it out to find the distance using the map scale.

♦ **Catch features.** These are features that indicate that you have missed a turn or have traveled too far. If circumstances make a destination difficult to find, know what roads or features are beyond the location. That way you will know whether you have traveled too far when you reach the catch feature you have chosen.

♦ **Confirm location by elevation.** Altimeters are a useful way to help confirm your location on a map. Compare altimeter elevation readings with map markings. Remember, a GPS receiver's altimeter may not be as accurate as a manual barometric altimeter.

♦ **Dead reckoning.** This is used to confirm your location by recording your travels from a last known position. It requires keeping track of every distance and bearing traveled. Starting from a known position, record your route on a map or in a journal.

This is an ideal way to back up a GPS receiver when traveling in unknown territory.

♦ **Directions from nature.** Remember the basics: The sun rises in the east, moves to the south, and then sets in the west. At night, find the North Star; also, the points on a crest moon point south.

♦ **Night navigation.** When traveling in darkness, remember that our natural night vision takes about 30 minutes to fully develop. Red LED lights or flashlight filters work great for producing adequate light without losing night vision. Besides using GPS, keep track of time and use pacing to maintain your position. Remember, pacing steps will be considerably shorter at night, and be sure that your compass glows in the dark.

♦ **Reverse perspective.** While traveling, remember to turn around and look for the reverse perspective. This is what the road or trail will look like when you return. Every few minutes, take a 360° scan. Notice the scenery and landmarks in every direction, paying special attention to what it looks like behind you.

♦ **Trail markers.** Manually back up your track log the old-fashioned way by blazing a trail with markers. Use natural resources like bending twigs or placing rocks. Draw arrows in the dirt with a stick or cut marks in tree bark. Homemade marking kits work great and are easy to make using thumbtacks and colored survey ribbon. Do not forget to remove the markers on the return leg.

♦ **Triangulation.** You learned how to use triangulation to confirm the location of a cache. In this application, your location can be confirmed by shooting a bearing to at least two or more different surrounding landmarks. A current location is determined by plotting the intersection of the bearings on a map.

The Least You Need to Know

♦ Various map options are available to ensure that you use the correct maps for the job.

♦ Pay attention to important collar information and the coordinate system used on your topographic map.

- On most 7.5-minute topographic maps, each contour line indicates a change in elevation by 40 feet. Taking the time to learn how to read contour lines and other map features will greatly enhance your navigation skills.

- Pacing is a fun and remarkably accurate way to measure distances in the field by counting your stride. A stride is two complete and normal steps that often average five feet, depending on your height.

- Using a map ruler is a fun and easy way to plot caches on a paper topo map.

- When geocaching or trekking, traditional map and compass navigation skills enhance the use of GPS, and will be critical if your electronic gear fails.

Chapter **13**

Computers

In This Chapter

- ◆ Learn how computers can save, transfer, and organize travel data
- ◆ Learn how to track your current location on computer map software
- ◆ Learn how to make GPS receivers and computers work together
- ◆ Learn to find more caches faster with help from your portable

Now that you know your grid lines from your contour lines, it's time to get your computer into the act.

If you're already geocaching, you likely know how to use a computer. However, you may not be aware of just how well computers and GPS units work together. Through the use of map software programs and GPS units, computers can be highly useful navigation tools. Whether at home or in the field, you can plan your trip by studying where you're going and how to get there. When you get back home, you can save a log of your travels and even share them with your friends.

This chapter covers how useful desktop and mobile computers are when it comes to GPS and navigation. There are many practical uses from converting a personal data assistant (PDA) into a receiver to trip planning with a map database. This chapter shows you how to transfer and save data. You'll also learn how to determine how steep your next hike might be and how to transfer your location onto a computer map. Finally, this chapter covers how to connect all of this gear to make it work, and how you can find more caches faster with help from your mobile computer.

GPS with Computers

GPS and computers go together as naturally as geocaching and adventure. There are many applications for using computers in navigation, with or without a GPS device. Computers can run highly detailed mapping software and can even be transformed into GPS receivers. Desktop computers work great for trip planning, whereas laptops and handheld PDAs are more easily taken into the field for more versatility.

Eureka!

To use a GPS receiver with other electronic devices, purchase one with a data port compatible with National Marine Electronics Association (NMEA) protocols. The NMEA has established a universal electronic standard to allow compatibility between GPS receivers and other electronic gear.

GPS receivers can be used with computers and other electronic devices such as cameras and amateur radios.

Computers are used as a tool for navigation in four ways: as a receiver, as a map database, for data transfer and management, and for real-time tracking.

As a GPS Receiver

Laptop and handheld computers are easily converted into GPS receivers through kits that include software and a remote antenna. The advantage of doing so includes the ability to use computer equipment you already own and carry it with you. Computers have large color screens and virtually unlimited memory compared to GPS receivers. In addition, a greater number of higher-quality map programs are available for computers as opposed to GPS units.

It might be possible to save a little money by not duplicating gear. Keep in mind, however, that laptop and PDA setups do not have nearly the durability of a standard GPS receiver. Moisture and vibration can quickly disable the electronics. Computer-based setups are best for vehicle-based applications due to high power consumption and limited durability.

Eureka!

Protective case manufacturers like Pelican make special water- and shockproof cases to protect PDAs, cell phones, and other electronic gear.

Personal handheld devices work great as a mobile database. Jason the Dino Hunter's PDA is loaded with caches to find and it's ready to go.

Jack W. Peters

Map Databases

One of the benefits of having a computer along is that one CD-ROM can store more map data than your glove box could ever dream. A single CD can include highly detailed data on a favorite region or general highway map information for a whole country. The convenience of having highway, regional, and topographic maps in such a compact format is great. Plus you don't have to fold them!

Despite the convenience of computer maps, they will not likely replace paper maps anytime soon. Paper maps are easier to read while bouncing down the road, and they don't require batteries.

Data Transfer and Management

For geocaching, mobile computers work great for storing downloaded caches. (You can never have too many to find!) Computer-based mapping software is ideal to manage navigation data and for trip planning. Before visiting an area, check it out on a map first. Geocache data can be loaded into mapping programs to find target-rich environments. Cache locations and other points of interest can be easily analyzed to help determine where to go and how to get there.

Besides creating and storing information, data can be transferred between GPS receivers and computers. Waypoints and routes created by trip-planning software can be easily transferred from a computer to a GPS receiver for use in the field. Waypoints, tracks, and route data saved in the field by a receiver can be transferred back to a computer. Electronically transferring this data saves considerable time and reduces the risk of error from manually entering the information.

Another benefit of this feature is the ability to share GPS data with a friend. Waypoints for your favorite caches and outdoor areas can be easily saved and transferred. Track logs and routes work great for documenting your travels. Plug a friend's receiver into your computer and he or she can follow in your bootsteps.

Real-Time Tracking

Real-time tracking is a fascinating way to use your receiver. An icon of your location appears in the center of your digital map. There is definitely a "cool" factor to seeing your movements on the computer screen. Your position normally remains in the center of the screen while the map moves as you travel.

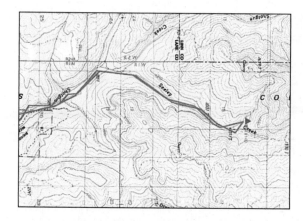

The map shows a real-time track log to and from a cache.

Jack W. Peters

An advantage of this option is that a small-screened receiver provides your location and direction of travel on a larger color computer screen. This is helpful if you are using a receiver without a basemap. It also provides two different screens of data. The driver can monitor the GPS receiver for information like speed and compass bearing, while the passenger watches your position on the computer.

To set up this feature, plug your receiver's data cable into an open port on a laptop or PDA. After the hardware is connected, settings are required in the receiver and computer mapping software to allow GPS track-log data to be transferred to the computer program. Most map software will support real-time tracking.

Setup menu options in both the GPS receivers and map software programs provide various interface options. The primary interface for real-time tracking and other receiver/computer functions is NMEA mode. As previously mentioned, the National Marine Electronics Association established this mode for electronic and navigation product compatibly. In the map software program, be sure to select the correct data port used for the data transfer. The next setup option is the baud rate. This is the rate at which electronic data is sent. The primary baud rate for real-time tracking is 4800. An incorrect baud rate is one of the primary reasons for interface

Dead Batteries

When driving, computers, cell phones, and GPS receivers can grow beyond distractions to serious hazards. Don't let the use of this gear get you into an accident. Let your passenger manage the electronics while you keep your eyes on the road.

failure. It may take a little experimenting to get the right settings, but it's worth the effort when you see your location appear on the computer screen.

Mapping Software

Mapping software is available in a variety of applications from many sources. It is a very practical application for your receiver because most brands provide so many useful options.

The following are examples of the options available:

♦ **Creating waypoints and routes.** Moving a cursor on map programs instantly provides coordinate information based on the cursor's location on the map. Waypoints are created with a simple click of a mouse. Routes are easily created after waypoints are saved. Waypoints appear on the map and can be customized with names, colors, and symbols.

♦ **Real-time tracking.** Using a GPS receiver to transfer a live track log into computer mapping software.

♦ **Recording travel history.** Track logs recorded in the field can be transferred back to a computer and saved as a recorded history of your travels. Computers provide virtually unlimited storage compared to the limited memory available in most receivers.

♦ **Search feature.** Most map programs provide a search feature allowing parks, towns, and other landmarks to be found instantly.

♦ **Terrain analysis.** Moving a cursor over a map instantly provides elevation. Connecting two points instantly provides an elevation profile, distance, or bearing.

♦ **Transferring waypoints, routes, and track logs.** Through the use of a data cable, data can be transferred back and forth between a receiver and a computer.

The following subsections provide a rundown of the types of map software.

GPS Company Software

GPS manufacturers provide proprietary mapping software that works exclusively with their brand of receivers. Additional map detail can be purchased on CD-ROM to enhance the unit's own basemap. For example, topographic, city, or nautical information is purchased to upload into a receiver. Programs are available for major cities, regional areas, various countries, and other parts of the world.

Besides upgrading a receiver's basemap, the software can be used on a PC and is helpful for organizing trips with the ability to transfer waypoints, routes, and track logs. The latest software programs include commercial metro or travel information such as the location of restaurants, hotels, and gas stations. The data uploaded into the receiver is limited only by the unit's megabyte capacity. Receivers accepting memory cards have unlimited memory potential through the use of large-capacity or multiple cards.

Aftermarket Software

Traditional map manufacturers like DeLorme and *National Geographic* provide electronic maps on CD-ROM for use with computers and PDA devices. These programs work great for planning trips as well as for creating, transferring, and saving travel data. They include a number of neat features like the ability to convert trails and roads into routes, and some provide a 3D display of your map data. They cannot, however, be used to enhance a GPS receiver's existing basemap.

The U.S. Geological Survey offers digital maps known as digital raster graphic (DRG). DRGs are standard topographic maps scanned and made available in an electronic TIFF file format. A 7.5-minute DRG averages 8 megabytes. These maps can be combined with other digital media such as photographic or satellite data for a unique perspective.

Map companies offer large topographic maps with your favorite location in the center. This is helpful in avoiding the problem of hiking into a map's corner, or having to bring multiple maps because the subject area is on the boundary. These maps can include any coordinate grid lines desired, and most are printed on waterproof paper. Map kiosk centers are becoming popular in outdoor stores. These centers are capable of instantly printing topographic maps of your favorite areas.

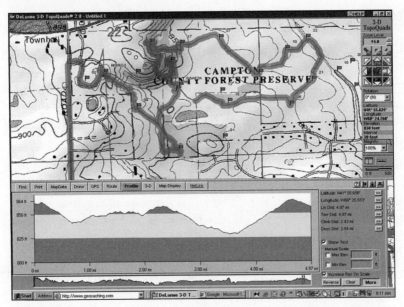

Using DeLorme software, the map shows a track log and waypoints from the Micro Dash event in St. Charles, Illinois.

DeLorme

Online Map Services

Online map services like Topozone.com enable you to instantly conduct an Internet search to obtain a map of any area of interest. These are similar to or the same map services available on the Geocache.com information page. Coordinates are displayed in any format selected and are easily transferred from one to the other. Coordinates to navigational targets can be entered and then maps can be printed in varied detail with the target displayed. Most of these services are free and are very helpful by providing quick and accurate mapping information.

> **Eureka!**
>
> You can use aerial photography similar to what intelligence agencies have been using for years. Geocache information pages on Geocaching.com include a link to obtain aerial photography. Various companies, such as TerraServer.com and Spaceimaging.com, offer satellite photo coverage for 60 countries, with detail down to as close as 1 meter.

Terrain Analysis

One of the primary benefits of using digital maps is the ability to study terrain. Regardless of software type, most brands provide features to allow you to study the ground before you get there. Knowing such factors as elevation and slope will make it easier to plan your trip. Determining how steep trails and roads are may make a difference in whether you can hike or drive there, or even help you determine whether you can bring children along for the hike.

Selecting two points with a click of a mouse can immediately provide distance bearing or elevation profiling. Maptech's Terrain Navigator software provides a unique 3D perspective of any selected area. In 3D mode, the area map can be rotated, tilted, and viewed from any bearing or elevation. A selected area can also be viewed in a topo map or aerial photo view format.

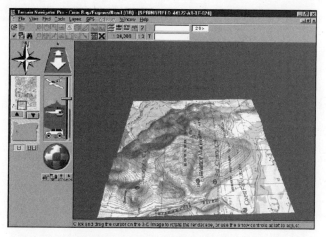

Electronic maps, such as this example from Maptech, provide many helpful features, including three-dimensional viewing.

Maptech

In the preceding example, a group of caches are profiled in the Mount Pisgah area. The cache locations were entered and then Maptech's 3D mode was activated to analyze the surrounding terrain. These high-tech tools are excellent for making flat maps come alive and making them much easier to interpret. Studying this information is as interesting as it is practical. Knowing what to expect can help avoid errors in calculating travel time and difficulty.

Component Wiring

Hopefully, the next receiver you buy will include a data cable. If not, check the owner's manual or customer support for your brand and model to ensure that you buy the right one. The cable will connect with a plug unique to your receiver's brand on one end, and a standard female DB-9 (serial) connector for the computer. Preferably, there will be a third set of wires to provide power to the receiver when the data port is utilized. These data/power cables can be purchased from the manufacturer or from an aftermarket company.

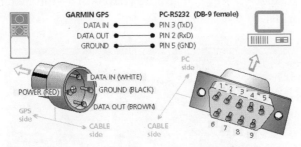

Typical Garmin wiring for a computer interface.

Dr. Thomas Vonesch

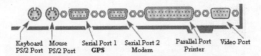

Many computers have a set of connectors like this one on their back side. Yours may have USB ports, or it may have larger serial ports. When you shop for a cable, make sure you can describe the connectors to a salesperson.

GPS Trackmaker

Ideally, your computer looks something like this. Plug the GPS data cable into serial port one, or some other unused port to avoid interference. If you are using an older computer, some modifications are required. If the computer has a 25-pin DB-25 serial port only, you'll need an adapter to match the wiring sequence to the nine-pin DB-9.

If the computer has no serial ports, you'll need an adapter to convert your cable for use with a USB port, or use a PCMCIA port with a PCMCIA PC card. A computer/electronic supply store should be able to provide whatever adapter is needed to get your gear connected.

GPS receivers of the same brand can transfer data such as waypoints, track logs, and routes from unit to unit with the correct data cable. The receiver unit is placed in "Host mode," whereas the sending unit is set up to transfer information by selecting a data transfer mode from the menu options.

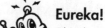

Eureka!

Check your GPS receiver's manufacturer's website to determine the latest version of operating software or firmware that is available for your receiver. Manufacturers often update this software to fix bugs and make other improvements. Your receiver can be easily upgraded through an online download. There is typically no cost, and it only takes a few minutes.

Taking Computers Geocaching

Laptop computers may be a little bulky to pack on a geocaching road trip, but they are definitely getting smaller and faster. They also have the power to manage your serious cache hunt outings.

Neal "Logscaler" Weathers and "Red" have logged more than 1,000 caches and counting. They find taking a laptop along proves helpful in a number of ways. These include storing waypoint information for a large number of geocaches which provides many options for spontaneous geocaching while away from the Internet. "We take the laptop with us just in case we get a "wild hair" to take off to track down some caches."

Here are some practical ways to use a portable computer for serious geocache hunting.

Load Lots of Maps

Most computers provide enough storage to load a number of mapping software programs. This will provide a useful variety of mapping options ranging from detailed topographic to street and trip planning. This software will allow you to keep those badly folded paper maps in the glove box (but don't throw them out yet), for an often quicker way to find the best access to the next cache.

Caches by the Thousand!

Once you decide on the area in which you want to go hunting, you can request a pocket query from Geocaching.com to get a GPX file of the caches in that area. At any time, you can have several hundred to thousands of caches stored in your computer with waypoints and a cache web page for each cache.

A list of waypoints is selected from the GPX files containing the geocache information. This list is transferred into a GPS data-transfer program like EasyGPS for Groundspeak to allow the waypoint data to be downloaded into a GPS receiver. The GPX file data is then used to select cache information pages. Folders are created in the laptop to contain and save both the waypoint list and cache information page data. Cache waypoint list data can then be downloaded into a mapping software program like *National Geographic* Topo! The cache locations appear across the computer screen. This is helpful to see where the caches are located and how they are located in relationship to each other. This visual information makes it easy to pick and choose which caches look like fun to go after.

Time for Real-Time Tracking

Finding your "live" location on mapping computer software is as easy as connecting your GPS receiver and computer with a data cable and selecting the correct GPS and computer settings for real-time tracking. This feature is great for indicating your exact location in relation to all of the caches you want to find. It also helps select which roads to take and where to turn to find each cache more efficiently. Using the receiver's GOTO feature indicates how far you are from each cache you want to find. Having all of this data allows you to more easily plan the order in which the caches will be found.

Some Final Computer Bytes

With all this technology and the trip-planning features of mapping software, there is no doubt that bringing along a computer will allow you to get around much faster and more efficiently. It will also enable you to find more caches than you could have ever done before.

Bringing along a computer can have other benefits, too. It can help you do things like storing photos from a digital camera and making notes for logging all of those caches you found for when you get back to civilization. On some computers, you can even plug in your cell phone for Internet access to download more caches!

Remember that electronics do not hold up well to abuse. Vibration and moisture can easily send your expensive gear on a one-way ticket to the service shop. Also remember that thieves often target computer and electronic gear so be sure to secure them and keep them out of site when out on the trail.

You must remember to use caution and not allow these electronics to become a dangerous distraction. Regardless of how you're traveling, taking your eyes off the road for a second to watch a screen can result in a serious crash. Allow a passenger to run the GPS and other gear so you can concentrate on driving, or pull over to do it yourself.

Eureka!

Some computer manufacturers make gear for extreme outdoor use, like the military-grade Panasonic Toughbook.

The Least You Need to Know

◆ You can convert your portable computer into a GPS receiver.

◆ The NMEA electronic format will allow you to use your receiver with other gear including computers, cameras, and radios, so make sure to look for NMEA compatibility with any equipment you buy.

◆ Using a computer will allow you the advantage of using mapping software as well as more easily manage waypoints, routes, and track logs.

◆ You can see your current location "live" on a computer map using real-time tracking.

◆ You'll be able to find more caches faster than you ever have before by organizing cache listings in a portable computer.

Part 4

Welcome to the Community

By now you're out there finding caches with the best of them. Each travel bug you plant goes on journeys more epic than a Cecil B. DeMille movie, and you can read a map better than you can read your own handwriting. So what's left? If you're ready to go to the next level, Part 4 is for you.

Learn about the geocaching community: fun-loving people like you, getting together and finding caches in nearly every country in the world. Learn about setting up your own geocaching group and how you can take your favorite hobby on vacation.

If you've found every cache within 100 miles and need a bigger challenge, it might be time to pit your skills against other geocachers in a friendly competition. Find out about some of the major geocaching events around the country and learn how to put on an event of your own.

Next we take a look into the future to see where GPS technology is going and what effect it will have on how GPS games are played. Finally we cover how geocachers come up with creative ways to push the envelope to help evolve the game to its next level. Maybe you'll even pioneer the next big GPS recreation trend!

Chapter 14

Geocaching Groups, Forums, and Travel

In This Chapter

- ◆ Geocaching groups and clubs around the world (maybe even in your area)
- ◆ Geocaching discussion forums
- ◆ Event caches help geocachers get together
- ◆ Opportunities to geocache abroad
- ◆ Learn to travel smart with GPS gear

When you think of geocaching, an image comes to mind of possibly one or two people out by themselves on a lonely isolated trail. In certain cases, that's true. Geocaching is a great way to get away from it all and find a trail that will get you away from everyone else. For many people, geocaching is a way to spend some quality time alone or with a friend for a tranquil outing in the woods. And yet, as you may have discovered by now, geocaching is more than an activity. With geocaching, much of the enjoyment may be found within its extensive community of participants.

Geocachers are an international group of fun-loving people made up of every age, sex, race, and background. Most geocachers will agree that the next best thing to finding a well-hidden cache is sharing the adventure with other geocachers. Just as geocaching will take you to places you would have never seen, it will also allow you to meet interesting people with whom you may not have come into contact otherwise.

It's great fun to meet other geocachers, whether on the trail or at one of the many geocaching events. It is especially enjoyable the first time you get to associate a face and personality to the geocaching handle of someone you've met online in discussion forums or chat, or through cache logs. You may find that a geocacher who goes by "Fresh Meat" is actually a very nice guy. You'll also find that many geocachers are not too different from you. Many geocachers have busy lives with family, children, and careers. But in all of life's chaos, they take the time to seek out a cache or two, and they also take time to get together with each other to share the many experiences of geocaching.

Since the inception of the sport, many geocachers have established friendships, teams, groups, and organizations; these allow them to get even more enjoyment from geocaching. Some have even found love through geocaching and proposed marriage using a specially placed cache! Geocachers spend hours online and offline discussing all aspects of geocaching from rules and policy to adventures and experiences.

In this chapter, you'll learn how geocachers use online forums, clubs, and events to plan get-togethers. Packing your suitcase for work or play? This chapter also covers how you can play the game and meet new people no matter where you travel.

Geocaching Groups

The Internet was a key element in the development of geocaching and has been equally responsible for its rapid growth. The web is used in a number of ways, ranging from informing new players about the sport and listing the available caches to allowing geocachers to keep in contact and discuss their favorite hobby. The following subsections discuss some of these online groups and forums.

Internet Groups

A quick search on the Internet provides hundreds of geocaching-related groups. Groups such as those hosted by Yahoo! provide an excellent format for geocachers. Groups are quick, easy, and free to set up. Each group gets a home page with a number of features, including a message bulletin board, a calendar, a member list, and the ability to post photos and links. These groups share information related to geocaching through e-mails and bulletin board posts. They can be a great resource for geocachers to keep up on local geocaching topics within their community. The following is a quick sampling of the groups found on Yahoo!:

California_geocaching. For California geocachers to share ideas and tips about geocaching

Geocaching_florida. For those of us in the state of Florida who enjoy geocaching

Geocaching_ut. A group for geocaching enthusiasts in Utah

Geocaching_be. The geocaching group from Belgium

Geocaching_america. A hangout for geocachers across America

Geocaching-hispano. *Ganas de aventura y un terminal GPS es todo lo que necesitas para practicar esta innovadora "búsqueda del tesoro."*

Geocaching_uk. For people interested in GPS geocaching in the United Kingdom

Geocaching_danmark. *Denne gruppe er til diskussion af geocaching i Danmark*

Geocaching_group. For GPS-using geocachers

GeoCaching_atlantic_canada. Dedicated to geocaching in the Atlantic Canada area

Geocaching_ireland. Dedicated to Geocaching in Ireland

Geocaching.com Discussion Forums

Geocaching.com provides a large ongoing bulletin board forum for geocachers to discuss practically every topic you can think of relating to geocaching and GPS. Discussion forums include announcements, getting started, general discussion, travel bugs, GPS, stories, and events. Discussion forums are also categorized by region throughout the United States and by various countries around the world.

These discussion forums start off by someone asking a question or making an announcement or comment. Then others respond and the conversation continues in the form of a discussion thread. A discussion thread is the topic that ties a string of conversation together.

These forums are filled with geocaching's colorful characters, many of whom are the pioneers of the sport and who helped evolve the sport into what it is today. Geocaching continues to evolve because it is participants like you who test the latest gear and the newest game idea. The forums are a place to share ideas and information to see just where the game will take us next. It's easy to get lost for hours in the ongoing discussions and it is a fun way to learn everything you ever wondered about the sport.

After a little while in the forums, you will begin to become familiar with the personalities of many of the geocachers who post and participate frequently. If you have a question and post it in the discussion forums, you will likely receive your answer within minutes, or you might get *markwelled*.

Geo-Lingo

Often in the Geocaching.com discussion forums, you may be **markwelled** when you ask a question. "Markwelling" (verb) refers to when someone points you to a discussion in the past that answers your questions. Markwelling originates from geocacher Markwell, who would often direct new geocachers to existing topics.

The Geocaching.com forums are a great place to learn about breaking developments in the GPS-based gaming circles, such as new unit releases, fixes, contests, and a variety of other issues related to geocaching. With hundreds of thousands of posts and a searchable format, they can be a great place to start for those with a lot of questions or a hunger to expand their knowledge of geocaching.

Club Websites

Many of the more established geocaching clubs have developed their own websites. Most of these sites are quite elaborate, complete with helpful information and a number of other resources. Most clubs represent regional or metro areas, so they're helpful to keep members informed about the latest news and events in their neck of the woods. They help out new geocachers by providing the basic information to get newbies started. These personalized sites really help build club identity; they can be used to promote events and you can post the group's photos and members' articles on these sites.

You can find links to the various geocaching clubs on the state cache listing web pages on Geocaching.com. A few of the many club websites to check out are:

- **Georgia Geocachers Association.** www.ggaonline.org/index.html

- **Southern California Geocachers.** www.scgeocachers.org/

- **Texas Geocaching Association.** www.texasgeocaching.com/

- **Maryland Geocaching Society.** www.mdgps.net

- **Michigan Geocaching Organization.** www.mi-geocaching.org/

- **Washington State Geocaching Association.** www.geocachingwa.org

- **Utah Association of Geocachers.** www.utahgeocachers.com/

- **Wisconsin Geocaching Association.** www.wi-geocaching.com/

- **Arizona Geocaching.** www.azgeocaching.com/

- **Geocachers of Kentucky.** www.geocky.org/

- **Colorado Association of Geocaching Enthusiasts.** www.coloradogeocaching.com

Starting Your Own Geocaching Group

So there are geocachers in your area but no group yet? This might be the ideal time to start your own club. Being part of a local group is a great way to meet fellow cachers as well as get out more often by planning events and outings. An organization also enables you to promote the activity and provide a positive public image through projects such as trail maintenance or "cache in-trash out" events.

The first step is to get the locals together. An easy way to do this is by hosting an event cache. This is a cache where participants find a social event instead of a cache container. Find a family-friendly park or pizza parlor, record the coordinates, and post the event on Geocaching.com. Event caches are covered in more detail later in this chapter.

Publicize the event by posting notices in local, regional, and Geocaching.com discussion forums, and send invitations to people finding caches in the area. You could even post notices at outdoor stores or with other organizations. At the event, provide name tags to help people start to get to know each other. Have fun, eat, and do a little caching. Afterward, make sure you have everyone's name, phone number, and e-mail address so that you can organize the group and plan the next event.

When you have a group of people interested, start a website or use a group forum (for instance, Yahoo! Groups). Use your cyber homebase to post membership information, photos, resources, and details of the next event. Group message boards allow members to post information and keep in touch. Be creative with your events and the member list will continue to grow. There are a lot of fun and interesting things for a group to do: hide a group cache, have a barbecue, camp out, invite special guests, host training seminars, visit historical or interesting outdoor places, and organize community projects. Involve members by asking them to come up with ideas and help plan the next events.

As your group grows, give it some organization. Its structure could be very informal, as long as projects are assigned to members who will follow through to keep things going. At some point, you'll need a leader, a treasurer, and someone organized enough to keep track of everything. The group can raise a little money to pay for web fees or t-shirts.

The main thing is for everyone to have fun. Don't bog the group down with meetings, politics, or business. People go geocaching to get away from those things. Use the get-togethers as an opportunity to meet fellow geocachers and get out more often.

Event Caches

In the wild west, mountain men had an annual rendezvous. It was an opportunity for trappers and traders to get together to blow off a little steam after a long cold winter of isolation. Geocachers have a similar idea. But instead of drinking whiskey and blasting off black-powder rifles, we eat pizza and picnic together with our families. We still have fun, however, because these events are a great way to get together after many solitary geocaching trips. They are also a neat way to make new friends and see who is behind all of those unusual geo-names.

Oregon's Emerald Valley Cachers are a social group. The gang takes a break during a backyard barbecue to find a microcache.

Tara "Geniustara" Negelhout

An event cache is set up much like a regular cache, except participants follow coordinates to the party. The events are held at family-friendly places like pizza parlors, parks, or backyard barbecues. To throw an event cache, choose a date and time, and then save the coordinates of the location. Log on to Geocaching.com to post the cache, selecting the Event Cache option. Enter the date of the event in the Date Placed field.

This future date places the cache at the top of a state cache search and places it on the Geocaching.com Event Cache calendar.

> **Eureka!**
> Love on the trail? You might be surprised how many couples find more than caches out in the wilderness. Geocaching has become a way for singles to meet, and several couples have actually proposed to each other at cache locations! Who needs an expensive wedding when you can get hitched at your favorite cache?

Taking Your Hobby on the Road

The best part of traveling is exploring new places. If you are heading off to unfamiliar territory, you're going to bring your GPS receiver along anyway, right? Traveling with your GPS is a great way to take the worry and guesswork out of getting to where you want to go and back again. Saving lots of waypoints makes travel easier and is a fun way to document your trip.

There's no reason to leave behind your favorite hobby either. Because there are caches everywhere, there should be no problem getting a list of caches to find to take with you. Besides, by now you have probably already found all the caches within 50 miles of your place. There is a big world to see and, luckily, it's covered in geocaches!

Bored to tears by endless company meetings or another trip to the in-laws? Sounds like a good time to get down to some geocaching business. So the next time you travel, think of it as an opportunity to see some new country and improve your stats by picking off a few more caches.

Most people place caches in areas that they consider to be special. So when you travel, check out the local caches and you are likely to find some exceptional places and adventures.

Geocaching Vacations

Most people go on vacation to relax, see new sights, and maybe play in the sun. Geocachers like all of that stuff, too, but vacations are a great opportunity to hide travel bugs! After all, how much lying around can you do? Before you get too sunburned at the pool, grab your gear and find some caches.

Traveling by yourself and don't want to go caching alone? No problem there either. Get on the web and find a group in the area to get out the word that you're coming to town. Chances are good you'll get a caching buddy and a tour guide for all the cache-finding and sightseeing a tourist can handle. Besides, you don't want to hang out with other tourists, do you? It's the locals who know where all the really cool stuff to see is anyway.

What about a geocaching cruise, exotic ports of call with caches along the way? It was only a matter of time, and as of this writing a major cruise is being planned. It includes seven days in the Western Caribbean on the Carnival ship *Inspiration*. On this cruise there are 41 caches to find at ports of call that include Grand Cayman, Costa Maya, Cozumel, Mexico, and Belize City, Belize. That sounds like our kind of vacation!

Travelin' Bugs

If you're traveling very far, be sure to snag a travel bug or two to take with you—especially if you are going to an area with a major or international airport. If the bug has a goal to travel somewhere different, drop it off at a *travel bug hotel*. These are popular cache sites next to major airports, making travel bugs easy to find and take overseas. Then, possibly, the next traveler can pick it up to get it closer to its destination.

Some travel bugs ask that you take them along on vacation. To show how quickly these can move around, have a look at the progress of the "Family Bug" travel bug.

> **Geo-Lingo**
> **Travel bug hotels** are caches set up primarily for the purpose of holding travel bugs for transfer. Feel free to drop one off or pick one up when you visit these locations.

The bug was released in Memphis, Tennessee, with the goal of going on vacation to as many places as possible. Finders of the bug attach vacation souvenirs to show where it has been.

Set in the wilds of Chickasaw Bluffs, Tennessee, after three months of travel, it's seen the birth home of Elvis, the Florida Keys, and ended up in Holland, Michigan, 1,947 miles later.

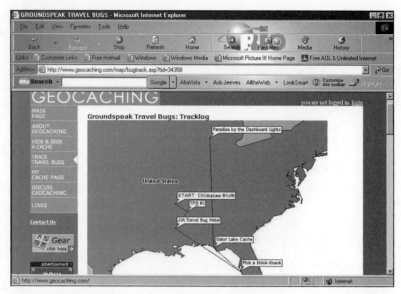

The travels of a vacation travel bug after a few months in the wild.

Groundspeak

Meaningful Places

Much of the enjoyment of travel is to visit places of special meaning, like historical sites, awesome vistas, or places that represent our families' roots. These places inspire us and help us appreciate our ancestors who contributed so much to what our lives are today. Through geocaching, travelers have the opportunity to see and experience these locations they would probably never see otherwise.

If the site is local, hiding a traditional or offset cache is a way to allow travelers to appreciate a unique area. Place information in the cache explaining why you chose this location, why it's special, and what visitors should look for to appreciate its history.

When traveling to such locations, planting a traditional-type cache is discouraged and generally not permitted if you are unable to maintain it. Virtual caches are great, however, to bring others to special sites. Persons who find the site are asked questions to verify they were there. Often this requires an answer available only at the physical location, such as information on a monument's plaque.

This is exactly what Pat and Stacy "2mooses" McDougall did for their trip to Scotland. They traveled throughout Scotland seeking caches and history of their ancestral tie to the MacDougall Clan. They also took the time to hide a couple of caches of their own, including one near Castle Gylen in Kerrera.

A virtual cache is placed at a monument in Islay, Scotland, honoring sailors lost at sea.

Patrick McDougall

Monumental Heights is a virtual cache placed in Islay, Scotland. It was placed at a spectacularly situated memorial to the hundreds of men who lost their lives nearby in two separate incidents at sea in 1918. "On Fame's eternal camping ground, their silent tents are spread, while glory keeps with solemn round, the bivouac of the dead."

To claim the cache, visitors are asked a couple of questions about the memorial plaque and are asked to pause for a moment of quiet thought in remembrance of the men whose lives were lost in the cold waters off Islay.

Packing for Vacation Caching

Self-described nerd Markus explains a dilemma that many of us have. "Let's see, swimsuit, sunblock, sunglasses, ... When you're a technology-obsessed nerd, it's not quite so simple." Markus assembled all the electronic gear needed for a trip of fun and geocaching across the desert southwest of the United States. Obviously, most of us do not require this many electronics, but it's a fun example of techno-travel accessorizing. Besides, even this much gear is still lighter than a bag of golf clubs!

Imagine how much fun it is to try to get this stuff through airport security!

Markus Wandal

Approximately top left to bottom right, we have:

- Laptop computer for storing digital pictures, GPS data, and GPS mapping software
- Power supply and line cord for the laptop
- Power inverter, to use line-powered gadgets in the car
- Cigarette lighter plug expander
- Compact flash adapter, for reading digital camera memory cards
- GPS receiver case (a cell phone case)
- Digital camera (Canon S100) and case
- Spare digital camera batteries
- Charger for digital camera batteries
- Spare batteries for headlamp.
- LED headlamp (Petzl Tikka)
- Spare batteries for GPS receiver.
- GPS receiver (Garmin eTrex Summit)
- Cigarette lighter extension cord
- AC extension cord (for use with power inverter)
- AC multiplug
- Charging base for FRS radios
- Belt clips for FRS radios
- FRS radios (Motorola T5725)
- Auto power/data cable for GPS

Ah, the modern convenience of it all.

International Considerations

When traveling internationally to geocache, it makes sense to pack some additional resources to help you find your way around and adjust to the local customs and requirements. Some of these items may include guidebooks, language translators, power translators, and international maps (both electronic and traditional printed maps).

You may also want to post a topic to the International section of the Geocaching.com discussion forums for the country to which you are traveling. You can ask locals for cool cache recommendations or even tips on local travel, restaurants, and other accommodations.

Flying with GPS

As great as the temptation might seem, don't turn your receiver on while flying on a commercial plane without first asking the flight attendants. Although seeing where you are as you fly over a country may sound like fun, this sort of thing is often frowned on by airline crews. Their common response is that receivers and other electronic devices could interfere with the plane's own navigation system. There is most likely no harm done, but in the days of heightened security there is no reason to cause concern or draw unnecessary attention to yourself.

If flying with GPS receivers, computers, and cameras, it is often best to pack them in a sturdy case and check them in. This helps avoid security problems and can help prevent the gear from becoming lost or stolen.

Dead Batteries

Use a GPS receiver in the wrong place at the wrong time and you could be considered a spy. In 1997, a Qualcomm wireless communication engineer was charged with espionage by Russian authorities. Richard L. Bliss was using a GPS receiver while installing a cellular phone system in the city of Rostov-on-Don. The Russian agents that arrested him insisted he was spying on secret sites.

Use Some GPS Discretion

Before firing up that trusty receiver, be aware of your surroundings and who might be watching you. Do not use it around any areas where it might appear as if you are a spy. For example, you may wish to avoid using your GPS or other electronics in close proximity to embassies, military bases, and other prominent government buildings. Obviously, some parts of the world are more sensitive to this than others. The last thing you want to do is extend your trip by lengthy interrogations at the local jail. You might also discover that the officials have determined your gear is nicer than theirs, so this time they will let you off with a warning and relieve you of that unnecessary travel baggage.

The Least You Need to Know

♦ Participation in a group is a great way to keep in contact with fellow cachers and be a positive influence in your community.

♦ Use geocaching forums to keep up on the latest news and developments in an ever-evolving sport.

♦ Traveling is an opportunity to find more geocaches!

♦ Bringing travel bugs along can liven up your next vacation.

♦ Use caution when using your GPS unit while traveling abroad to avoid security problems, and avoid using it around sensitive areas such as embassies and government buildings.

15

Geocaching Events and Competitions

In This Chapter

◆ Are you ready for the challenge?

◆ Geocaching competition

◆ Preparing to enter an event

◆ Organizing your own event

Do you have a competitive spirit? Does the need to be the best and win define your very existence? Well, you're in luck because there are growing opportunities to test your geo-skills against the fastest cache finders around. Since the beginning of the sport, participants have come up with ideas and events to bring geocachers together for a little friendly competition.

This chapter covers some of the events available for participation and discusses how you and your teammates might prepare to enter a competitive event. Who knows, you just might want to organize your own tournament. This chapter provides some tips for doing that, too.

Events and Competition

One of the neat things about geocaching is it is what you make it. It can be as peaceful as a quiet stroll on a scenic path, or as grueling as a non-stop race to a mountaintop struggling against others and the clock to find as many caches as you can. Competitive events may not be for everyone, but they're great for those with the need to test their abilities and endurance to the fullest.

Eureka!
Check the Events section on the home page of Geocaching.com to find out about upcoming geocaching events and competitions in your area.

One of the factors of competing in these events is that you really have to know your gear and hone your navigation abilities. In timed events, participants have to know exactly how to enter and retrieve GPS data. You also have to make quick decisions on what routes to take from reading a map and compass. There's not much time to stop and think about anything, and making a mistake will likely cost you and your team valuable time. Competitive events are often physically demanding. They may require running up and down hills or covering a substantial distance. Knowing how to use your GPS receiver is one thing, but have you ever had to do it in a sprint? Geocachers are not used to being in that much of a hurry!

If you think you're up for the challenge, here is a rundown on some of the events held across the United States.

GPS Goldrush

The Goldrush may be geocaching's largest annual event. In 2002, it took place on Killington Mountain, Vermont, the largest ski mountain in the northeastern United States. Participants traveled from 10 states and Canada to participate in last year's event and compete for $13,000 in cash and prizes.

Participants are given waypoints known as prize coordinates to program into their GPS receivers. At the end of the day, participants return to base camp to cash in their prize cards for thousands of dollars in prizes.

Congratulations to the GeoPups, a two-member team who took home the first-place trophy in 2002.

The event's territory spanned 7 mountains, 20,000 vertical feet, and more than 2,000 acres of trails and forest. This terrain required participants to be in top shape to even think about winning. Event staff was shocked by the number of participants who climbed above the 1,000-vertical-foot mark to find 3 point targets. One of the top prizes was on Killington Peak, 1.93 miles away and 2,000 vertical feet above the starting point!

The Foxhall Geocaching Challenge was the sport's first known official prize money event.

Foxhall Farm

Midwest Invitational Geocaching Competition

The Missouri Geocachers Association is presenting the first-ever Midwest Invitational Geocaching Competition beginning in March 2004. Event promoters say participants should prepare themselves for a weekend packed with high-level excitement and fun. "This will be a huge event and will be a strong competition by those who know how to geocache."

There will be many different timed events set up for individuals and teams. Teams will compete in a multicache event requiring them to solve puzzles and decipher clues to get through a 20-waypoint course spread throughout one of Missouri's most scenic parks. Individual events will include two 10-waypoint courses over two days. The courses will be divided by difficulty. Course A will be a course for beginners to intermediates, and course B will be designed for intermediate to expert cachers.

For more information, check out www.mogeo.com.

Eureka! _____

In May 2001, the Foxhall Geocaching Challenge was the sport's first known official prize money event. Erick Kobres of Georgia won overall, taking home $5,000! The Memorial Day weekend event near Atlanta, Georgia, drew cache seekers from all over the eastern half of the United States.

GPS Orienteering Events

Orienteering groups maintain courses where participants compete using a map and compass. They negotiate the course to search for control point markers. When a marker is found, participants mark their cards with the letter listed on each control point.

Geocaching meeting orienteering.

Kevin Shipley

Some event organizers are beginning to make these events geocacher-friendly by posting the coordinates for each control point. This is a great opportunity for geocachers to learn about orienteering and participate with a GPS unit.

The Chicago Area Orienteering Club has been promoting such activities as the third annual Snowgaine event. The name is taken from a winter version of ROGAINE (Rugged Outdoor Group Activity Involving Navigation and Endurance).

Geocachers received a list of latitude/longitude coordinates and a punch card used to prove that they found each location. Twenty-two controls are scattered over nearly 7 square miles (11 square kilometers) in a park known for its deep gullies, hostile vegetation, and up to 200-foot (60-meter) bluffs overlooking the Mississippi River. Each control was worth between one and five points, depending on its distance from the start and its difficulty to find. Competitors can visit the controls in any order they like as long as they are found within the six-hour time limit.

Texas State Geocaching Extravaganza

This event is hosted by the Longhorn Council of the Boy Scouts of America in conjunction with their annual spring orienteering meet.

The highlights of the two-day event include a timed hybrid orienteering-style multicache challenge. There are also six regulation orienteering courses. Awards are given by age category for each course. At night, there is a "murder mystery" cache hunt event, similar to a cross between a multicache and the game of Clue. Training seminars are also provided on various topics involving geocaching and orienteering.

Nevada Trophy—A Navigational Adventure

Do you like your competition a little more motorized? This event combines geocaching and off-road driving for both 4×4s and motorcycles. It is held in the northern Nevada desert around Lovelock. Each team includes two vehicles, paired up for safety. Participants have 12 hours to find more than 200 waypoints!

Team Cawte and Aguirre in action on the Trophy Course.

Off-Road Experience

The promoter, Michael Green of Off-Road Experience, states that the requirements are a sense of adventure, a GPS receiver, and a *Nevada DeLorme Atlas*. Sounds like a couple very sturdy off-road vehicles and the desire to chase down lots of waypoints in the desert would help, too. Sounds like fun to us.

For more information, check out www.offroadexperience.com/.

Entering Competitive Events

So do you and your cache-hunting friends have talent? Can you go out, rain or shine, day or night, and find well-hidden stashes like a well-oiled machine? Sounds like it's time to prove your stuff by entering the next event. We've put together some ideas to help improve your competitive edge.

Back to Basics

Most events are based on a time challenge where you race against the clock and others to find as many caches as possible within a specified time frame. This kind of competitive pressure leaves no room for error, or even much time to think. To be competitive, your navigation skills must be on autopilot. No time to fumble with the wrong buttons on your receiver or try to remember the degree of magnetic declination on your compass. Obtaining this kind of skill takes nothing short of lots of old-fashioned study and practice. You need to be absolutely proficient in the following areas, at least:

◆ **Know how to quickly enter waypoints in your receiver.** Often the clock is ticking when you're handed a list of targets. Practice loading 10 to 20 waypoints as fast as possible, and then check your accuracy to ensure all the numbers are correct. Remember that even one number off will send you hopelessly in the wrong direction.

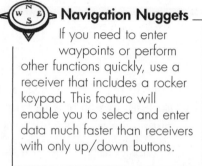 **Navigation Nuggets**

If you need to enter waypoints or perform other functions quickly, use a receiver that includes a rocker keypad. This feature will enable you to select and enter data much faster than receivers with only up/down buttons.

Team Magellan using GPS and maps to prep for an adventure race.

David Poleto

◆ **Know the magnetic declination for the area.** This can be confirmed by checking the difference in your receiver in the Setup menu between true and magnetic north. You can also check the scale at the bottom of a topographic map. If game instructions ask you to travel at a specific bearing, check to see whether they are referencing true or magnetic north, and know how to instantly adjust your compass accordingly.

♦ **Know the game field.** Study the area on a map to find trails and other access areas as well as barriers such as cliff walls and other obstacles. If possible, get out and walk the area's trails to commit as much of the area to memory as possible. Many times during the event you will be required to plot a course from point to point as quickly as possible. Having an understanding of the area will pay off both by saving time on travel routes and preventing you from hitting a wall of blackberries or falling off a cliff.

♦ **Check your pacing.** You should already know by now the number of your strides that make up 100 feet or 50 meters. Remember that inclines and other rough terrain will increase the number of steps to reach the same distance.

♦ **Get in shape.** Competitive events require brain and brawn. Dashing up and down hills in a hurry is a serious cardiovascular workout. We suggest you hit the gym before hitting the competitive trail.

Team Dynamics

Many events are set up for two- or three-person teams. This is a great opportunity to meet up with friends to see whether you can really work together as one high-performance cohesive unit (or at least see whether you can have fun together without killing each other). Here are some ideas to keep your team running and winning smoothly:

♦ **Practice with teammates.** Don't expect to work well with each other if the first time you go caching is the morning of the event. Whether having one or two teammates, it takes time and practice before getting into the groove of functioning efficiently.

♦ **Delegate based upon skills.** Part of what makes teams perform is that each member has specific skills that complement the group. Work together long enough to know each member's special abilities and use those skills to the fullest advantage. For example, one may be better at using a receiver and another better at finding hidden caches. Have members focus on the roles that best suit the team.

Geocachers pause for a photo at their annual event.

Tracy "CameraThyme" Galsim

Organizing Your Own Event

So is your group all fired up to compete, but there's no event to attend? This might be the right time to plan your own geo-bash! There is much planning to do, however, before pulling off a successful gathering. Here is a list of topics to cover to help your event run like clockwork and keep them coming back year after year.

- ◆ **The first rule is to make sure everyone has fun!** Keep things simple and the mood light. Even in seriously competitive games, don't let the atmosphere become so intense that it overrides the ability for contestants to simply enjoy themselves.

- ◆ **Organization is the key to everyone's sanity.** Before the event, post as many details as possible. For the event, put together a program explaining the details so that everyone knows where to be at what time. The idea is to remove any confusion or surprises.

- **Plan in advance**. Post major events at least six months in advance. This gives participants the opportunity to take the time off to attend. Also, campgrounds and lodging may be booked long in advance. Make sure lodging and camping is available on your weekend.

- **Location, location, location.** The success of your get-together will be highly dependent on the location you choose. Find a large park or outdoor area where you can get permission to hold the event. Reserve the location and secure whatever permit you need far in advance. Find an area that is interesting for geocaching (and, ideally, one that has access to camping). State parks often have scenic outdoor areas with campgrounds.

- **Boy Scouts to the rescue.** Recruit help from cachers and outdoor groups to assist with everything from catering to serving as game officials. The Boy Scouts of America do a great job. Your event can be a fundraiser for the Boy Scouts and a great educational opportunity for the scouts.

- **Get sponsors to provide prizes.** Start hitting up potential sponsors in advance to support your event. Tell them you will provide advertising in your program and at your event if they will send products you can give away. Offer to hang a banner or provide a link to their website. In exchange, you can score some good stuff to give away, allowing you to advertise that participants can win neat prizes like a new GPS receiver, mapping software, or a hotel getaway.

> **Eureka!**
> Many geo-events are adding educational opportunities by providing pregame seminars on various topics relating to navigation, GPS, and geocaching.

Game Time!

A variety of games helps keep events interesting and fun. You can offer a number of game variations to keep players on their toes. Here are some commonly used basics:

◆ **Traditional timed cache events.** Participants attempt to find as many caches as possible within a specified time limit. Caches contain a ticket or envelope taken by the finders to verify they were there. Some form of handicap system could be used to allow older and younger teams to compete with the highly experienced or athletic ones.

◆ **Hide and seek.** Participants provide their own cache containers and hide them for the officials to find. Players are judged by their creativity in creating and hiding the cache. Some players have become very innovative and have made custom cache containers out of hollowed logs and fake rocks. One cacher even used an old tortoise shell.

◆ **Puzzle caches.** Use your imagination to come up with games to keep players guessing and using their creativity. One example is to place items in caches that, when found, require participants to make something with the contents. Another idea might be to have players find envelopes containing trivia questions. Players receive points for questions answered correctly.

With creativity and good organization skills, your event will be one geocachers will look forward to year after year.

The Least You Need to Know

◆ Events and competitions are a great way to get together and test your caching skills.

◆ Check the Geocaching.com website Events section to find current happenings in your area.

◆ Know your gear, get in shape, and practice with teammates before entering a serious geocache event.

◆ Good organization is the key to throwing successful geocache events.

Chapter 16

The Future of GPS Technology

In This Chapter

- Learn how GPS will improve and consolidate with other technologies
- Take geo-photos with geographic coordinates
- Learn how to track someone's position using radio signals
- Learn how making a 911 cellular phone call can alert emergency dispatchers to your location, and how GPS drives other personal safety technology

In the past 10 years, GPS has grown from a curious set of initials to a household word. Unless you've been living in a cave, which is about the only place they don't work, almost everyone has some idea of what GPS is and how it works. A once-obscure military technology now has some effect on nearly everyone's lives. Hikers, racers, scientists, soldiers, pilots, emergency medical technicians, and engineers—the number of persons and professions using GPS is growing rapidly with no end in sight.

As the technology continues to reduce in size and price, more people will be packing receivers for both work and play.

We know that GPS is an extremely useful outdoor tool, but you might not know what other uses it has, or how it might be used in the future. GPS integrated with other technology will enable you to do neat stuff like mark your photographs with geographic coordinates. You might also be able to find a friend's position using amateur radio and a portable computer. A GPS chip in a cellular phone will provide an emergency operator with your position. In this chapter, you will learn how the technology is used in unique applications and how these other uses may tie in with geocaching.

Jay is ready to go with a handheld computer full of caches. Someday soon, computers, cell phones, receivers, and radios will all be combined into one device.

Jack W. Peters

Trends and Possibilities

With electronic technology, time is on our side. It wasn't that long ago when brick-sized cell phones cost hundreds of dollars. It was even more recently that lumbering, single-channel, no-map receivers cost thousands of dollars. Isn't technology great? Cell phones are practically free, and powerful receivers cost $100! Thankfully, because technology is constantly changing, gear will only get better, smaller, and cheaper.

It will not be that long from now when we will ask, "Remember when we used to pack around a cell phone, mobile radio, PDA, GPS, and digital camera?" It will not be long until all these devices will soon be merged into one. These devices are pairing already. Garmin's iQue is a Palm PDA and a GPS receiver. Garmin has also made a cell phone/receiver combo. PDAs can double as cell phones, and cellular companies are including walkie-talkie radio features and cameras in their phones.

This is all good news to us travelers and geocachers. Our computer will be able to give us turn-by-turn directions to wherever we want to go. From a practical standpoint, getting lost should be much more difficult, and getting out of trouble will be easier with improved communication services.

Even though GPS gear has evolved quickly, much room for improvement still exists. We know the equipment will continue to get better, and accuracy will improve, but there is nothing wrong with being a little impatient. Besides, it gets system and gear developers thinking. Here's a wish list of improvements we hope to see in the near future:

- ◆ Standardized features such as universal remote antenna jacks and data storage memory cards.

- ◆ Larger color screens with improved resolution and contrast.

- ◆ Faster computer processors, and PC-based operating systems that will accept aftermarket mapping software.

- ◆ Improved rechargeable battery pods to eliminate expensive disposable batteries.

- ◆ Increased WAAS-style radio-frequency enhancements to improve accuracy under and around obstacles.

- ◆ Military accuracy for civilian receivers.

- ◆ More wireless technology to eliminate data cables.

- ◆ Standardized, low-cost memory cards like those used by digital cameras.

- Ruggedized and waterproof PDAs and mobile computers.

- Satellite-based systems for communication and Internet access that replace cellular phone towers.

- Service providers to provide GM's OnStar-style services for our own equipment. Using independent devices would make updating and moving the system from vehicle to vehicle easier and less expensive.

GPS and Personal Training

Has all that computer time got you a little flabby? Need to tone up to find caches a little faster? GPS can help out there, too. Garmin has released a personal training aid, the Forerunner 201. The Forerunner 201 offers athletes an easy-to-read display, and integrated GPS sensor that provides precise speed, distance, and pace data.

GPS can even help you get into shape.

Image used courtesy of Garmin Ltd. or its affiliates. Copyright Garmin Ltd. or its affiliates.

The device is small, light, and waterproof enough to fit on an ergonomic wristband. The unit's Virtual Partner feature enables you to set a personal training goal by configuring the Virtual Partner's pace and workout distance. A graphic display comparing your performance to that of the Virtual Partner's will let you know whether you're keeping up the pace.

Bluetooth

A recent approach to incorporating GPS technology is the use of GPS as a wireless peripheral. Similar to a wireless printer or fax machine, the GPS unit sends information wirelessly to your device through *Bluetooth*. Bluetooth wireless networking technology is based on the same frequency used in cordless phones. This is the same technology that allows networking and data transfer between desktop computers, mobile computers, and cell phones. For example, if these devices are outfitted with a Bluetooth radio frequency chip, an electronic address book database can be loaded into a cell phone without cables.

Geo-Lingo

The term **Bluetooth** came from tenth-century Danish Viking Harold Bluetooth. He was known for his ability to get different people to communicate with each other.

There are several unique benefits when a GPS receiver is combined with Bluetooth technology. For example, to use most GPS units you need to hold them a certain way for optimal satellite reception. A Bluetooth-based GPS device could be kept in a backpack or in a location within satellite view, while your favorite PDA receives the data and acts as a comfortable, familiar interface. The technology will eventually allow more than one device to receive this data, such as a cell phone, a laptop, or a friend's PDA. It will also be a convenient way to transfer waypoints (such as geocaches) between your computer and your GPS unit without requiring a special cable.

Bluetooth technology will enable us to integrate much of this same technology using third-party devices. At some point, vehicles will be equipped with computer central processing units (CPUs) that will communicate with our navigation and communication gear. We will be able to subscribe to services that could provide Internet access, navigation, roadside assistance, and vehicle diagnostics.

Imagine driving on a cross-country road trip. You'll be able to download hundreds of caches to find in every new area you travel. Then your vehicle will help you find them. Hopefully, your car won't make it too easy to find the cache. After all, it could take much of the fun out of geocaching. (Maybe too much technology is not always a good thing.)

GPS and Digital Photos

Because many digital cameras have input jacks, there must be some way to plug in a GPS receiver to document the location of photos, right? Good thinking. With a little homework and a data cable, you can create photos stamped or watermarked with geographic coordinates and the date and time.

Adding geographic coordinates is a neat way to document your photos.

George Malina

The use of digital cameras has grown along with geocaching and the Internet. Although nonprofessional digital images typically provide lower resolution as compared to 35mm film, these snapshots work great for taking lots of pictures without high film and development costs. Images are usually saved in a compressed format to keep their size down, making them ideal for sending by e-mail.

Currently, around a dozen digital cameras, such as the Kodak DC290, use the Digita operating system (DigitaOS). This system enables cameras to take advantage of a scripting language built into the operating system to communicate with computers and electronics like GPS receivers.

There are currently DigitaOS cameras available from Kodak, Minolta, Hewlett Packard, and Pentax.

If you are using a DigitaOS camera, we can show you one way to attach your camera to your GPS receiver.

In the receiver's Setup menu, set the baud rate to 9600. Set the receiver's output to Text. One challenge may be connecting a cable between the camera and receiver. Both digital cameras and GPS receivers include a data cable for a connection to a computer. Each of the cables includes a female DB-9 serial connector. A gender changer is necessary to mate the two connectors. The problem with this system is that it leaves you with 8 feet of cable with a bulky connector in the middle. A cleaner way to go is to solder your own custom cable.

Kodak DC290 digital camera with a Garmin III Plus connected by a custom-made data cable. A mounting system was made to hold the camera and receiver with a piece of aluminum. The camera is attached with a quarter-inch bolt, and the receiver is attached using the Ram Mount. The whole rig can be attached to a tripod.

George Malina

Here is the wiring code for a Kodak-Garmin combination:

Kodak	Garmin
Pin 4 Ground(-)	Pin 1 Ground(-)
Pin 5 Data In	Pin 2 Data Out
Pin 3 Data Out	Pin 3 Data In
Pin 4 (not used)	Pin 4 Power(+)

The Digita operating system runs text scripts that are saved to a system directory on the camera's compact Flash card. These scripts enable you to automate most of the camera's functions and to interact with a computer or receiver. The camera's script requests a text string from the receiver and writes it to the image. The text will appear like this:

@030716150820N4152850W08806622G

It is confusing to read until it is broken down into separate components:

◆ The date is 030716 (July 16, 2003).

◆ The time in UTC is 150820 (3:08:20 P.M.).

◆ Latitude is N 41° 52.850'.

◆ Longitude is W 088° 06.622'.

As George Malina says, "It's kinda geeky cool!" and we agree. This geo-photo feature has many applications. Anyone from land surveyors to accident-scene investigators could use this technology. For us geocachers, it's a fun way to document the caches and other places we visit. For even more detail, use your compass to document what degree the camera is pointing.

GPS Radio Tracking

No one can find your position using standard recreational GPS gear. However, under certain circumstances, it would be great if they could. Fortunately, a receiver can be converted into a tracking device through the use of radio- or satellite-based communication equipment. This technology is used to track assets and sometimes persons around the world. GPS-based tracking opens up a whole can of "privacy issue" worms, but you can also imagine the practical benefits of being able to track and locate someone or something else, and maybe even having someone find you in an emergency. Naturally, geocachers are always thinking up the next cool game possibility. The ability to track objects and people in real time presents many opportunities for both business and recreation. Although you can use tracking technology to manage a business supply chain, it can also be used for many other things from tracking criminals to, on occasion, a cheating spouse.

Recently, Garmin introduced "peer-to-peer" tracking with its line of Rino GPS receiver radio tracker units. Besides being GPS receivers, Rinos are radios operating on the Family Radio Service (FRS) and General Mobile Radio Service (GMRS) bands. The radio signal is used to broadcast the receiver's location to other units within radio-frequency range. That means a group of geocachers can be out and about in the countryside and everyone who is in radio range will appear on each other's screen. These radios have limited range, however, because of their low power and because their signals are not rebroadcast through a *repeater*. If you're in a group traveling in the same area, it's great to see your position in the middle of the screen, and the location of the others around you. These units can definitely make meeting up for lunch a whole lot easier.

> **Geo-Lingo**
>
> Mobile radios broadcast in simplex or duplex. Simplex means that radios transmit directly to each other. Their range is limited to line of sight or less. Radios operating in duplex use a **repeater** to rebroadcast the transmission over a much larger area. Many mountaintops include an antenna called a "repeater." To use the repeater, the user dials the radio to the correct frequency. This allows persons even with low-power hand-held radios to easily speak to others across mountains and valleys.

Amateur radio buffs have been using this same technology to track people and vehicles since 1992. Automatic Position Reporting System (APRS) uses a GPS and VHF radio frequencies to broadcast and track one's position. A terminal node controller (TNC) is used to digitize GPS coordinates in the NMEA format for radio transmission. Software decodes these digital transmissions to display the tracked object's location on a computer screen's map. The primary national designated frequencies for this transmission are on VHF 144.390 and on UHF 445.925.

The APRS system is made up of mobile tracking and base stations. Mobile stations are persons or vehicles being tracked. This can range from search dogs to helicopters, nearly anyone or anything that a receiver and radio can be attached to. The location of objects can be entered manually (as when tracking tornadoes, for instance). Stationary objects such as base and weather stations can also be programmed to appear on the map screen.

Base stations are desktop or mobile computers used to track mobile stations. It's possible to create base stations that can track and are trackable (for instance, a VHF radio and APRS software). No receiver is needed after the base station's coordinates have been programmed into the APRS software. A mobile tracking station will appear on all base stations in the form of the user's call sign within its broadcast range. GPS digital location data continues to transmit, providing base stations with updated location data. Base stations can also send and receive text messages similar to e-mail. Messages are addressed using amateur radio call signs or sent to everyone in range as a bulletin.

APRS software is available in various versions based on the computer application and the basemap used. APRS operation software is shareware. It is obtained by downloading it from the Internet or ordering the program from a specific version's author. For a small fee, the software becomes fully functional when it is registered.

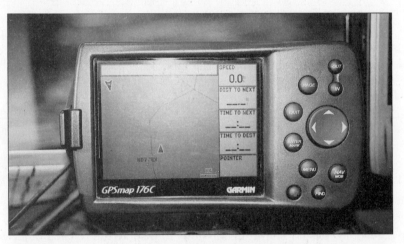

A Kenwood TM A700D with a built-in TNC and APRS firmware provides a Garmin 176 C with the location of a nearby friend, represented by his radio call sign.

Jack W. Peters

APRS can work in simplex mode, but as repeaters greatly extend the range of voice transmissions, APRS digipeaters work the same way to expand the system into a larger network. Digipeaters, whether located on mountain peaks or on home computers, rebroadcast data from all mobile trackers and base stations within range. Special Internet digipeaters can feed local data to the Internet for retrieval anywhere in the world. The network is also expanding through the use of satellites.

This kind of power and versatility makes the APRS ideal for finding friends in the outdoors and for emergency management. It may also be a vehicle for a high-tech game. Perhaps one day players will attempt to find a mobile cache as occasional clues are broadcast to the searchers. If an Internet digipeater is used, spectators could watch the game field in real time all around the world.

For more information on amateur radio use and APRS, check out these websites:

- ◆ **ARRL American Relay League.** www.arrl.org

- ◆ **Northwest APRS.** www.nwaprs.org

- ◆ **Tucson Amateur Packet Radio.** www.tapr.org

Eureka!

Some amateur radio manufactures such as Kenwood have developed handheld and mobile radios that include a built-in TNC and firmware to support APRS. The radio and GPS receiver connected with a data cord make up a complete unit, eliminating the need for a computer.

Eureka!

Amateur "HAM" radios are ideal for backcountry communications. Handheld radios are 5 watts, but their range is substantial by transmitting through repeaters. Most mobile radios are 50 watts. Compare that to CB radios, which are limited to only 4 watts. A license is required, but it is easy and inexpensive to obtain.

Safety and Security Services

GPS has been used for some time to monitor the movement of vehicles, such as tractor trailers, delivery trucks, and other commercial vehicles. Until very recently, the cost was too prohibitive to bring the technology to the average consumer. The reduction in the cost and size of GPS receiver hardware has resulted in innovations in the safety and security business, resulting in new products that impact positively on our daily lives.

The General Motors OnStar system is an excellent example of the integration of computers, GPS, and communications. This system is offered in new GM vehicles and provides such practical creature comforts as navigation, telephone, emergency notification, vehicle tracking, and systems management (such as unlocking doors or activating the lights and horn to assist police in finding a stolen vehicle). GPS technology is intricately involved in every aspect of the process, providing peace of mind for those who use the service.

Wristwatch-sized personal tracking devices are also growing in popularity. This microsized gear includes a GPS chip and transmitter. It is used for keeping tabs on children, pets, Alzheimer's patients, and even criminals placed on house arrest. This technology will become more accessible and affordable over time.

Wherify Wireless, for example, offers a watch that can be locked onto a child's wrist. At any time, parents can go online and find out where their child is located. Also, if the child is in distress, he or she can push a button that will result in an immediate 911 call.

It's not unlikely to think that this same technology will be available through mobile phones—possibly a service we could turn on or off, allowing the user's positions to appear during a phone call. However the technology evolves, personal privacy will need to be addressed and protected before it becomes a part of mainstream society.

As it becomes a larger part of our lives, expect GPS to take a larger role in securing personal assets (and even our loved ones).

GPS and Cell Phones

As of October 2001, the United States Federal Communications Commission (FCC) mandated that cellular phones sold in the United States include the ability to obtain a user's location during an emergency 911 call. This feature is known as enhanced-911 or E-911. The requirement is that phones be equipped with the Auto Location

Identification (ALI) feature. The original requirement was the ability to locate a caller within 125 meters, 67 percent of the time. This original requirement could be met through cellular tower network triangulation.

The FCC E-911 requirement is the ability to locate a caller within 50 meters, 67 percent of the time. This increased accuracy is possible through cellular phones equipped with GPS chips capable of providing a specific longitude/latitude coordinate address. Upon dialing 911, the phone obtains a satellite fix that allows emergency dispatch centers or public safety answering points (PSAPs) to receive the caller's coordinates. This is great news for us cachers. We now know that we may be found quickly if we experience an emergency within cell range. Unfortunately, many areas of the country do not yet have this service in place. The federal requirement is that the system be operational across the United States by 2005.

Personal Locator Beacons (PLBs)

Need to be rescued beyond the very limited range of cell phones? You just might need to add a personal locator beacon (PLB) to your pack. PLBs are essentially a smaller version of the emergency locator transmitter device used in aviation and boating for years. The gear is about the size of a TV remote control and costs approximately $600 to $1,000.

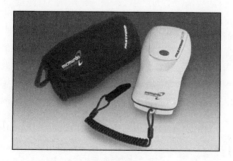

Handheld PLB uses satellite technology to send a distress signal worldwide.

McMurdo Pains Wessex

PLBs work on the international distress signal frequency of 406 MHz. This frequency allows the satellites to locate the user's position anywhere on the earth. They are accurate to within 3 miles. PLBs also include a 121.5-MHz transmitter to allow search-and-rescue crews to home in on the person's exact location. Some PLB models include a GPS chip or allow a GPS receiver to be connected to provide a more exact location, typically within 100 feet.

After years of bureaucratic delays, as of July 1, 2003, the U.S. government finally approved the use of PLBs within the United States. This lifesaving technology has been used around the world in such countries as Canada, Australia, and Europe since the early 1990s. PLBs have been allowed in Alaska in a test program since 1994. Its use there is credited for successful search-and-rescue missions involving 378 registered PLBs saving hundreds of lives. "It takes the search out of search and rescue," said Paul Burke, who helped develop and manage the Alaska test program.

The U.S. Mission Control Center manages the system under the National Oceanic and Atmospheric Administration (NOAA). Distress calls are routed through the Air Force Rescue Coordination Center (AFRCC). The AFRCC then directs the information to the search area's local law enforcement agency. Typically, search-and-rescue resources are managed by the sheriff's office in each county in the United States. "It will change the way search and rescue is done in the United States," states AFCC Commander Lt. Col. Scott Morgan.

Upon purchasing a PLB, you register your name, address, family contact, medical history, and other relevant information with the NOAA. There is no cost for this service, and updates can be made at any time. This way, if the beacon goes off, emergency crews know exactly who they are looking for and any special medical conditions the person may have. Anyone foolish enough to set one off as a hoax will be facing federal charges with the potential for 6 years in prison, a $250,000 fine, and restitution for search costs.

PLBs are good news for outdoor enthusiasts (much like the release of GPS receivers to the public 10 years ago). PLBs are a great example of how GPS and satellite technology will continue to help save lives.

The Least You Need to Know

- Technology will continue to improve, and get smaller and cheaper.
- Bluetooth technology makes gear more compatible through wireless data transfer.

- ◆ Taking geo-photos is a fun way to document your travels.

- ◆ Peer-to-peer and APRS tracking are great ways to keep track of your geo-mates in the field.

- ◆ By 2005, a 911 cellular phone call in the United States should alert emergency dispatchers to your exact location.

Chapter 17

The Future of GPS Entertainment

In This Chapter

- Where the sport has been and what the future might hold
- How geocaching-style challenges are finding their way into traditional games
- The current and potential role of GPS in adventure racing
- Geocaching and environmental ethics
- Some final thoughts for ongoing geo-success

We might not know exactly how geocaching will grow and evolve, but because cachers are a creative bunch, we know it definitely will. The quest to develop new games and make existing games more challenging will be ongoing. The popularity of GPS and the Internet will only continue to grow. One interest complements the other, driving the sport as more people discover the adventure of geocaching and GPS games.

This final chapter looks at how the sport is evolving and where it might go from here. This chapter covers how geocaching-style challenges are being introduced into other activities and how GPS challenges could be used in future events. Could geocaching-style games enter the mass media by being included on international race or survivor shows? Anything is possible, and it will be fun to see what the future holds for our favorite outdoor activity.

From 0 to 80,000 in 3 Years

It's incredible to think how quickly geocaching has developed and grown in its first three years. It has gone from a single cache hidden in rural Oregon to more than 80,000 caches being found in nearly every corner of the world. It is estimated that there are about 200,000 new GPS users around the world per month, and by 2010 the number of people using GPS is estimated to reach 50 million.

With that kind of growth in GPS use, it's no wonder that geocaching continues to be one of the fastest-growing games in history. What will the next three or six years bring, and can the sport continue to grow at its rapid rate? We agree that it will continue to grow and evolve as long as participants continue to take care of outdoor areas and leave a positive impression on everyone they meet.

Integration into Other Games

As the sport increases in popularity, participants will continue to find ways to incorporate GPS skills or challenges into traditional activities. This is a great way to introduce new players to geocaching and to spice up traditional games. Here's a look at some interesting examples we ran across.

Poker Runs

This is a good game for event activities. Hide a series of caches that contain playing cards. Participants visit a group of the caches, taking a card from each. The person who has the best poker hand at the end wins a prize. Car clubs have played this type of game for years, but using GPS adds a fun new twist.

Golf

Geo-golf is also a fun game for events. A course of 9 to 18 waypoint golf holes is set up. Participants use a scorecard and find each waypoint. Then they right down the closest distance they get to each hole. The measurement is recorded in feet or meters, with each set distance being a stroke. For example, every 4 feet could be 1 stroke. Waypoint holes placed over challenging terrain increase the level of difficulty. The person with the lowest score at the end of the game wins.

Paintball

Do you need to crank up your adrenaline rush a few notches higher than golf? Adventure junkies have developed ways to combine two of their favorite sports for some serious action. Paintball involves teams playing capture-the-flag-style games with paintball guns. There are many game variations, but the basic idea is to seek out, find, and capture the opposing team's flag without getting covered with paint. Geocachers have come up with game scenarios in which the flag stations are provided as waypoints. Another possibility is to restrict ammo to just a few paintballs per player. The object then is to find paintball ammo caches before the opposing team.

Morse Code

GPS and amateur radios go together as good as geocaching and old ammo cans. A number of geo-hams are busy trying to come up with ideas to combine amateur radio with caching. One common idea is to incorporate Morse code to provide cache location clues. These dots and dashes can be provided on the cache information page or as part of a multicache. All but the entry-level amateur radio exam requires knowing Morse code. Including this element in caching is a fun way to learn and practice the skill.

Hero Hunting

Historians have been documenting the burial places of Civil War veterans for many years. Now geocachers can partake in the ultimate history lesson by finding and listing coordinates of grave markers or monuments of significant military, political, and historical people.

Games Built In?

GPS manufacturer Garmin International now includes a game pack in some of its new receivers, including in the Geko and Rino. These geo-location games turn outdoor areas into virtual game boards. The games were first introduced on the Rino series, which includes two-way radio communication. Several of the games take advantage of the integrated navigation and communication technologies.

The Geko 201 contains four geo-location games: Virtual Maze, Memory Race, Nibbons, and Geko Smak. Participants need an area of roughly 360 square feet to play. Virtual Maze is similar to a "real-world" version of the popular Pac-Man video game. The player walks through a labyrinth on the screen in search of markers. The goal is to collect all the flags within the maze in the fastest time possible. Multiple players can compete against each other on the same maze by synchronizing the start of the game.

The Memory Race game requires concentration as players attempt to match different symbols inside treasure chests within a grid system. Gamers can choose higher levels of difficulty and larger playing areas for more enjoyment.

Nibbons is a game of navigational strategy. Players travel to a numeric marker, leaving behind an electronic breadcrumb track log. After reaching the marker, they need to walk to the next sequential marker. The catch is trying to reach the next marker without crossing your tracks. If you do, you'll have to start over.

Geko Smak is a game based on the Whack-a-Mole carnival game. The object is to "smack" virtual lizards before they disappear from your display. The lizards appear within close proximity to your current location, and you smack them by pressing the OK key when you reach them. The game gets progressively more difficult at higher stages as lizards appear quicker and farther apart.

Both Garmin and Groundspeak consider geo-location games to be in their infancy and are developing more games to enhance GPS-based outdoor activities.

Theme Events

Large theme and puzzle cache events are an interesting touch to a sometimes solitary sport. These are event caches that include a major caching challenge. An example of this type of event is the annual get-together known as the Champoeg Rendezvous. Pronounced Shampoo-ee, this event is located at an Oregon campground not too far from the sport's roots, between Portland and Salem. Geocachers take over a section of the campground to take part in various caching games and relax around the campfire. The event is concluded by a huge campout-style geo-bash. It was the main event, however, that will keep geocachers talking about this party for years. Planners Fractal and Soup put together what has to be the most elaborate geocaching game in history, known as Broken Arrow. This event took nine months to develop, and all who attended agreed these guys should win an award for their hard work in organizing such an event.

Elaborate theme cache events add a whole new dynamic to the sport. Do not miss the opportunity to check one out if someone from your area is creative enough to host one.

Fractal and Soup

One hour. One chance.

On the afternoon of May 31st, 2003, Dr. Isotope's plan to change the world will begin, and the Broken Arrow will be his weapon of choice. But there is another man with a plan of his own: Voss Piety. He will stop at nothing to take control of the Broken Arrow and use it to make sure that his vision becomes a reality. Which of these two men can you trust?

Either way, the Broken Arrow will count down to 0, and you're going to get 60 minutes to try and stop it. How do you stop it? That's the big mystery, isn't it? Fail, and the world changes forever, leaving Dr. Isotope or Voss Piety in control.

Succeed, and you can find a cache. Both Dr. Isotope and Voss Piety have people on their side … common geocachers just like you. They will try and stop you from disarming the Broken Arrow, but you won't have any idea who they are. You must ask yourself: Whom can I trust?

—From the Broken Arrow cache page, Geocaching.com

Can the geocachers find the clues in time to save the world?

Fractal and Soup

Geocachers had the time of their lives trying to save their lives and the world. How will event organizers with such creative imaginations outdo themselves? October 2003 involved the Halloween extravaganza Blood, Bath & Beyond.

Gary "Fractal," one of the creative forces behind these events, said, "I used to be a very introverted person, struggling to find a way to express myself creatively."

That was before he discovered geocaching a couple of years ago. Now he enjoys getting before a group of people and challenging them to solve one of his inventive puzzle caches (such as defusing a nuclear bomb).

Inspired by movie themes, he has created elaborate caches based on movies such as Jodie Foster's *Contact*. His puzzle cache, The Game, involved participants finding multiple clues during a wild two-hour ride on Portland, Oregon's, light rail system. His creativity has brought positive responses from around the world. "All the support has been wonderful. I have finally found a great way to express myself and give people enjoyment at the same time."

Fractal's efforts prove the sport is limited only by your imagination.

What will these guys come up with next?

Fractal and Soup

Racing Games

Extreme outdoor racing games such as the Eco-Challenge have gained popularity over the past few years. Mark Burnett, producer of both the Eco-Challenge and CBS's *Survivor*, has taken a lot of what makes geocaching popular and moved it to prime time. The Eco-Challenge is an international multisport endurance competition during which teams travel over land, water, and mountains using kayaks, mountain bikes, and sheer guts and determination. Navigation and outdoor skills are a must, and GPS use has been limited to managing the team's arrival at

Eureka!
Adventure racing has been around for years but has recently become more popular with the interest in extreme sports and television coverage of the Eco-Challenge. These events can last one day to a week, and are an exciting way of combining navigation skills and strategy with running, mountain biking, climbing, and kayaking.

checkpoints. Each team carries a receiver, but it can be used for emergencies only.

Many of these multisport endurance-type races follow a similar format. The race can take days to complete as teams choose navigation routes to travel from checkpoint to checkpoint. Because they are a navigational challenge, strategy and planning can be as important as physical endurance. These games are a natural for GPS use, but have been slow to adapt, requiring competitors to rely on traditional map and compass skills.

Team Magellan at the Four Winds USA Adventure Race.

David Poleto

GPS manufacturer Magellan has recognized the growing interest of using GPS in such sports as adventure racing. The company sponsored the Four Winds USA Adventure Race based out of Park City, Utah, and supplied the receivers for the event. Basemaps were eliminated to avoid providing too much of an advantage. Teams were required to save various checkpoints as waypoints to verify they were there.

Magellan also sponsors an adventure race team. David Poleto, captain of Team Magellan says, "Adventure racing is an amazing sport! Proper preparation is crucial to being successful in the sport. You must use every tool available to give you an edge over the other teams. GPS is not only an indispensable tool when used in racing, it also gives them an edge while training." Their team has discovered huge benefits by including GPS technology in training and race preparation. "With the ability to store multiple routes, input waypoint checkpoints, and monitor speed of travel, we have developed training courses to hone our team's skills and have seen huge advances in our race results."

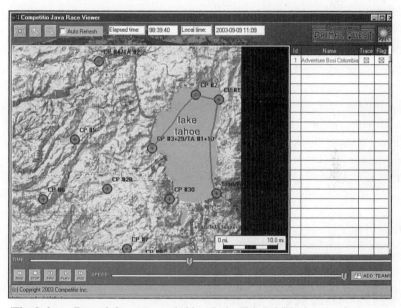

The Subaru Primal Quest event held at Lake Tahoe, Nevada, attaches tracking devices to race teams to track their progress in real time.

www.SubaruPrimalQuest.com

With the popularity of adventure racing and reality TV programs, we doubt whether it will be long before GPS games and challenges are included. As these programs become more competitive and sophisticated, GPS is the natural solution to make the events more challenging and interesting. Could it be that sometime in the future on a TV near you, you could see contestants packing GPS receivers on *Survivor* or *The Amazing Race?*

What about our favorite traditional race events? Could it be possible that GPS challenges will find their way into such events as the Great Iditarod race in Alaska, or other off-road, rally, or yachting events? These types of competitions are already influenced and managed by GPS technology. It may not be long before the inclusion of geocaching-style games becomes part of the natural evolution of these sports.

Geocaching events and competitions are already using ideas from these various races and programs. Tonja and Dan "geoGryffindor" Muret incorporated the "Amazing Geocache" at their last event. It is a mix between the *Amazing Race* and *Survivor,* and is a unique way to test your outdoor knowledge.

The game starts when players pick a card that includes cache coordinates. Next you go find the cache to pick up a sealed envelope. On the envelope is a question with three possible answers, each with a set of coordinates to a new cache. The correct answer and a correct set of coordinates are inside the envelope. Every correct answer scores two points. You get docked a point if you have to peek inside for the answer. Answer the question wrong and you're off and running to coordinates where no cache exists. This can be a real stumper depending on the difficulty of the caches. Players can spend a lot of time looking, and if they are not absolutely sure of the answer, they start to second-guess themselves. They become tempted to open the envelope, reducing their chances for a higher score.

Environmental Ethics

The issue of environmental ethics and access is critical because geocaching as well as other outdoor activities require access to park, rural, and wilderness lands. Those of us who enjoy venturing into the outdoors are frequently faced with challenges. Such challenges include individuals and organizations that would prefer all wilderness lands be closed to public access. Many of these individuals are concerned about the impact of a particular activity on the environment. Although their intentions may be good, most geocachers would agree that it is unreasonable to deny access to everyone.

We should be permitted to enjoy the outdoors as long as we do so responsibly. Another challenge faced by outdoor enthusiasts lies in dealing with the very small percentage of individuals who care nothing about the outdoors or anything else. Some people lack consideration for the environment and often use wilderness areas as garbage dumps or for criminal activities. These people give the rest of us a bad name. Unfortunately, sometimes their actions can lead to private and public land managers limiting access to the lands.

As a community, geocachers must practice good environmental policy and educate those who do not. Otherwise, the land managers may have good cause to lock the access gates. If we continue to treat the environment with respect, outdoor and wilderness areas will likely be accessible for generations to come.

Geocaching is an activity that can be conducted with no or minimal impact to the local environment. In fact, geocaching may have less of an impact than many other outdoor activities. It is also fair to say that as a group, geocachers are environmentally conscious. Geocachers are a global community composed primarily of individuals with a strong appreciation of nature. Through a demonstrated appreciation of nature and a lot of education, geocachers have worked with landowners and managers to open parks and other lands to geocaching.

As geocaching continues to develop, we must continue working to overcome any negative preconceptions. Many people are unfamiliar with geocaching, and some have preconceived notions about what it is and is not. Some might have the image of geocachers digging holes and stashing junk. We need to work at educating the public, whether we are out on a trail as individuals or taking part in community projects within our geocaching club. It's a matter of letting others know that we do not dig holes, leave garbage, or bushwhack. If there is a problem with a cache or there is a path being worn to it, we will move the cache. Our strength has always been our ability to take responsibility for ourselves as part of the geocaching community.

To maintain its positive image, the geocaching community must regulate itself and remember that actions speak louder than words. Many people will judge the geocaching community, positively or negatively, based on what they actually see happening in the field. Their perception will be based on how we conduct ourselves on the trail. Are we courteous or suspicious? Do we leave garbage behind, or help take out a little extra (cache-in, trash-out)? This is why working within groups and clubs can be so important. Through numbers and positive effort, we can really be effective in cleaning up local areas through cache-in, trash-out events. Groups can also help with community and outdoor projects (for instance, by taking youth groups to a park to teach them about GPS and geocaching or by repairing a hiking trail at a favorite park).

Local cachers help create and manage their own geocaching park.

Friends of Haw Ridge Park

A group of cachers in Oak Ridge, Tennessee, took the initiative to create their own geocaching park. The Friends of Haw Ridge Park worked with the City of Oak Ridge Recreations and Parks to establish their own area filled with geocaches. The terrain is wooded and hilly, and the trails rough, but the caches are placed near the trails to eliminate the need for bushwhacking.

The park is accessible by mountain bike and canoe, and some caches are reachable by boat. The park supports a variety of trees, plants, and wildlife.

The park, and its partnership between a private group of geocachers and a government agency, is an excellent example of how land can be managed and used for the greater good of all.

Where Do We Go from Here?

Thanks again for taking the time to learn about geocaching and using GPS. We are excited about the opportunity to offer this book, and appreciate having you along to learn and enjoy it. Regardless of what happens in geocaching, we hope to leave you with three final thoughts:

◆ First, the sport has grown rapidly and maintained a positive reputation because geocachers honestly care about their hobby. Most go out of their way to ensure that no one says anything negative about its players or their impact on the outdoors. In fact, geocaching has been covered by hundreds of media outlets around the world with very positive feedback. This kind of coverage will remain only as long as we continue to self-regulate the sport and each other. That means picking up after ourselves and, unfortunately, sometimes others, as well as leaving everyone we meet with a positive impression of the game and those who play it. It is an awesome responsibility, but you can rest assured that geocachers are up to the task.

◆ Second, remember to have fun. With all the high-tech twists and turns that game variations may take, remember the basics. You got hooked on this activity because it is so enjoyable to enter the coordinates to some unknown location and then bring friends, family, and children along for the adventure. Don't forget the simple joy of getting into the outdoors, leaving all the worldly problems behind. Getting out on the trail is truly good therapy and one of life's simple pleasures. Never let life get so busy that you forget to take time to go outside and play!

◆ Finally, remember that like life, the enjoyment of the sport often lies in the journey as much as the destination. Geocaching allows us to be alone to reflect about what is really important or to participate with a group of friends and share in the experience. Geocaching also allows us to see beautiful places and meet great people and share in a multitude of experiences along the way.

Enjoy! We hope to meet you sometime, somewhere on the trail.

Happy geocaching!

The Least You Need to Know

- ◆ Geocaching is a fun activity with a promising future.

- ◆ The excitement and challenge of geocaching will continue to influence traditional games and sports.

- ◆ Major theme event caches make for an exciting opportunity to get together and share the experience.

- ◆ GPS makes extreme sports and races even better.

- ◆ The success of the sport will have much to do with the community's environmental responsibility.

- ◆ Good positive fun with family and friends is key to the long-term success of geocaching.

Appendix A

Resource Directory

Amateur Radio and APRS Tracking

Northwest APRS Group: www.nwaprs.org

Tucson Amateur Packet Radio: www.tapr.org

Rutgers University: aprs.rutgers.edu

ARRL American Relay League: www.arrl.org/

Compass Manufacturers

The Brunton Co.
620 E. Monroe Avenue
Riverton, WY 82501
Phone: 1-800-443-4871
Website: www.brunton.com

Silva, from JWA
1326 Willow Road
Sturtevant, WI 53177
Phone: 1-888-245-4986
Website: www.jwa.com

Suunto USA
2151 Las Palmas Drive, G
Carlsbad, CA 92009
Phone: 1-800-543-9124
Website: www.suuntousa.com

Geocaching

Geocaching.com: www.geocaching.com

Groundspeak Forums: forums.groundspeak.com

GPS Games

Armchair Treasure Hunt Club: www.treasureclub.net/

Benchmark Hunting: www.geocaching.com/mark/

Geodashing: www.geodashing.org

Euro Bill Tracker: www.eurobilltracker.com/

International Orienteering Organization: www.orienteering.org/

Letterboxing North America: www.letterboxing.org/

MinuteWar: www.minutewar.org/

The Degree Confluence Project: www.confluence.org/

Where's George: www.wheresgeorge.com/

GPS Information

GPS Navigator Magazine.com: www.gpsnavmag.com

Joe Mehaffey and Jack Yeazel's GPS site: www.GPSInformation.net

GPS Manufacturers

The Brunton Co.
620 E. Monroe Avenue
Riverton, WY 82501
Phone: 1-800-443-4871
Website: www.brunton.com

Cobra Electronics
6500 West Cortland Street
Chicago, IL 60707
Phone: 773-889-3087
Website: www.cobra.com

Garmin International
1200 E. 151st Street
Olathe, KS 66062
Phone: 1-800-800-1020
Website: www.garmin.com

Lowrance Electronics, Inc.
12000 E. Skelly Drive
Tulsa, OK 74128
Phone: 1-800-324-1354
Website: www.lowrance.com

Thales Navigation (Magellan GPS)
960 Overland Court
San Dimas, CA 91773
Phone: 909-394-5000
Website: www.magellangps.com

Master list of GPS manufacturers: gauss.gge.unb.ca/manufact.htm

GPS Groups

Cache Across America: groups.yahoo.com/group/CacheAcrossAmerica/

Geocache GPS Treasure Hunt Game: groups.yahoo.com/group/
geocachegpstreasurehuntgame/

Groundspeak Forums: forums.groundspeak.com

The newsgroup where geocaching began: news://sci.geo.satellite-nav

Geocaching Software

A list of software applications that support GPX and LOC file formats: www.geocaching.com/waypoints

EasyGPS for Groundspeak (GPX/LOC), a great (free) application for managing both LOC and GPX file types: www.geocaching.com/waypoints/download.aspx

Mac GPS Pro—(LOC) Shareware application for Mac OS 6 through Mac OS 9 and natively on Mac OS X: www.macgpspro.com/

Geocaching Pocket Queries (GPX/eBook)—Create customized cache queries you can have generated on a daily or weekly basis. They are in a format you can bring along with you on cache hunts on your GPS and/or PDA.: www.geocaching.com/pocket/

GPS Babel—A free console-based application for converting LOC and GPX to various other formats. Source code available: http://gpsbabel.sourceforge.net/

GPX Spinner (GPX)—Geocaching-specific shareware application that can convert GPX files to iSolo and Plucker format: www.gpxspinner.com/

Watcher (GPX)—Geocaching-specific-freeware application that helps you manage your Pocket Query GPX files: http://clayjar.com/gc/watcher/

GPS Software

DeLorme
PO Box 298
Yarmouth, ME 04096
Phone: 1-800-452-5931
Website: www.delorme.com

Fugawi
95 St. Clair Avenue West, Suite 1406
Toronto, Ontario M4V 1N6 Canada
Website: www.fugawi.com

TopoGrafix
PO Box 783
Medford, MA 02155
Website: www.topografix.com

Maptech
10 Industrial Way
Amesbury, MA 01913
Phone: 1-888-839-5551
Website: www.maptech.com

National Geographic Maps
375 Alabama Street, Suite 400
San Francisco, CA 94110
Phone: 415-558-8700
Website: www.topo.com

Ozi Explorer: www.oziexplorer.com

Government Resources

Australia Travel Advisories: www.dfat.gov.au/travel/

Canadian Bureau of Consular Affairs: www.voyage.gc.ca
Phone: 613-944-6788

United Kingdom Travel Advisories: www.fco.gov.uk/travel/

United States Department of State, Bureau of Consular Affairs
Office of American Citizens Services, Room 4817 N.S.
2201 'C' Street NW
Washington, DC 20520
Phone: 202-647-5225 or 202-647-5226
Website: //travel.state.gov/

Assistance to Americans arrested abroad: //travel.state.gov/arrest.html

Doctors and hospitals abroad: //travel.state.gov/acs.html#medical

Embassies and consulates: //travel.state.gov/links.html

Embassies with attorneys: //travel.state.gov/judicial_assistance. html#attorneys

Medical information, including lists of air ambulance and travel insurance companies: //travel.state.gov/medical.html

Road safety abroad: //travel.state.gov/road_safety.html

Travel warnings abroad: //travel.state.gov/travel_warnings.html

Welfare/whereabouts of Americans overseas: //travel.state.gov/ where.html

United States Embassy in Mexico: www.usembassy-mexico.gov/ eacs.html

United States Census Bureau (search for city information including latitude/longitude coordinates): www.census.gov/cgi-bin/gazetteer

Map Resources

TerraServer USA, Satellite photography: //terraserver-usa.com

Topozone: www.topozone.com

Trackmaker: www.gpstm.com

Map Ruler, Finding Coordinates

Topo Companion and Coordinator Map Rulers

Map Rulers for Lat/Long and UTM

GPSNavigatorMagazine.com
PO Box 841
Eugene, OR 97440
Phone: 866-405-5GPS (477)
Website: www.gpsnavmag.com

UTM Converter (converts UTM and lat/long):
www.cellspark.com/UTM.html

Paper Map Resources

Canada Map Office
Department of Energy, Mines, and Resources
615 Booth Street
Ottawa, Ontario K1A0E9 Canada
Phone: 1-800-465-6277

National Oceanic and Atmospheric Administration

National Ocean Survey Map and Chart Information
Distribution Branch N/CG33
Riverdale, Maryland 20737
Phone: 303-436-6990

The Earth Science Information Center Headquarters
Phone: 1-800-USA-MAPS

U.S. Geological Survey
507 National Center
Reston, VA 22092
Website: www.usgs.gov/

Search for international city information, including latitude/longitude
coordinates

Getty Thesaurus of Geographic Names: www.getty.edu/research/
conducting_research/vocabularies/tgn

United States Census Bureau: www.census.gov/cgi-bin/gazetteer

Training

Bill Burke's 4-Wheeling America
307 N. Ash Street
Fruita, CO 81521
Phone: 970-858-3468
Website: www.bb4wa.com

Off-road driving and expedition planning

GPS Navigator Magazine.com
PO Box 841
Eugene, OR 97440 USA
Phone: 866-405-5GPS (477)
Website: www.gpsnavmag.com
E-mail: info@gpsnavmag.com

GPS navigation and off-road travel training and adventure

Kacey Smith, BajaGPS Guide
Website: www.bajagpsguide.com

GPS navigation and Mexico off-road travel

Navigation Northwest Hood Consulting & Services
Rick Hood, Edmonds, WA
Phone: 425-640-8134
Website: www.hoodcs.com

Weather

National Weather Service: www.nws.noaa.gov

The Weather Channel: www.weather.com

Appendix B

Glossary

agonic line The only location on the globe where magnetic north and true north are the same.

aiming off Bypassing an obstacle to reach the intended target, or deliberately aiming off to one side to help ensure a known direction of travel to reach the target, such as finding a vehicle parked on a roadway.

almanac data The information broadcast from GPS satellites used by the GPS receiver for computing its location.

altimeter A gauge for measuring elevation.

amateur radio Also known as ham radio. Based on licensing privileges, various bands and frequencies are used for local, regional, or international communications. Handheld radios are 5 watts, but their range is substantial by transmitting through repeaters. Mobile radios are primarily 50 watts. (Compare that to CB radios, which are limited to only 4 watts.) A license is required through the FCC, but it is easy and inexpensive to obtain.

APRS (Automatic Position Reporting System) GPS is combined with ham radios to provide mobile stations that are tracked by a computer using mapping software.

archive This is usually seen when you own a cache. Archiving involves deleting your cache from the active listings on the website. This usually occurs when you are not going to replace a cache after it has been removed. You can temporarily disable it as the cache owner if you plan to activate it again within a month.

attack points One or more landmarks used to reach a navigational target.

autorouting GPS function that provides turn-by-turn directions to a waypoint. Directions may be in the form of arrows or automated voice commands.

azimuth Evolved into the same definition as a bearing.

back bearing Reversing a bearing for a return trip. It is 180° in the opposite direction.

baseline navigation Baseline or handrail terrain features are linear reference points, such as roads, rivers, and power lines.

bearing (BRG) A direction measured by a compass degree needed to travel to stay on a course. Also known as an azimuth.

benchmark hunting The search for NGS (National Geodetic Survey) navigation survey markers. These markers document elevation or latitude/longitude points. Survey markers can be found with GPS or by following written instructions provided by the NGS.

Bureau of Land Management (BLM) A U.S government agency within the Department of the Interior. They manage 262 million acres of America's public lands, located primarily in 12 western states.

cache (geocache term) Pronounced "cash," in geocaching it is a hidden container filled with a logbook and pencil/pen and, possibly, prizes. Caches were often used by explorers, miners, etc. to hide foodstuffs and other items for emergency purposes. People still hide caches of supplies today for similar reasons.

cardinal points The primary compass points: N, E, S, and W. The intercardinal points are NE, SE, SW, and NW.

chart A map of a waterway typically indicating depth and hazards.

chromes   From the term "crow miles" or "as the crow flies." GPS receivers calculate distances in a direct line to the target. Actual ground travel is often double the distance.

CITO (cache in, trash out)   When out geocaching, take a bag with you and pick up trash along the way.

contour interval (CI)   The distance, typically 40 to 100 feet, between topo map contour lines.

contour lines   The light brown lines on a topo map, which indicate a distance, usually in feet, above sea level.

course   A direction traveled between two points, or to reach a destination.

course-deviation indicator (CDI)   Used to measure the degree of cross-track error.

cross-track error (XTE)   The distance traveled off-course. This is measured by a CDI, a course-deviation indicator.

datum   A datum is a global survey system used to create maps. They are titled from the year they were created. The two primary datums are NAD 27 or WGS 84. Latitude and longitude are calculated differently for each datum. Geocaching uses the WGS 84 datum for all caches, although many maps still use NAD 27. Failing to set the GPS receiver to the correct datum can cause inaccuracies in excess of 1,000 meters.

decimal minutes   Geocaching uses this format of the latitude/longitude system, in which seconds are not shown. This is represented in the GPS receiver as HDDD° MM.MMM'. HDDD means hemisphere and degrees. MM.MMM' are minutes in the decimal format.

declination   The deference in degrees between magnetic north and true north.

Degree Confluence Project, The   Another GPS-based hobby involving visiting points where the latitude and longitude are integers (e.g., N 42° 00.000 W 088° 00.000) and reporting your visit.

DGPS (differential correction)   A system to improve GPS accuracy through ground-based radio transmitters to correct existing GPS signals for accuracy averaging 5 meters.

DOP number The dilution of precision number indicates the quality of the satellite signals received. The smaller the number, the better the satellite geometry.

EPE number The estimated position error number is based on satellite geometry with a reading that provides an estimate of accuracy in feet.

estimated time en route (ETE) The amount of time needed to reach the destination based on current speed and course.

estimated time of arrival (ETA) The time scheduled to arrive based on current speed and course.

Force (The Force) The ability to instinctively know where a cache is hidden when you get within a certain proximity.

FTF (first to find) Scoring a FTF is confirmed by being the first person to record "FTF" into the cache's logbook or online entry.

Garminites Those who favor the Garmin brand GPS receivers.

geo-coin Small minted coins with the geocaching logo on one side and a customized impression on the other. Trackable through Geocaching.com.

GPS An acronym for global positioning system. GPS is the global, satellite-based navigation system operated by the U.S. Government. With the use of a GPS receiver, you can find your position anywhere in the world, and it is the basis for the game of geocaching.

GPSr A GPS receiver.

GPSr food Batteries.

heading A marine term to describe a desired direction of travel.

hitchhiker A hitchhiker is an item that is placed in a cache with instructions to relocate it to other caches. Sometimes they have logbooks attached so you can log their travels. Travel bugs and geo-coins are examples of hitchhikers.

index line The dark brown line on a topo map, which indicates elevation. This is typically the fourth or fifth line and is numbered in feet.

index map A master chart used by the USGS to select a topographic map.

latitude/longitude system   The world's primary navigation system, in which distances are measured in degrees, minutes, and seconds. Horizontal latitude lines measure north/south coordinates. Vertical longitude lines measure east/west coordinates.

letterboxing   A game similar to geocaching that started in the United Kingdom more than 100 years ago. The boxes are found by following clues and using a map and compass (www.letterboxing.org).

loose bearings   The GPS receiver's compass feature does not work in the stationary position. This causes the direction arrow to point in various directions. The bearing reading will still be correct, and a compass will be required to stay on track.

Maggies   Those who favor the Magellan brand GPS receivers.

man overboard (MOB)   A GPS receiver function allowing a waypoint to be quickly saved in an emergency situation. This is typically done by holding down the GoTo button.

markwelling (verb)   When a response to a new post in the online forums points you to a similar topic discussed previously. Named after the resident archivist on the Geocaching.com discussion boards, Markwell.

McToys   Originally a negative term for trinket toys of little value left in caches, it's now used as generic slang for geocache treasures. Known as McToys from the infamous McDonald's Happy Meals toys.

muggles (or geo-muggles)   A nongeocacher we meet in the field who wonders what we're doing, or someone who accidentally finds a cache. Based on "muggle" (a nonmagical person) from the *Harry Potter* series. They are often puzzled looking, but are usually harmless.

nautical mile   6,080 feet or 1.152 of a statute mile.

navigation or "nav" target   The desired location or waypoint to be reached.

neocacher   An inexperienced geocacher or a "newbie."

NMEA (National Marine Electronics Association)   A universal electronic standard established to allow GPS, radios, and computers to exchange navigational data.

north: grid   Vertical map grid lines that may deviate from true north.

    magnetic   Direction of compass needle as it points to magnetic north.

    true   Direction to the actual North Pole.

orienteering   A sport in which competitors race from point to point using a map and compass.

pacing   A method of tracking distances by counting footsteps. A pace is one step. A stride is 2 steps, typically about 5 feet.

PDA   A personal digital assistant, such as a Palm Pilot.

prominent features   All major landmarks, being man-made or natural, including mountains, highways, waterways, and bridges.

real-time tracking   A GPS receiver is connected to a computer loaded with mapping software. The user's current location is displayed on a computer screen as an icon centered on the digital-moving map.

ROT13   The encryption method utilized by the encrypted hints or logs on Geocaching.com.

route   A series of waypoints listed in sequence from start to finish.

selective availability (SA)   A degree of inaccuracy programmed by the U.S. government causing civilian receivers to be off as much as 100 meters. SA was discontinued in May 2000.

simulation mode   The format that allows the review and programming of information without the receiver attempting to search for satellites.

spoiler   Text that gives away too many details of a cache location, spoiling the experience for the next cachers who want to find it. Also used to describe a person who gives away details to other geocachers.

statute mile   A standard ground mile with the distance of 5,280 feet. Established by the ancient Romans, its distance represented 5,000 Roman Legionnaire paces.

terrain association   A way to orient a map to actual terrain by matching up prominent features and baseline features.

TFTC   Thanks for the cache.

TNLN (took nothing, left nothing)   Usually found in cache log-books by folks who enjoy the thrill of the hunt more than the material contents of the cache.

TNLNSL   Took nothing, left nothing, signed logbook.

TNSL   Took nothing, signed logbook.

topographic or topo map   A detailed small-scale map showing eleva-tion with contour lines.

track (TRK)   The actual direction currently being traveled to reach a nav target.

track logs   An electronic breadcrumb trail that is stored and displayed by a receiver, indicating a path traveled.

trade items   The most commonly used term (after treasure) for items found in a cache.

travel bug   A special hitchhiker produced by Groundspeak, trackable on Geocaching.com.

triangulation   Confirms a location by shooting a bearing to more than one surrounding land mark. Effective in the field or on a map.

UBBCode   UBBCode tags enable you to add formatting (bold, italics) and other information (e-mails, URLs) to your messages in the Geocaching.com online forums without learning HTML. They were created by Infopop, who run the Groundspeak forum software. More info on UBBCode can be found on their website.

universal time coordinated (UTC)   This is a universal time standard based on some point in the world. Many GPS receivers use the UTC at Greenwich, England.

Universal Transverse Mercator (UTM)   A worldwide navigation system that measures the globe's coordinates using meters and kilome-ters.

U.S. Forest Service (USFS)   A U.S. government agency of the Department of Agriculture. The USFS manages 191 million acres of national forests, grasslands, and prairies. These public lands are gener-ally geocaching-friendly, except for designated wilderness areas, and other specially designated botanical, wildlife, and archaeological sites.

UTM system (Universal Transverse Mercator) The world's second primary navigation coordinate system. Often considered an easier system to use because it uses metric meters and kilometers instead of degrees, minutes, and seconds.

variation Another term for magnetic declination.

velocity made good (VMG) When traveling on course, it is the speed and direction calculation used by the receiver's computer to determine ETA.

virtual cache Adapted from "virtual reality," these caches are a distinct, unique object on the planet. Nothing is traded except photos and experiences.

WAAS (wide-area augmentation system) Developed to improve GPS accuracy in the United States to within 3 meters 95 percent of the time through additional radio signals broadcast by 25 ground stations and 2 satellites.

watch list A list of users on Geocaching.com who are watching a particular hitchhiker or cache. When a listing is logged, users on the watch list are notified by e-mail.

waypoint A selected point-of-interest location that can be saved, stored, and recalled from the GPS receiver's memory. Cache locations are saved as waypoints.

Navigation and Map References

Distance

- 1 inch   25.4 millimeters   2.54 centimeters
- 1 foot   12 inches   30.48 centimeters
- 1 yard   3 feet   .914 meter
- 1 mile (statute) 5,280 feet 1,760 yards 1.609 kilometers
- 1 nautical mile   6,080 feet 1,853 kilometers 1.15 of a mile
- 1 millimeter   .039 inch   .1 centimeter
- 1 centimeter   .394 inch   10 millimeters
- 1 meter   39.37 inches   3.28 feet
- 1 kilometer   3,280.8 feet   .62 mile   1,000 meters
- 1 acre 43,560 sq. feet, approx. 208.7' × 208.7'

Map Scales

- 1:500,000   1 inch = 8 miles
- 1:250,000   1 inch = 4 miles
- 1:150,000   1 inch = 2.4 miles
- 1:62,000 (15 minute)   1 inch = 1 mile
- 1:24,000 (7.5 minute)   1 inch = 2,000 feet (topo size)

UTM

Each grid is 1,000 meters (1 kilometer) square.

Latitude/Longitude

- Latitude lines run horizontally and measure north-south coordinates.

- Longitude lines run vertically intersecting the poles to measure east-west coordinates.

- 1° (degree) = 60' (minutes), 1' (minute) = 60'' (seconds).

- 1 degree = 69.05 statute miles = 111 kilometers.

- 1 minute = 1 nautical mile or 1.15 statute miles = 1.85 kilometers.

- 1 second = 100 feet = 30.83 meters.

* Distances apply to latitude, but only to longitude at the equator.

Township, Range, Section

- A township equals 36 square miles.

- Each square mile is a section. Each section is numbered from 1 to 36. Section 1 begins in the northeast corner as the numbers proceed west, then east, alternately down each row, ending with 36 in the southeast corner.

◆ Each township has a TOWNSHIP AND RANGE designation to define its 36-square-mile area.

◆ The horizontal rows are the township designation.

◆ The vertical rows are the range designation.

Sections are divided into quarters, which are further quartered to describe a property location: for example, SE ¼, NW ¼, Section 23, T.1 S., R.1 E., of the Salt Lake Base Line.

Cache Log Sheet

GEOCACHING.COM

Geocache Name: _____

Placed by: _____

Contact Info: _____

Take something, leave something, sign the log.

Found by: _____   Date: _____
Notes:_____
_____
_____
_____

Found by: _____   Date: _____
Notes:_____
_____
_____
_____

Found by: _____   Date: _____
Notes:_____
_____
_____
_____

Found by: _____   Date: _____
Notes:_____
_____
_____
_____

Found by: _____   Date: _____
Notes:_____
_____
_____
_____

Found by: _____   Date: _____
Notes:_____
_____
_____
_____

Geocache Notification Sheet

This Is a GEOCACHE

Congratulations, you've found it! (Intentionally or not!)

The name of this geocache is _____.

This container is for the game of *geocaching*. It is a modern hide-and-seek game played by adventure-loving global positioning system (GPS) users around the world. A GPS user hides a cache or treasure (this container) and publishes the exact coordinates on the Internet. This is so other GPS users (like you) can go on a treasure hunt to find it.

The rules are simple! If you take an item, you must also leave something in return (but nothing illegal or harmful). Then write about your visit in the logbook.

IF YOU FOUND THIS CONTAINER BY ACCIDENT:

Great! You can join in on the fun! We do ask the following:

Please don't move or vandalize this container.

Go ahead and take something if you like. But also leave something.

If this container needs to be relocated, please contact me and I will do so immediately. My contact information is:

_____

For more information, and to let us know you were successful in finding this geocache, please go online and visit www.geocaching.com.

Travel Itinerary

Critical Information to Leave Behind

❏ Ranger station   ❏ Family/friends   ❏ At trailhead

Trip Date & Time: _____ Return Date & Time: _____

Destination: _____

Geocache(s): _____

Location Description: _____

Route Taken: _____

_____

Coordinates: _____

Motels/Campgrounds: _____

Comm. Ham: Frequencies _____ Cell ( ) _____

Sat. Ph. ( ) _____ CB: Ch. 1_____, Ch. 2 _____ FM: _____

Persons:

Name _____ Contact Phone _____

_____

_____

Vehicles:

Make _____   Model _____

Color _____   License Plate _____

_____

Photocopy this page courtesy of Alpha Books

Gear Checklist

For Geocaching, Camping, and Outdoor Adventure

- ❏ Ax
- ❏ Batteries
- ❏ Binoculars
- ❏ Camera and film
- ❏ Clothing, two sets minimum
- ❏ Cooking kit and utensils
- ❏ Dog stuff
- ❏ Energy bars
- ❏ Firewood
- ❏ Flashlights and batteries
- ❏ Glasses, contacts
- ❏ GPS and accessories
- ❏ Bar-B-Q or grill
- ❏ Beverages
- ❏ Boots and socks
- ❏ Cell, 2-way, CB
- ❏ Compass
- ❏ Cooler and ice
- ❏ Emergency blanket
- ❏ Fire extinguisher
- ❏ First-aid/snakebite kit
- ❏ Gas and oil
- ❏ Gloves
- ❏ Hat

- ❏ Insect repellent
- ❏ Licenses (game)
- ❏ Knife, large and small
- ❏ Maps, general and topo
- ❏ Money: cash/credit cards/ traveler checks
- ❏ Passport
- ❏ Rope
- ❏ Signal mirror and whistle
- ❏ Snow chains
- ❏ Sun block, lip balm
- ❏ Swimwear
- ❏ Tent
- ❏ Toolbox
- ❏ Water
- ❏ _____
- ❏ _____

- ❏ Jackets (light/heavy)
- ❏ Kid stuff
- ❏ Lantern and fuel
- ❏ Medication
- ❏ Notepad and pencil

- ❏ Propane gas
- ❏ Shovel
- ❏ Sleeping bags and pillows
- ❏ Stove and fuel
- ❏ Sunglasses
- ❏ Tarp
- ❏ Toiletries
- ❏ Toothbrush and paste
- ❏ Waterproof matches
- ❏ _____
- ❏ _____

❏ Meals:

Breakfast: _____

Lunch: _____

Dinner: _____

Snacks: _____

Photocopy these pages courtesy of Alpha Books

Index

C

D

H

S

Check Out These
Best-Sellers

Grammar and Style
SECOND EDITION

1-59257-115-8
$16.95

Buying and Selling a Home
FOURTH EDITION

1-59257-120-4
$18.95

Being a Groom
SECOND EDITION

0-02-864456-5
$9.95

Learning Spanish
THIRD EDITION

0-02-864451-4
$18.95

Personal Finance in Your 20s & 30s
SECOND EDITION

0-02-864374-7
$19.95

Organizing Your Life
FOURTH EDITION

1-59257-413-0
$16.95

Total Nutrition
FOURTH EDITION

1-59257-439-4
$18.95

Positive Dog Training

0-02-864463-8
$14.95

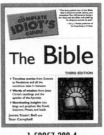

The Bible
THIRD EDITION

1-59257-389-4
$18.95

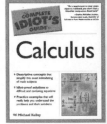

Calculus

0-02-864365-8
$18.95

Music Theory
SECOND EDITION

1-59257-437-8
$19.95

The Perfect Resume
THIRD EDITION

0-02-864440-9
$14.95

Playing the Guitar
SECOND EDITION

0-02-864244-9
$21.95

Manga

1-59257-335-5
$19.95

Knitting and Crocheting
SECOND EDITION
Illustrated

1-59257-089-5
$16.95

More than *450 titles* available at booksellers and online retailers everywhere

www.idiotsguides.com

ALPHA